# THE DANGER OF EQUALITY

*By the same Author*

POLITICAL PSYCHOLOGY
*The Revolutionary Ideas of the Marquis de Sade* (1934)
*The Life and Ideas of the Marquis de Sade* (3rd edition 1964)

TRAVEL
*Africa Dances* (1935)
*Bali and Angkor* (1936)
*Hot Strip Tease* (1938)

POLITICAL SATIRE
*Nobody Talks Politics* (1936)

SOCIAL ANTHROPOLOGY
*Himalayan Village—a study of the Lepchas of Sikkim* (1938)
*The Americans—a study in national character* (1948)
*Exploring English Character* (1955)
*Death, Grief, & Mourning in Contemporary Britain* (1965)

in collaboration with Dr. John Rickman
*The People of Great Russia—a psychological study* (1949)

# THE DANGER OF EQUALITY
*and other essays*

by
GEOFFREY GORER

THE CRESSET PRESS

© GEOFFREY GORER, 1966
*Published in Great Britain by
The Cresset Press Ltd., 11 Fitzroy Square, London W.1
First published 1966*

*Printed in Great Britain
at the St. Ann's Press,
Park Road, Altrincham*

# ACKNOWLEDGEMENTS

'Justification by Numbers' was originally published in the *American Scholar*.

'Pride, Shame, and Guilt', 'The Remaking of Man', 'Dionysus and the Welfare State', 'Nature, Science, and Dr. Kinsey', and 'Man to Man' were originally published in *Encounter*.

'The Anatomy of a Dream Man' and 'Mirror, Mirror on the Wall' were originally published in *Lilliput*.

'The Uses of Pornography' was originally published in the *London Magazine* and included in *Does Pornography Matter?* edited by C. H. Rolph and published by Routledge and Kegan Paul. 'Poor Honey' was originally published in the *London Magazine*.

'The Perils of Hypergamy' was originally published in the *New Statesman*.

'The Euro-American Way of Life' was originally published in the *New York Times Sunday Magazine*.

'Woman's Place' was originally published in the *Observer*.

'The Erotic Myth of America' was originally published in the *Partisan Review*.

'An Anthropologist Considers Retirement' was written for the Institute of Directors' conference on Problems of Retirement. A text was privately published by the Institute.

'The Marquis de Sade: Sado-Masochism and Theatricality' was written for the Menninger Foundation, Topeka, Kansas.

'On Falling in Love' was written for radio station RIAS.

'Cultural Community and Cultural Diversity in the North Atlantic Nations' was written for the ninth national conference of the U.S. National Commission for Unesco.

In several cases the articles or lectures have been modified or expanded for this book.

## CONTENTS

|  | Acknowledgements | v |
|---|---|---|
| I. | Kind Invitations: an Introduction | 3 |

### PART ONE: HUMAN SOCIETIES

| II. | The Concept of National Character | 9 |
|---|---|---|
| III. | Pride, Shame, and Guilt | 24 |
| IV. | The Remaking of Man | 39 |
| V. | Cultural Community and Cultural Diversity in the North Atlantic Nations | 48 |
| VI. | The Danger of Equality | 63 |
| VII. | A Reconsideration of the Functions of Class Distinctions | 72 |

### PART TWO: PHASES OF HUMAN LIFE

| VIII. | Adolescence in Different Cultures | 91 |
|---|---|---|
| IX. | Dionysus and the Welfare State | 105 |
| X. | The Euro-American Way of Life | 112 |
| XI. | The Anatomy of a Dream Man | 119 |
| XII. | On Falling in Love | 126 |
| XIII. | Woman's Place | 133 |
| XIV. | Mirror, Mirror on the Wall | 142 |
| XV. | An Anthropologist Considers Retirement | 150 |

### PART THREE: QUESTIONS OF SEX

| XVI. | Justification by Numbers | 165 |
|---|---|---|
| XVII. | Nature, Science, and Dr. Kinsey | 172 |
| XVIII. | Man to Man | 184 |

## Contents

| | | |
|---|---|---|
| XIX. | The Marquis de Sade: Sado-Masochism and Theatricality | 193 |
| XX. | The Uses of Pornography | 217 |

### Part Four: Books and Writers

| | | |
|---|---|---|
| XXI. | The Erotic Myth of America | 235 |
| XXII. | The Perils of Hypergamy | 242 |
| XXIII. | Poor Honey—Some Notes on Jane Austen and her Mother | 248 |

*Kind Invitations*

An Introduction
*(1966)*

# I

## Kind Invitations

### An Introduction
### *(1966)*

I IMAGINE IT is common experience for anybody in Britain or the United States who has acquired even a minor reputation as a writer or lecturer to receive unsolicited invitations to contribute to a series or symposium. This has been my experience over the last 15 years, and I am very grateful to the various editors and organizers who have sent me such kind invitations; well over half the essays in this book were written because the editors or convenors suggested the topic. I am particularly grateful to the British Institute of Directors for asking me to consider the institution of retirement, to the United States National Commission for Unesco for making me think about the implications of the phrase 'the North Atlantic Community', to the Menninger Foundation of Topeka, Kansas, for getting me to organize my thoughts on the relationship of sado-masochism and theatricality, and to Mr. C. H. Rolph and Messrs. Routledge and Kegan Paul for asking for an essay on the uses of pornography. Without the stimulus of these invitations I should probably never have considered paying careful attention to any of these topics; I think I have learned something, and hope that I have been able to convey what I learned.

A second stimulus was provided by books I was asked to review. Up till the last two years I wrote quite a lot of book reviews—perhaps 20 to 25 a year; the vast majority of these were short and ephemeral pieces. In the magazine *Encounter*, however, particularly while Mr. Irving Kristol was editor, I was able to write review-articles on various subjects which interested me, taking a book as the point of departure for exploring some topic. Of the pieces I have chosen to reprint in this collection three out of the five were suggested by Mr. Kristol.

Most of the invitations one receives, of course, ask one to repeat again something one has already written or said (at least, this is my experience); this requires little work, and may be profitable, either financially or because the make-up of the audience is stimulating; but I do not find this engenders new ideas, though the questions from lecture audiences are useful in indicating where one has failed in communication.

Out of the quite considerable number of articles I have written or lectures I have given in the last 15 years, I have made a selection of those which seem to me to have some continuing validity and interest. I have grouped them into four sections: those dealing with human societies, those dealing with the phases of human life, those dealing with questions of sex, and those dealing with books. This final section is really self-indulgent. I do not consider myself a qualified literary critic; I wrote the last paper out of love of the subject.

I became a 'sex expert' (hideous phrase!) purely by accident. I was in New York, participating in the Columbia University Research in Contemporary Cultures Project, in 1948 when the first Kinsey report, *Sexual Behavior in the Human Male* by Kinsey, Pomeroy and Martin, was published. The person who was to review it for the *New York Herald Tribune* book section was unable to fulfil the commitment; and I was asked, at very short notice, to provide a review. I thought this was a challenge I should accept. My review was not a favourable one; and, as it happened, this was the first published reasoned criticism that the book received. Because of the novelty of the approach at that period, I was asked to repeat the same theme again and again (I am only reprinting one of these variations) and came into contact with the odd saintly old men who had made the study of sex their life work at a period when it was still academically and socially dangerous to do so. In order to be able to hold my own in the various symposia and meetings resulting from these contacts I had to do a good deal of reading of the relevant literature; but I did not, and do not, have the training in physiology which would equip me for contributing to the topic except as a

## *An Introduction*

social anthropologist. The five essays in the third section represent all that I want to preserve on these subjects.

Although the topics of the essays are very various, and the subject-matter of some may appear trivial, it is my hope that two themes can be seen informing all, or nearly all, of them: the illumination that the comparative data of social anthropology can bring to bear on contemporary social problems, and the fact that all human social behaviour is susceptible to systematic analysis.

I should regret it if any of these pieces were interpreted as favouring or criticizing any political party in this country or elsewhere. This has certainly not been my intention. In some of the essays in the first two sections I have tried to analyse the climate of opinion, the general consensus, on various subjects in Great Britain and elsewhere; occasionally, one party voices this consensus with more emphasis than the other; but it is my belief that this is only a difference of emphasis, not of values or implicit assumptions.

*January*, 1966                                     GEOFFREY GORER

# PART ONE

*Human Societies*

II

## The Concept of National Character
*(1962)*

i

IT IS MY contention that people's characters—their motives, their predispositions, their values—can be described from three observational viewpoints: as human beings, as members of the genus *homo sapiens*, where the point of contrast is with other animal species; as unique individuals, where the point of contrast is with all other human beings whatsoever, with the possible exception of unseparated identical twins; and as members of a society, where the point of contrast is with members of other societies. The study of the human race is the province of the physiologists, the geneticists, the ethologists, the physical anthropologists; the study of the individual is the province of the psychologist or psychiatrist, to a certain extent of the doctor; the study of members of a society is the province of the sociologists and social anthropologists. These various disciplines, these contrasting observational viewpoints, could and should be complementary, each enriching the concepts of the other two; but unfortunately to date this has not generally been the case; in particular, the implications of membership of a society have been generally ignored.

To describe the psychological implications of the membership of a society, I have been forced to use the rather unfortunate phrase of 'national character'. I call this phrase unfortunate because the term of reference is not the nation-state, the political entity, but the society, and the two are frequently not coterminous. A political nation may be composed of several societies —witness Great Britain, composed of (probably) five societies: English, Welsh, Lowland Scots, Highland Scots, and Irish; or conversely, a society may be split into two or more nations by a political frontier or frontiers as, for example, the Kurds. But the term 'social character', which would be more apposite, has already been pre-empted by the social psychologists for some aspects of individual character which can be observed in the behaviour of small groups; and, since the term national character is already in the literature, I shall continue to use it, with the *caveat* that my frame of reference is social, not political.

Nor shall I try here to give a full definition of the term 'society', which is a most vexed and complicated problem. Components of all societies are the fact that they are relatively enduring associations of people of both sexes and all ages who are in direct or mediated relationships with one another, these relationships being structured into institutions; and in the greater number of cases these societies are located on some fixed area of the earth's surface. This location is not invariable; the gypsies are a striking example of a society without geographical location. Typically, the personnel of a society is recruited by birth from adult parents of the same society; but again there are instances to the contrary—the United States at certain times of its history, Canada, Australia, New Zealand, Israel, where much of the personnel has been recruited as adults.

Although it is so difficult to produce a verbal definition of society which will cover all known instances, it is in practice seldom difficult to discover by inspection and interrogation the society or societies to which any group of people belong. Membership of a society is always articulate among those who can speak; one definition of a society might be 'the largest group of people who mutually describe one another by the same term, the largest group habitually included in the first person plural, We'. The one exception to this definition is the political identification by continents which have arisen in the last decade or so—Asians, Africans and so on; but, as I have already stated, no single definition of society will cover all cases.

All human beings are members of some specific society, the only possible exception being the indifferently authenticated stories of wolf-children; there is no such person as that popular figment of the speculative imagination, the 'natural' man, the man uncontaminated by society. Nor is there any good ground for supposing that, even in the remotest past, *homo sapiens* lived without some rudimentary form of society; articulate speech, a biological characteristic of *homo sapiens*, implies a society; and the very long dependent phase of the human young demands a settled organization, almost certainly including mainly monogamous marriage whose preservation was socially sanctioned, for the successful rearing of enough children to replace the adults. Speculations about 'the origin of society' which posit a group of 'pre-social' adults should be treated as mythology, as 'Just-So' stories, whether they are written by Aristotle or Rousseau, Locke or Freud.

Consequently the phrase 'human nature' can only be properly used to describe the characteristics of man as a species, characteristics resulting from human physiology and neurology, and a few highly abstract characteristics of human psychology which have been discovered in all non-defective human beings: the processes of learning (many of which are shared with other mammals); dreams, which seem always to manifest the principles isolated by Freud; the derivatives of the long dependency of the young on adults; and speech. Of any human being (defectives, other than idiots, are only a partial exception) we can be sure that he or she was dependent as a child on adults, learns, dreams, and speaks; how the dependency of infancy and childhood was treated, how and what they learn, the contents of their dreams and the language they speak are predominantly determined by the society of which they are members. The variations of individual character are selected from the repertoire which the society makes available.

ii

Of these four universal human characteristics—dependency, learning, dreaming, speaking—speech is the least esoteric, the least involved in theoretical disputes; and I should like for a little to discuss language both directly and analogically. The greater number of human societies have a single language which can be used by all its members for inter-communication; and most usually one language is specific to one society. As with all generalizations about human societies, there are some obvious exceptions: quite a number of societies have a secondary esoteric language which is used by only a section of the population; and colonizing countries establish settlements which continue to use the language of the mother country while developing their idiosyncratic institutions. While these exceptions must be kept in mind, it can be stated that a language is a feature of every society, and that this language will structure the universe for its users in a way which will not be exactly paralleled by the users of any other language.

Linguists distinguish three basic components in all human languages: phonemes, vocabulary and syntax. The phonemes are the group of sounds selected, as it would seem, quite arbitrarily out of the total of sounds which the human vocal apparatus is capable of producing, to be meaningful in a specific language. The vocabulary represents the way the sounds are organized into permanent and relatively unambiguous groups—into words. Syntax represents the way the words are organized into patterns of relatively unambiguous communication.

Analogically, from the social point of view, these three elements can be considered to represent three stages of generalization. Although the phonemes are the simplest element, they are also the most individual; I think it is very rare for a person not to recognize the voice of a person he knows, even if he cannot distinguish the words, from the phonemes, the intonation or accent. Phonemes can be considered the analogue of individual psychology.

No recorded language is so simple that the total vocabulary is available to every speaker. Besides the vocabulary which is shared in common, each group within the society has its own specialized vocabulary which it uses for inter-communication within the group: technical vocabularies in the first place, but also esoteric vocabularies, and the private vocabularies of family jokes and allusions. Vocabularies sustain in-groups. Analogically, the study of vocabularies parallels the study of institutions, of social classes, of regional variations and of similar groupings within a society.

## The Concept of National Character

By contrast the syntax, the grammar, is common to all the speakers of a language with very minor variations; moreover it is learned very early in life, without either pupil or teacher being fully conscious or articulate about what is being communicated. Analogically, the study of syntax corresponds fairly closely with the study of national character; both are a search for the patterns which underlie and organize an almost infinite variation of behaviour.

Syntax, it may be remarked parenthetically, is one of the most remarkable and complex of all human inventions, so complex that, as far as is known, only once in human history up to the beginning of this century has the syntax of a language been fully analysed and described. This was done for Sanskrit a couple of millennia ago; and this Sanskrit grammar has subsequently been adapted for all Indo-European languages (and indeed for others too) with increasingly less precision and more arbitrariness, until the contemporary grammars of all languages studied today—apart from those of professional linguists—are presented as imperfect copies of the Platonic ideal of Sanskrit, so that the student has to learn parrot-fashion long lists of 'irregular' forms and modifiers, because the rules and generalizations derived from Sanskrit correspond so imperfectly with any contemporary practice. It is tempting to say that the views of 'human nature' which are so frequently advanced stand in much the same relation to the facts they are purporting to describe as do the rules of Sanskrit grammar to those of any living language.

While I am being parenthetical, I should like to express my surprise at the fashion in which the various groups of linguistic philosophers, such as the logical positivists, treat the syntax of their own language, or at most two or three related languages, as though it represented a human universal. They play their clever games with linguistic forms, particularly verbal modifiers, as though these were part of the structure of the universe. It strikes me as a somewhat provincial attitude.

Although syntax is so complicated, every non-defective human child learns the syntax of his native language very early in life, certainly in the first seven years. I do not think any detailed studies have been made of precisely how a child does acquire his syntax, to parallel the few careful studies which have been made as to the way he acquires his vocabulary. And within very small limits, the syntax is the same for all the speakers of the language. In a complex society there may be some minor variants in the syntax employed by people from different regions or social groups; and, if one region or group has higher prestige than the remainder, its syntax may be considered more correct or elegant than those of other regions or groups. But these variants are very minor, compared with the difference of phonemes or vocabulary which habitually distinguish classes and regions, when these are distinguished by speech. You would practically need two groups of phonemic signs to transcribe, say, the Cockney and Somerset dialects of English; there would be relatively little overlap in the vocabularies of an English barrow-boy and an English metaphysician; but the syntax of these four groups would be practically identical. None of them, to take simple examples from related languages, will give every noun a gender as the French do, employ the habitual sentence construction of the Germans, or relate all temporal modifications of verbs to the present, as do the Russians.

### iii

When a linguist starts the study and analysis of an unknown language, his technical equipment is a sensitive recording skill for putting down on paper the sounds he hears, and the comparative knowledge of the components of many languages, in the light of which he can be certain that this unknown language is organized into coherent and consistent patterns by syntax. He may well have no clue for any aspect of the syntax, but he has no doubt that the syntax does exist, can be analysed and, if correctly analysed, will be found to underlie any statement by any speaker of the language. He will then start to take dictation from any native-born speaker of the language willing to talk to him; he will subsequently take texts from people in different social positions—men and women, young and old, high status and low status and so on—to see what variants, if any, are found among these groups. He will try for a social scatter, but not for a statistical sample; the patterns, which all his previous experience assures him exist, will be demonstrated by all native-born speakers of the language.

The assumptions which underlie research into national character are completely analogous. The linguist assumes that patterns will regulate such topics as the relationship of actor to action and what is acted on; the indication of time of action; possession, direction and location; the connection between attribute and object and so on. The student of national character assumes that patterns will regulate such topics as subordination and superordination, authority and deference; attitudes to equals; the mechanisms of internal and social control; attitudes to pleasure or pain; expressiveness and impassivity; the funny, the ridiculous and the obscene; the scale of values, and so on. His immediate data are not spoken sentences but completed sequences of action, preferably observed, or else recounted by the actor or described by an onlooker. Works of art and imagination, in those societies which possess them, are treated as relevant data, though their relationship to the national character of their audience is a matter for investigation.

Apparently nowadays it is necessary to be defensive about the scientific implications of any deductions based upon the perception of pattern. For most people today 'science' is a synonym for physics and chemistry, and all scientific statements must approximate to mathematical statements of distribution. Most statements about the inanimate world fall into this category, with the possible exception of crystallography; but nearly all the organized knowledge of living matter is based on the recognition of pattern —genetics, physiology, ethology, electroencephalography, psychology. If the pattern is visible in space, so that its components can be measured, or can be translated into visual equivalents— such as electroencephalograms or chromosome-maps—then the fact that it is fundamentally patterns which are being studied can be overlooked. But if a pattern cannot be translated into a visual, and so measurable, form, or if it has a very large number of components, then any statement about such patterns is 'unscientific', 'impressionistic', 'literary'. In the present climate of opinion, such adverse judgements seem almost inevitable.

It must be admitted, too, that the ability to discover and be articulate about such patterns depends on a type of skill which somewhat resembles a type of aesthetic discrimination or skill in diagnosis. There are numerous groups of artifacts—paintings, pottery, textiles and so on—which are composed of a very large number of elements and of which no two may be exact duplicates. Specialists in these objects can usually locate them fairly unambiguously in place and time by discerning the pattern underlying the extremely heterogenous details. In such contexts the pattern is usually called 'style'. Once a style has been identified, the identifier can usually be articulate enough about the elements which compose it so that its recognition can be taught to others and can be demonstrated; but the process by which the existence of a style which links these heterogenous objects is first apprehended is certainly an obscure one, and would seem to depend on an idiosyncratic gift. Once the concept of style is admitted, just as once the concept of syntax is admitted, there will be people who will be able to discern whether, in any group of artifacts or sentences, one or more styles or syntaxes are represented.

iv

I have given two analogies to national character: the syntax of any language and the aesthetic style of elaborate artifacts produced at a certain place over a certain time. I should now perhaps try to state more directly what I understand by national character.

The most concise definition of national character that I can give is that it is a description of the learned motives, attitudes and predispositions which are shared by the members of a society, and which are manifested in their behaviour and are the bases of reference by which they judge their own conduct and that of others. These motives, attitudes and predispositions may be conscious or unconscious, articulate or inarticulate. They are coherently related to one another.

The study of national character is the study of motives underlying behaviour, not of the behaviour itself; and it is a study of

## The Concept of National Character

learned motives, not of innate drives or instincts. I can perhaps make this distinction clearer by a consideration of the elaboration of a universal innate drive, hunger.

To keep alive, any member of the genus *homo sapiens* needs certain quantities of food. The nutritionists can define on a fairly abstract level the chemical constituents of the food necessary to maintain health and growth. At regular intervals human beings will feel pangs of hunger. But within limits social learning will determine how long these intervals before feeling hunger are and when in the twenty-four hours in the day they will occur. As far as I know, no society in which there is not an actual shortage of food has restricted its members to one meal a day; but there seems to be a gamut of from two meals to seven or eight in the twenty-four hours. Whereas people in one society may habitually fast for eight or nine hours before being conscious of hunger, in another they may only go for two or three.

This patterning of hunger is *not* an aspect of national character; nor is the selection of the available foods within the area which the society has decided are suitable for human beings. These are aspects of culture and can be determined by observation only; the determination of meal-times and the selection or rejection of various foods probably have origins in the past but it is almost impossible to discover them. People will tell you that it is impossible to do a day's hard work without a good meal inside one, or that it is impossible to do a day's hard work if one fills one's stomach before one starts; that milk and milk products are one of the most healthy of foods, or one of the most disgustingly repugnant of foods, or a food which is good in itself but will contaminate any other food it comes in contact with, and so on; but it is only very rarely that such beliefs can be accounted for.

But when one comes to the attitudes towards food and hunger, then one comes nearer the domain of national character. Hunger is a physiological response; the interpretation of the stomach cramps and other concomitants of hunger is to a very large extent patterned by the society in which an individual grows up. Mild hunger may be considered a pleasant and necessary precondition for providing a good appetite for a meal, or an unpleasant and frightening warning that the ordered routine of life is threatened, with anxiety which will mount steadily unless some sort of snack is forthcoming. Similarly, severe hunger may be an unpleasant feeling which a Proper Man will ignore or an intimation of catastrophe which threatens all other values including manhood itself.

These of course are only some of the variants of the ways in which a society can pattern the interpretation of the feeling of hunger, and they may appear trivial; but the reports of the behaviour of members of different societies under conditions of semi-starvation, such as for example the prison camps in Burma or Korea, suggest that this may be a major component of what is rather vaguely called 'morale'. And if soldiers have to be protected from quite mild hunger, the mobility of a force, the amount of transport it needs, and the size of its service 'tail' will all be affected.

v

It is not my intention to treat in any detail the ways in which different societies have patterned the attitudes towards the gratification or frustration of the various physiological needs and potentialities which characterize human beings. The subject is a vast one; for no society has been described in which these attitudes are not patterned, in which personal choice is allowed more than a very small range of alternatives out of the gamut which one society or another makes available.

One of the general characteristics of human beings appears to be that they learn by analogy, that two actions or processes are felt to be similar because they have some similar components. These components are often of a highly abstract nature—giving, withholding, joining, separating and so on; they are very often indicated by verbal metaphor. When we talk about 'getting our teeth into a problem' or 'digesting a piece of information' (for example) we are in some fashion making an analogy between abstract ideas and gobbets of food, between the way food sustains the body and ideas nourish the intelligence. This analogy—which at the most abstract level is concerned with 'taking in' or 'receptivity'—would seem to be one of the more wide-spread; the elaboration of food in complicated cooking and the elaboration of ideas in a high evaluation of discussion occur together as paired characteristics in more than one society; France and China are well-known examples. One can also easily find pairs of the opposite tendencies: societies which disapprove of both fancy cooking and fancy talk.

Because of this human characteristic of drawing analogies, it is nearly always possible to find a connection between the typical physiological and family experiences which members of a society undergo in their first few years of life, and the social and political organizations and aspirations of the society, its values and its ethics, its techniques for social control and self-control and so on. But though these connections can be found, it is not necessary to do so, or at least to make these connections explicit. It is in the first place a research technique; by tracing out as exactly as is possible the lessons and experiences which the newborn members of the society receive in their first years of life, one is dealing with a far smaller number of variables than would be the case if one only examined adult values and aspirations, and these are variables which can be compared from one society to another; and by holding on to the sheet-anchor of the human body and the small cohabiting family one avoids the risk of flying off into the empyrean, of imputing to societies aspirations and notions which cannot be related to the behaviour of any identified human beings: the danger of getting bogged down in the mysticism of 'the racial unconscious', the 'super-organic', and all the other high-sounding phrases which can so easily be used as a substitute for clear statements and precise observation. But, as I have said, the use of these analogies is above all a research technique; it is not necessary, from the point of view of communication perhaps not even desirable, to spell them out in detail. Such detail is useful and necessary for the psychologist, the sociologist, the anthropologist; for people outside these disciplines, it is the description of coherent patterns of adult values, predispositions and attitudes which gives relevance to the study of national character.

## vi

The concept of national character becomes relevant in any situation which involves people reared in more than one society; and in any theoretical statement about human behaviour or motivation which is meant to have validity beyond the society in which it is made. If both speaker and audience (or however the situation be structured) are members of the same society, then the implications of national character can be left unspoken and implicit; but as soon as more than one society is involved, then explicitness becomes essential if inter-communication is to be successful. The most immediately important setting for cross-national communication is international politics.

I think it would be generally agreed that our predominant values as a society are safety, justice, and a modicum of prosperity; and we believe that, if these goals are achieved for all, or the great majority, of the citizens, they will be contented, honest and law-abiding, supervising their own conduct and that of their neighbours with a lively conscience, internalized standards of right and wrong which they will apply in all circumstances. Now I think this true of the English today, and not only true of the English as a nation, but of the English as individuals and as family-members; in their private lives the concept of justice is given the synonym of fairness; and 'it's not fair' is the one reproach against which we nearly all think we have to defend ourselves.

I repeat, I think this is true of the English; but I also think that it is true of very few other peoples, and that most of our difficulties in dealing with foreign peoples derive from our acting on the assumption that they share our motives, our values, our national character. Of course, this ascribing of one's own motives and values to others is not a peculiarly English failing; it is nearly universal. Where people are very conscious of their physical appearance, they may ascribe different motives and values to people with a different skin-colour; but these motives and values are nearly always diabolized, and represent the rejected aspects of their own character, rather than any objective

## The Concept of National Character

assessment of the national characters of the people they are describing. What the Boers, for example, say about the African Negroes can tell us, if we can interpret, quite a lot about the Boers but nothing about the Africans; what recently independent people say about colonizers is similarly informative about the speakers.

This colour-consciousness apart, the belief that all people share one's own motives, values and aspirations is very generally held: it underlies the two great missionary movements of today (as it has always underlain the missionary movements of the past): communism and democracy. Both these movements make assumptions about 'human nature' which have justification in their countries of origin but, I would argue, no universal validity. Russian communism assumes that people are unable to control themselves, and feel safest and most secure when they are strictly controlled and supervised; Anglo-American democracy assumes that most people are capable of controlling themselves and of regulating their own conduct, and feel safest and most secure when the apparatus of external control and supervision is kept to the lowest possible strength.

To the best of my knowledge, neither of these assumptions has universal validity; and I believe that the democratic assumption is the more limited in its application. The democratic assumption is founded on the belief that most of the citizens have a strict conscience based on categorical imperatives of right conduct, in the light of which individuals will control and judge their own behaviour and regulate that of their fellows. As far as all the evidence available to me goes, the strict conscience is one of the rarer components of individual and national character; although it has been reported for one or two primitive societies (such as the Manus of the Admiralty Islands) it seems to have become wide-spread only in the last three or four centuries in countries where the state religion has been some form of reformed Christianity—Protestantism or reformed Catholicism—which has placed the responsibility for personal conduct—for salvation—on the individual without intermediary between himself and his God, and has made parents answerable for the character of their children. A *sine qua non* for the development of a strict conscience would appear to be that parents should demand absolute standards of conduct from their children and should consistently reward and punish, give and withhold love to their children in accordance with their children's adherence to these standards. This type of parental behaviour is uncommon; in most societies parents either maintain an even attitude towards their children, or vary capriciously according to the parents' feelings at the moment, rather than in response to the children's behaviour.

If the strict conscience which is the basis of our type of democracy is rare, the sense of sin which seems to underlie Russian character, whether Czarist or Communist, is even more uncommon; indeed it has not, so far, been reported for any other society. What is idiosyncratic about this sense of sin is its all-or-none character: either you are completely in the right, blissfully enveloped in the protecting arms of God or History; or, if you deviate even to the slightest degree, you are completely in the wrong, damned, lost, execrable. One step off the right path, and disaster follows, as one misplaced rock will produce an avalanche; but most people do not know the right path, and can only be safe under the surveillance of guides who have made a special study of Truth. Only with such supervision can one be safe from the potential dangers of one's own strength and one's own ignorance. Where the Truth exists and is known, compromise is essentially a dereliction to be abhorred and to be resisted as much as may be.

Far more general than either a strict conscience or a sense of sin is a concern for renown. This may take a great variety of forms but seems to fall into two major classes: a desire to increase one's renown in the eyes of one's fellows, a sense of pride; and a fear of losing one's renown in the eyes of one's fellows, a sense of shame. Because we have had numerous dealings with the people of Japan and China we do pay some acknowledgement to the sense of shame; but we call it 'face', and by using this pseudo-ethnological term, we reduce the strongest emotion which such people recognize to a quaint and superficial feeling of no great importance. At the present time, it is probably the most dangerous word in the political vocabulary.

When the desire to increase renown—the sense of pride—is

## The Concept of National Character

the major motive of a society, we find it very hard indeed to reach even an intellectual understanding; it seems to us contrary to common sense that renown should really be preferred to our values of safety, justice or prosperity, that all these will be willingly hazarded to gain fame or wipe away an insult. Very many of the difficulties which have bedevilled our international relations in recent years have sprung from our failure to recognize the strength of the sense of pride of the people we are dealing with and the paramount importance they give to it.

III

*Pride, Shame, and Guilt*
*(1959)*

QUITE A NUMBER of anthropologists, and a few psycho-analysts who have used anthropological data or themselves experienced non-European cultures (notably Erik Erikson) have classified societies according to the predominance of one or another mechanism of internal or social control, the mechanism by which people regulate their own conduct, and which others can invoke to obviate or to punish conduct which transgresses the norms prevalent in a given society at a given period. These mechanisms fall into three major categories: a sense of sin, a sense of shame or pride, and a sense of guilt.

Ontogenetically, in the life of a human being, these three mechanisms represent a temporal sequence. A sense of sin is the most primitive, probably developing before the achievement of coherent speech. It is an all-or-none affair; either one is overwhelmed with sin, completely worthless, wicked, and unloveable, or one is blissfully innocent, oceanically enveloped in a loving universe. A sense of shame or pride on the other hand is based on speech, on the expressed or imagined judgements of identified others: one's self-esteem, one's feeling of being at rights with the world, depends on the esteem of others, of the world. With a sense of guilt we are all, in the Western world, familiar; we introject absolute standards of right and wrong; a part of ourselves sits, as it were, in judgement on our behaviour and even our impulses, and punishes us with feelings of anxiety and guilt if we transgress these internalized imperatives, even though there be no chance of these transgressions becoming known to anyone else. According to orthodox Freudian theory, this sense of guilt, this self-regulating internal conscience, develops after the completion of the Oedipal phase, around the age of six or seven. It seems probable that everybody who has developed a sense of guilt has also passed through the earlier stages, and has at least residual senses of sin, shame and pride; but it is by no means certain that in those societies which rely predominantly on these latter mechanisms most people also develop a sense of guilt.

This distinction is not merely of academic psychological interest. When we talk about democracy, we habitually mean the types of democracy which have developed in the predominantly Protestant societies on either side of the Northern Atlantic; and these democracies depend for their continuing functioning on the fact that the great majority of their citizens have a lively sense of guilt, so that they will supervise their own conduct in the light of categorical imperatives, and will not give way to the temptations inherent in any position of power, influence or prestige. People can be trusted to function properly without continuous supervision from others, because they supervise themselves. Bureaucracy, whether of government or business, works adequately and fairly because of these internalized controls in the great majority of their members. In the absence of these internalized controls as the major self-regulating mechanism, it is, to say the least, uncertain whether the spirit of a modern democracy can survive, even though the forms can be readily exported and imported.

It can, indeed, be argued that the ways in which any society can be organized in a relatively permanent fashion are dependent on the mechanisms of internal control which are most prevalent among the members of that society; but when I have advanced this hypothesis to audiences in Britain or America who have a sense of guilt, I have always been conscious of a failure to communicate to them what is implied by 'shame' or 'pride' as a predominant mechanism. With us these feelings have, comparatively, little strength; there are enclaves, such as the public schools, or the traditional armed services, where these mechanisms are more frequently evoked, and counter-mores groups, criminals or fascists, who suppress from consciousness the feelings of guilt; but for the vast majority shame and pride are fairly intermittent painful or pleasant feelings, not the motives by which we would build our lives; and it is, apparently, very difficult to imagine that members of other societies feel very differently.

Incidentally, there is much less difficulty in communicating what is implied in a sense of sin. Even though, among Protestants, 'sin' is most frequently used to signify guilt in an ecclesiastic setting, the great nineteenth-century Russian novelists are well known, and their descriptions of a sense of sin convincing. The only society which has been investigated which used a sense of sin as a major mechanism of social control was the traditional peasant society of Czarist Great Russia.

Pride and shame have had no Tolstoi, no Dostoievski. When I have been asked to recommend books which would give a feeling of what was meant by a 'shame culture' or a 'pride culture', my choice has so far been limited either to ethnographic monographs, which tend to lack the literary graces that can command belief, or else the classical Chinese novels such as *Golden Lotus* or *Dream of the Red Chamber* which are so exotic in detail, and so distant in time and place, that they too fail to carry conviction. But this gap is now filled, at least as far as a 'pride culture' is concerned, by Milovan Djilas's quite remarkable autobiography, *Land Without Justice*,[1] with its vivid account of traditional Montenegrin life.

This book has a number of merits apart from the aspects I am dealing with here. It is beautifully written, and one can believe that the anonymous translator has, as William Jovanovitch says in the preface, caught Djilas's evocative poetic style. It throws considerable illumination on the historical development of Yugoslavia in the years covered by the story, 1911–1928: and the other writings and present fate of the author make it an important political document. But these aspects are not my concern now; I want to try to isolate those features of traditional Montenegrin society into which Djilas was born and in which he spent the first ten years of his life and which seem to me to convey, more vividly than any book I have ever read, what is implied in being a member of a 'pride' culture.

---

[1] Methuen. Published in the U.S.A. by Harcourt Brace and Co., 1959.

## Pride, Shame, and Guilt

Montenegro is a desolate, barren, mountainous country in which the first towns were built in the second half of the nineteenth century. Through most of modern times it was vaguely under Turkish suzerainty, the frontier where Christian and Moslem met and massacred one another, for a few decades an independent kingdom. It had no exploited natural resources; the sparse population subsisted on a very primitive level of agriculture and herding, supplemented by loot and booty. A money economy, apparently, started operating in the last quarter of the nineteenth century, and literacy came in the twentieth. Djilas tells us that his mother learned to read in 1940, at the age of sixty. The only art which was at all developed was that of the folk bard, the *guslar*. 'This land may not be good for living, but it is fine for telling tales.'

When Djilas was a schoolboy, around 1921, the old bards, the *guslars*, were already a rarity, though there was one old man in the same townlet as the school.

> Listening to his songs, I, like others, lived with the deeds of folk epic and tales. I was intoxicated most of all by the feeling that I, too, was a part of that great narrative, which shone through the living present, the past, and the future of nations. There was something austere and exalted in the often monotonous repetition of images and phrases in the *guslar*'s chant. Again and again, he depicted the trials and misfortunes through which we must live as a people, and showed us how to become men—to sing, to make merry, to keen, to create, to invent, to produce, and, above all, to guard our honour and our good name.

In this short quotation are summarized many of the themes which characterize a culture built on pride, such as that of Montenegro. First, perhaps, is the idiosyncratic attitude to *time*, the constant awareness of oneself as a link between the remembered past, and the expected future, with *renown*, public speech or song, as the bridge which alone can link past, present and future. Next is the emphasis on the *proper way of acting*—no deed is intrinsically good or bad in itself (this is the most obvious contrast with the categorical imperatives of a culture founded on a sense of guilt); it is how the deed is done, to whom, and under what circumstances, which determine whether it is a subsequent source of *pride* or *shame*. Finally, in the list of the qualities which make for a proper man, there is a complete absence of what we should consider moral or civic virtues; the man is not enjoined to be righteous or just or charitable, to prosper or to be a good citizen; he should do well those things that a man must do in public, and, above all, guard his *honour* and his *good name*.

In Montenegro this meant murder, of the right man in the right place in the right fashion. Not only were Christians (in any religious sense of the word, this is a misnomer; practice of the Orthodox faith was nearly non-existent) and Moslems constantly killing one another in ambush and small affrays; Christians, organized into patrilineal clans and tribes, carried on perpetual blood feuds with their hereditary enemies.

> The word blood meant something different in the language I learned in childhood from what it means today, especially the blood of one's clan and tribe. It meant the life we lived, a life that flowed from generations of forebears who still lived in the tales handed down. Their blood coursed in all the members of the clan, and in us, too. Someone had now spilled that eternal blood, and it had to be avenged if we wished to keep from drowning in shame before the other clans. Such a yearning has no limits in space, no end in time. . . .
>
> Vengeance—this is a breath of life one shares from the cradle with one's fellow clansmen, in both good fortune and bad, vengeance from eternity. Vengeance was the debt we paid for the love and sacrifice our forebears and fellow clansmen bore for us. It was the defence of our honour and good name and the guarantee of our maidens. It was our pride before others; our blood was not water that one could spill. It was, moreover, our pastures and springs—more beautiful than anyone else's—our family feasts and births. . . .
>
> Vengeance is not hatred, but the wildest and sweetest kind of drunkenness, both for those who must wreak vengeance and for those who wish to be avenged. . . .

## Pride, Shame, and Guilt

This land was never one to reward virtue, but it was always strong in taking revenge and punishing evil. Revenge is its greatest delight and glory. . . .

The story of any Montenegrin family is made up of traditions about the lives of ancestors who distinguished themselves in some special way, most frequently through heroism. These traditions, spiritually so close to one another, reach back into the remote past, to the legendary founders of clan and tribe. And since there are no unheroic tribes and clans, particularly in the eyes of their members, there is no family without its renowned heroes and leaders. . . .

My forebears were drummed into my head from earliest childhood, as was the case with all my countrymen. I can recite ten generations without knowing anything in particular about them. In that long line I am but a link, inserted only that I might form another to preserve the continuity of the family, the people, and the human race. Otherwise the earth would be an unpeopled desert with none to tell of it.

Where this concept of pride differs from the traditional aristocratic pattern of feudal Europe is that there is no division of the population into exhibitors and spectators, the knights and barons exhibiting their prowess, the common people observing and applauding. Here every male permanently holds both roles; every man may hope to be a hero, and he will be part of the consensus which will determine the heroic status of his fellows.

Moreover, your own heroism is to a considerable extent determined by the heroism of your enemy. It is here, perhaps more than in any other situation, that the contrast between the culture of pride and the culture of guilt is thrown into greatest emphasis. If we are to fight to kill, we must be filled with righteous anger, must feel assured that our enemy is so wicked and base that he has forfeited all human rights. It is impractical to love our enemies, impossible to admire them. But for the Montenegrins, as for some of the American Indians of the Great Plains, the best enemy was he whom one could admire with one's whole heart. Of an incident which occurred when he was seven, Djilas writes:

It was little wonder that we children mourned for Iso Boljetini. Father mourned him too, though he was proud that his group had felled him. It was a special kind of sorrow, admiration rather for a fearless hero of wild Albania who had fought to the end on a bare field and an empty road, neither begging nor forgiving, upright and without protection. There was this admiration in our sorrow, too. If one had to die, it would be good to fall like Iso Boljetini. Let it be remembered, at least by those who have seen and heard it.

Father Djilas took Boljetini's large Mauser, with its silver-mounted handle, and kept it as his most precious souvenir. It was the boast of the Montenegrin men that they got all their arms from their fallen enemies; but this was not so much for use as for reverence.

Boljetini is not the only enemy who was praised while Djilas was a small boy, and whose memory is celebrated in these pages. 'The greatest heroism was shown by the Moslem Huso Mehotin, a renowned freebooter against the Montenegrins.' Todor, the brigand and outlaw,

> never laughed much nor was he much of a talker. He was terrible only at first glance. He liked to play with children and did not even keep them from going through his ammunition and weapons. Towards the old people he was attentive and obliging. He was the soul of simple courage and goodness. [He was] one of the most distinguished rebels in all Montenegro.

Only with a noble enemy can one attain true heroism oneself. If the enemy has not made a good death, one has not oneself made a good name. The blood feuds were carried on with treachery, deceit and trickery—there are horrifying stories in the early sections of the book—but though these gratify revenge, they did not constitute heroism: they were not talked about. For Montenegrins 'something becomes not only great but remarkable only if it is sung about and praised.'

Silence is the sanction applied to deeds done in the wrong way, at the wrong time, or to the wrong person; and in bitter silence are preserved the unwitnessed shames one has suffered. When the Moslem Sandjak was being looted by the Christians, Uncle Mirko

> forced a Moslem child to squeeze through the bent bars of the window of a mosque and to hand him the carpets. This was charged to Uncle as a great sin and shame, like desecrating a church, and we never talked about it in our house.

When Djilas was three years old

> In honour of something, a cannon was to be fired. Everyone made a terrible face and stopped their ears as though something dangerous was going to fly into them. Father's orderly buried my head between his legs, and I stopped my ears myself. Why did he bury my head in so shameful a spot? I was ashamed because of this but I was afraid to pull away my head. I never told anyone about my shame, nor about the spot where my head had been buried.

Chronologically, this is the second clear memory of his life which Djilas recounts. The first memory is less unusual:

> A boy had locked a door from the inside and found himself stuck between the wall and the bed. Through the window, from the stairs, they promise him everything and beg him to open the door. He is no longer a little boy, they tell him, he is two years old. He comprehends. He would like to do this great deed, but he cannot get loose.

This first incident, the appeal to the little boy's pride in his growth, might have occurred in any society, though I should think it would not often be so vividly remembered; but consider the training which the little boy of three must have undergone to have felt the shame which is recounted in the incident of the cannon! Although Djilas does not detail this, it seems as though, as in traditional peasant Poland, the body is divided from birth into noble and shameful parts, in Poland the head being the noblest and the feet the most shameful.

The early training was extremely severe and consistent.

And Mother beats us. If she cannot catch us during the day, she beats us when we are asleep. The switch cuts into the flesh and one sleeps on. And when we awaken, she demands our promise that we will never again do what we did. Or else the beating is continued.

It would be easy to promise that we would not do what we did if only we could feel truly guilty for what we did. But since we do not feel guilty it is better to lose some sleep and endure the beating to the end.

It is not clear from the narrative whether this harsh beating of the little boys—Milovan must have been five or six, his brother a year or so older—was intended to make them yield, or to harden their wills, as though one were tempering hot iron, and the good mother's success was shown by her children not yielding to her. My impression is that the latter was the true aim: a boy-child must be made spiritually proud and unyielding as soon as possible. I also get the impression that no allowances were made for boys past infancy because of their youth: some feats are beyond their present strength and skill; but they should think and feel and command themselves like men. When Djilas was five, in 1916, one of the conquering Austrians

> told Father that he was under orders to escort him to the command post at Kolašin, supposedly to give some information. All of us at home already suspected, knew, that Father would not return. But nobody cried. Our pain was cold and full of hatred and scorn.

This tempering of the will produced a strong, shining, but very brittle character. While their pride was untarnished, the Montenegrins were most of them most of the time noble, generous and manly; but if their pride were broken they were without self-respect or self-restraint, without justice and without mercy. Everybody, it must be repeated, had a just source of pride:

> Just as every family in the village was proud of something, so every camp in the mountains was proud if its bull lorded

## Pride, Shame, and Guilt

it over the others, or if its lads could heave stones further or outleap the lads of other clans. Good house-holders as they were, my uncles valued their good cattle as much as their own good name.

There was a drought and famine in the country:

> Fear of starvation is frequently stronger with those who have something than with those who do not. Those who have, talk about how they have nothing. The others keep proudly silent and endure, as though they had some other great wealth, but wealth that cannot be eaten. . . .
> (Among the starving) were poor people who had no house; they lived, both summer and winter, in a shack. Yet Radovije held himself proudly, as though he were in the thick of a battle, holding aloft the flag which not even death would force him to let out of his hands. In his poverty the flag and pride were all that remained to him of his forebears.

This proud society was destroyed as a society when Montenegro was conquered by the Austrians and Bulgarians in 1915.

> A whole people—the Montenegrins—which understood life in terms of war and glory, stopped fighting. A people's army and state had ceased to be.
> The fall of the Montenegrin state did not blunt the forces of heroism and of manhood, and it seemed to sharpen others—forces of violence, untamed and unrestrained. . . . Men became bad, rotten, unwilling to give one another air to breathe. Bestiality and scandal at home, in the village, quickly crowded out of our minds the national tragedy. These vices were our own, Montenegrin and domestic.

It was not, it must be emphasized, the defeat which produced these vices and violence, it was having survived the defeat.

The grandeur of the holocaust of Mojkovac was not in victory, for there was none. The enemy was simply stopped, while the state dissolved at the same time. The grandeur of this battle lay in the expression of an undying and inexplicable heroism and sacrifice, which held that it was easier to die than to submit to shame—for in death there is neither defeat nor shame.

After the end of the war, a representative of the new state of Yugoslavia destroyed two rebel clans by making them survive shame.

Picking about forty of the arrested men . . . he had this group taken separately to the schoolhouse and beat them, one by one, with his own fists and boots, cuffing them and pulling their noses and whiskers. . . . The whole clan had been humbled, crushed. Boško then called them all to a meeting and established order and obedience.
The Rovčani were treated with cruelty and insult. Their houses were burned down; they were pillaged and beaten. The women had cats sewn in their skirts and the cats were beaten with rods. The soldiers mounted astride the backs of old men and forced them to carry them across the stream. Property and honour and the past—all these were trampled on.

This last quotation recalls a similar tale from Oceania, where the men were forced to stand under a bridge, while the women walked over the bridge, *over their heads*. This was so profoundly humiliating that the men refused to produce further children, and the tribe died out.
Nations, clans and individuals can be destroyed through shame, turned into vicious thieves and murderers, or reduced to docile robots, or to complete despair.

Mihailo was thrown in jail and beaten. From that time on, he began to withdraw from Communism and into himself, out of shame that he had been beaten. Everyone noticed and laughed.

Mihailo was Milovan Djilas' godfather. He had converted his godson to Communism when the boy was seven years old.
It is extraordinary that Djilas should be able to give so detailed a picture of a society which stopped its full functioning

before he was ten years old, and in which he only participated very intermittently after that age. At ten he was sent to live with relations in the small town of Kolašin to attend an elementary school, and then three years later to the larger town of Berane to high school. It is perhaps because this proud life practically stopped at the same time as he was sent away that it has remained so complete in his memory.

Another possible reason for this remarkably complete picture is that the life and values of the Montenegrin male seem to have been extraordinary simple and uncomplicated, so that there was little which a ten-year-old boy could not learn. He might not yet have developed the strength and skill necessary for the simple agriculture, hunting, herding, warfare, building; but there was practically nothing he could not understand. Some men might develop special gifts—Djilas's grandfather was a healer, Djilas himself was a poet, would, surely, have been a *guslar*—; but the way of a man was uncomplicated, devoted to the single aim of good repute.

The one male relationship which Djilas was too young to participate in, and whose role he consequently fails to make entirely clear, is 'blood brotherhood', the ceremonial bond between two otherwise related men. For Djilas this is the purest love of all, even purer than the love between brother and sister. In his schooldays he comes across such a pair:

> They were more than real brothers. Because of this kind of love, which had been a more frequent thing in earlier times, everyone held them in high regard and esteem, despite the fact that they were not particularly pleasant fellows. They were like a remnant of something long past and distant, a folk song that still walked the earth.

Somewhat uncommonly for a society in this stage of technical development, the roles of women seem to have been more complicated and various than were those of men. They apparently had an almost exclusive concern with the economy, with petty trading and techniques of production, which they had to carry on unaided. As a young boy, Djilas contrasts the behaviour of his own male kin with that of the Serbians, the Metešani, who 'did not beat their wives, or at least they did so only rarely. With them, a man did not regard it as shameful to take a woman's place in any task.'

Kinship dictated the way women should behave to any related male; before marriage they lived a life of strict rules which decreed that, with unrelated males 'they can dance and joke in public but must be virtuous and unapproachable in private.' They were allowed to be tender only with their brothers, and, in a different way, with their grandchildren.

> Montenegrin women love their brothers—even their cousins if they have no brothers—with a love that combines a feminine feeling at its purest and subtlest with a primeval determination to preserve the breed from which one has sprung. That tongue of stone and fire which knows no words of endearment becomes transformed in the mouth of a sister into an incredible softness and cooing. A sister is not something greater than a mother, or less—but different. She has a more direct and irrational warmth in her love for her brother. A sister will quarrel with her brother, but she will never break with him. She does not share with him in the property. The family has no obligation towards her, or she towards it. She simply gives and accepts love and goodness.

Although she treats some cousins as brothers, and in the absence of appropriate males may even occasionally perform an heroic deed in the blood feud—for other cousins, the Montenegrin girl was, before either were married, available as a partner in sexual games and exploration (not, apparently, including intercourse). Djilas does not make clear how these cousinly roles are differentiated, whether by the type of connecting relations, or by the distance from a common ancestor. A similar distinction is reported for the men who live in the hills of the Southern United States, where cousins are classified as 'kissin' cousins' and 'crackin' cousins'.

In marriage there seems to have been extremely little tenderness, with the stick in the hands of the husband and the 'tongue of stone and fire' in the mouth of the wife. Even when love was felt, it could not be demonstrated. Djilas recounts that when his

## Pride, Shame and Guilt

father returned from being a prisoner of war 'Mother, to hide her tears—for it was not becoming for a woman to show before others too much happiness at her husband's coming—ran out, into the woods.' From shame, too, she has to bear her children outside the house; and I have already described how severe she has to be as a mother.

If she bears sons, and they too have sons, she comes into her own.

> Grandmother was one of those Montenegrin women whom no calamity or catastrophe could keep from fulfilling the purpose her life was meant to fulfil—to breed male heirs and preserve from ruin the house into which she had come. . . . Without such women, and they were all like that, this people would not even exist.

If she only bears daughters, or is sterile, her life is completely miserable.

Djilas's grandmother was a 'wise woman', in contact with the frightening, non-Christian, supernatural world of evil spirits, witches and vampires. She was also able to call for supernatural help on the soul of a drowned man which 'was wandering over the earth, unshriven but just, seeking peace'. I know of no other instance of this belief.

Montenegrin women, it would appear, can cause embarrassment, and even shame, to their menfolk if they misbehave, but they cannot destroy their pride or their honour. Indeed the surname of Djilas, which means 'a jumper', comes from an over-frisky widow among the paternal ancestry.

> This irrepressible widow was named Djisna and her sons were named after her. At first they were angry, and blood was shed over that nickname, but none the less it held, as in the case of so many others. My grandfather Aleksa finally accepted the surname as his own. He could afford to do so because he was so renowned that his heroism denied any shame.

The fact that a man's honour could not be destroyed by his women-folk's misbehaviour put the Montenegrins into a stronger position than that of the traditional Greek peasants, whose honour, it may be rather coarsely said, was kept between the legs of their women-folk, particularly their sisters. Because their pride, their *filotimo*, is not in their own control, Greek men are, or were, far more vulnerable than the Montenegrins.

I have not treated this account of a vanished society of murderous mountaineers in such detail purely because of its intrinsic interest. It offers, I hope, a vivid paradigm of the psychological predispositions current, in one variation or another, in a great part of what are called 'the uncommitted nations', above all in the lands bordering the Eastern Mediterranean which were formerly under Turkish suzerainty, and the lands of further Asia which were or are under Chinese suzerainty or influence. In much of this world a concern for renown, the hope of heroic stature, and a duty to wipe out the shames of past history have far greater strength than the desire for prosperity and justice which we tend to consider the main motives which should govern the behaviour of politician and citizen alike. If our negotiators could develop some feeling for the great sensitivity of these people's pride, where an insulting phrase can outweigh millions of dollars of aid and scores of years of good administration; where the past is never really dead until old scores have been paid and past humiliations wiped clean—not necessarily with blood, but at least with words 'as soft as feathers on a wound': then much of the hostility and resentment which so needlessly bedevil our relationships with these people and governments could be avoided. As human animals, all men everywhere have the same basic needs; but as members of society they differ greatly in the value they put on different goals. If we can afford the respect to pride and shame that we demand for conscience the world will be an easier, and a safer, place to live in.

## IV

## *The Remaking of Man*
## *(1956)*

ONE OF THE most urgent problems—perhaps the most urgent problem—facing the world today is how to change the character and behaviour of adult human beings within a single generation. This problem of rapid transformation has underlaid every revolution (as opposed to *coups d'état*) at least from the time of the English Revolution in the seventeenth century, which sought to establish the Rule of the Saints by some modifications in the governing institutions and the laws they promulgated; and from this point of view every revolution has failed. The successful revolution will place power in the hands of members of a different group within the society, perhaps modify the distribution of property and the crimes which the law selects for punishment; but the character of the mass of the population, their attitudes and expectations, change apparently very little; as revolutions recede in history what appears most striking is the continuity of the society of the country, as the new institutions are adapted to the existing adult characters of the population, rather than the adult characters modified to the new institutions.

Up till the present century revolutions were typically concerned with the internal arrangements of one political unit, one country; but the nearly simultaneous development of world-wide communications and world-wide ideologies—democracy, socialism, communism—has posed the problem not merely of how to transform ourselves—whoever 'ourselves' may be—but how to transform others; in different settings these 'others' are the underdeveloped countries, or the uncommitted nations, or the Asian and African peoples, or even, with messianic exaltation, the whole world.

Simultaneously with the revolutions which so signally failed to establish the Rule of the Saints, or the Reign of Reason, or the Classless Society, a remarkably successful transformation (in most cases) was being effected in individual Europeans who left their countries of origin to populate the new 'white' dominions which were established in the less inhabited portions of the temperate zones; in the first instance the United States of America, and also, following similar patterns, Canada, Australia, New Zealand were able to accept large numbers of individuals or families from the most varied backgrounds and transform them within a generation into good citizens of their countries of adoption, with changed values, habits, and expectations.

This successful transformation of millions of immigrants into Americans, Canadians, or the like was conducted without theory, without much ratiocination, as it were, intuitively or unconsciously; claims were made for the evident superiority and attraction of democracy, freedom or opportunity, the American Constitution or British parliamentary government; but while the process was at its most vigorous, little attempt was made to discover how the transformations actually occurred, how the new values and expectations were adopted and maintained. Only when the flood of immigration had slowed down to a trickle was some attempt made to analyse the process of transformation for immigrants to the United States, and the key-role, in that particular setting, of the woman school-teacher as a model and exemplar of proper American behaviour pin-pointed.[1] In our original thinking, this role of the school-teacher, and the derivatives of this situation, were idiosyncratic to the culture of the United States; we did not, and do not, have comparable data for the processes of transformation within the British Commonwealth; and it did not seem possible at the time to extrapolate from this unique situation.

A further clue was provided by my hypothesis that the very great modifications in the behaviour of the English urban working classes in the nineteenth century from violence and lawlessness

[1] *And Keep Your Powder Dry*. By Margaret Mead, Chapter III (New York, 1942).
*The Americans*. By Geoffrey Gorer, Chapter III (London, 1948).

## The Remaking of Man

to gentleness and law-abiding resulted from the peculiar invention of the English police forces,[1] which provided in the policeman an exemplar of self-control which the mass of the population could emulate and use as a model. This hypothesis was not provable; it was based on the one hand on the historical facts of the transformation of urban behaviour, and, on the other, the very great admiration for and identification with the police which I discovered in my large samples.

These two hypotheses only dealt with portions of single societies —the new United States immigrants, the urban English working class; we had not, till now, a model, or even working hypotheses, of the way in which a whole society can be transformed within a single generation. With the publication of Margaret Mead's *New Lives for Old*,[2] the whole approach to the problem is radically altered, and our ability to think about the remaking of man in a single generation greatly enhanced; for this is an account of a society which has transformed itself within twenty-five years, and which Dr. Mead had studied in its primitive state. The leading men of today were the small boys of twenty-five years ago who were described in such vivid detail in *Growing Up in New Guinea* (New York and London, 1930).

This book, together with the associated more technical papers by Dr. Mead and Dr. Fortune, dealt with the Manus of the Admiralty Islands. In 1928, and for untold generations before that, the Manus could properly be described as 'primitives' or 'savages', people with a technology little more complicated than that of our Stone-Age ancestors, speaking an idiosyncratic language completely understood only by the few thousand members of their society, following a religion which no other society shared, in which the censorious ghosts of dead ancestors, communicating through mediums, punished every infringement of the rules governing economic and sexual transactions. They had trade relations with neighbouring tribes, bartering the results of their fishing for other foods and manufactures, and using the surplus acquired to accumulate the dogs' teeth and shell money

[1] *Exploring English Character.* By Geoffrey Gorer (London, 1955). Especially Chapter XIII and Appendix One.
[2] New York, Morrow, 1956. London, Gollancz, 1956.

necessary for liquidating the debts accrued to sponsors who had paid the heavy bride-price for a wife, and in turn becoming the sponsors of the marriages of other young men. Their only persistent contact with the greater world was the departure of some of the younger men for indentured labour on plantations where they would learn the lingua franca of Pidgin (or, as it is now called, Neo-Melanesian), earn money with a wider currency than dogs' teeth, and get a little knowledge of how other peoples ordered their lives. This was an experience for individual young men, and a subject for conversation; but when their period of indenture was finished, they returned to the treadmill of debts, taboos, and unceasing effort to which they saw no alternative. In 1928 the missions had not yet arrived, but they were approaching near enough so that the Manus could consider the alternatives offered; and the general consensus was that Roman Catholicism was the more desirable, since the privacy of auricular confession would be an undoubted gain over the public confession demanded by the family ghosts.

This rigid, competitive, angry adult society provided no role for the pre-adolescent boys; and their earlier years were spent in carefree, co-operative, relatively unstructured play until an arranged betrothal brought them as debtors into the adult world.

By 1953 the Manus had moved from their pile-dwellings to the neighbouring shore; the nearly naked, mop-haired savages dressed in trousers and shirts and had modern hair-cuts. They bought and sold their goods in the world market; they were members of a world religion, albeit in a dissident form, since there had been a dispute with the missionaries; as far as was possible they were using modern medicine; they had marriage by choice, without the payment of bride-price; they had formalized education, schooling in reading, writing, and arithmetic; and they were most enthusiastic followers of the forms of democratic government and democratic justice, with daily discussions at village meetings, most anxious to get their village council recognized by the Australian administration. To the best of their ability, and with a striking measure of success, they had transformed themselves into participants in the contemporary globe-encircling democratic world.

## The Remaking of Man

Dr. Mead's book describes and analyses the historical events which lead from stone-age Manus of 1928 to air-age Manus of 1953, recounts in absorbing detail the way of life and institutions of modern Manus, counter-pointing this with the way of life and institutions of Manus a generation earlier, following through the development of named and known, twice-studied individuals. This unique study is so rich in vivid information and illustration that no summary can do justice to it. The adjective 'unique' is justified because, although on occasion anthropologists have made return visits to a previously studied tribe, they have never studied the changes in identified individuals. No previous anthropological study has concentrated on the observation and analysis of change, though a hypothetical reconstruction of the past has been a feature of some field-studies. There is nothing in anthropological literature to which this double study of the Manus can be properly compared.

Although a summary is impossible, insight can be gained by a rather abstract tabulation of the conditions which accompanied this dramatic transformation. There would appear to be five of them.

(i) The Manus adults found their traditional culture irksome and restrictive. The young men, after their carefree boyhood, and perhaps experience on plantations, felt themselves caught in a trap. They knew vividly that other peoples' lives were arranged in other ways. They were predisposed to change, if they could see how this could be achieved.

(ii) The Admiralty Islands, where the Manus dwell, were used as a major American base during the war, nearly a million young American men passing through the area. The distinctions of American social class are chiefly maintained by women, and this womanless group of Americans presented a vivid model of fraternal egalitarianism. The great attention paid by the American authorities to the health not only of their own troops but also of the Manus assistants was a continuous lesson in the value given by members of a democracy to the life of each individual. The easy generosity of the Americans (often enough with 'Uncle

Sam's' property) taught a revolutionary new attitude towards material possessions and provided plenty of material, perhaps especially sawn wood, with which the Manus could build the settings for a new sort of life.

(iii) Many tribes in New Guinea participated in apocalyptic 'Cargo cults'; the common feature of these cults is that prophets or other people in trance state that if all the old belongings are destroyed in suitable sacrifices, the ancestors will bring ships loaded with the desired goods of the white men as a reward. In some areas these cults caused a great deal of loss and many difficulties for the administering authorities. In Manus the cult, which was called The Noise, only lasted a few days; but during those days all the objects of material magic were thrown into the sea; the old black magic was jettisoned, save the magic of one old man; his magic was verbal and he had nothing to throw away. The Manus moved from their pile-dwellings to a completely new village on the shore.

(iv) A charismatic political leader of genius, Paliau, was available to give form and direction to the vague aspirations towards a dignified and democratic way of life.

(v) Some of the local Australian administrators were sympathetic and helpful in the implementation of the new Manus way of life, though they had to counter suspicion and hostility from some of their superiors.

Put even more briefly, the Manus had a predisposition to change; they were presented with a model of a way of life which they considered superior; they made a sudden and complete break with their old way of life; they had a leader to give the new way of life direction; and they were sympathetically helped by the representatives of higher authority with whom they were in most direct contact. The availability of a man of Paliau's genius is obviously an unpredictable accident which cannot be generalized; but the other four conditions—readiness for change, the presentation of a model for study and observation, the sudden and complete break with the past, nurture and support

## The Remaking of Man

during the first years of the new life—would seem to provide a paradigm of the way in which men may be changed in a single generation.

The first and fourth conditions require little comment. Unless there is a willingness to change a traditional way of life, all changes will be resented and resisted; unless the economically and militarily superior neighbours or administering powers nurture and support the new society or new aspirants they can have only slight chance of survival. The other two conditions are, however, much more novel and controversial.

In her concluding chapter Dr. Mead particularly stresses the desirability of rapid and complete change, as contrasted with the gradual handing over of small selected portions of the superior culture. She uses the illustration of clothing the naked. If cloth is provided for people who have previously lacked it, they will quickly become dirty and shabby unless at the same time a continuous supply of soap is assured, and the necessary implements and materials for mending and replacing clothes, and irons for smoothing them made available. The houses of the previously naked will become disorderly slums unless containers—cupboards or chests-of-drawers—are provided to hold the clothes not in use, and lines for drying the newly-washed garments. If shoes are provided as well as clothes, then chairs and tables will be necessary as the floor will no longer be suitable for sitting on. And so on. The transmission of selected aspects of a culture may well be degrading to the receivers; the complete and sudden change from the old to the new, the transmission of the totality as far as is practical, is far more likely to achieve success. In the case of the individual immigrants to whom I referred earlier, the crossing of the ocean, the abandonment of all that was old and familiar, is a close analogue to the communal destruction of the past in the Cargo cult.

This is Dr. Mead's major conclusion, and I think it is true, important, and a new insight. I should like, however, to consider somewhat further the remaining component in the Manus transformation: the presentation of a model of a way of life which they considered superior.

The presence of a model—the American woman school-teacher,

the English policeman, the American army—is the unifying element in all the rapid transformations which we have been considering. It seems at least a theoretical possibility that the presence of a model is an essential prerequisite for the transformation of attitudes and character within a single generation; and the relative failure of idealistic revolutions to produce a comparable transformation may be due to the absence of models. All idealistic revolutions, of whatever complexion, proclaim high ideals of justice, equality, righteousness, and similar supreme values; but they none of them indicate in anything like adequate detail how ordinary men or women should modify their lives, their habits and expectations, to approximate more closely to these ideals. Consequently the men and women maintain their old habits and expectations in the new situations; and Soviet Russia establishes new boarding-schools for the sons of professional officers a generation after a revolution had sought to abolish hereditary privilege; Napoleon crowns himself a few years after the proclamation of the Rights of Man; the officials in a nationalized industry are at least as hard to approach or persuade as the displaced owner.

A second conclusion which can be drawn is that all the models so far discussed are in some sense incomplete. The American school-teacher and the English policeman were each adequate models for their own sex; but American men and English women have less satisfactory models for their roles. The Manus had no models for the behaviour of wives and mothers, beyond what they could see on the cinema or hear from New Guinea natives who had acted as servants to Australian families. Besides the American army, their only model was a community of missionary nuns.

This led the serious, exploring Manus into great perplexity. How should one commit adultery democratically? Possessiveness was bad, anger was bad, jealousy was bad, secrecy was bad, an obsessive desire was bad and disturbing; there must be some solution which would avoid all these undesirable emotions. They drew up their own rules for democratic adultery (Dr. Mead describes them in Chapter XII) which are simultaneously a paradigm and a parody of the results of theoretical planning.

## The Remaking of Man

The Manus rules for adultery have a sort of family resemblance to the East African ground-nut scheme or Lysenko's market gardening in the Arctic circle.

If, as is suggested by these data, models are essential for successful transformation, then pilot schemes and institutional inventions take on a greatly enhanced importance for the guidance both of 'under-developed' and 'over-developed' countries; if change is the more successful if it is as complete and rapid as possible, if progress is an escalator rather than a ramp, then our views of the momentum of progress will need considerable revision. At the moment these are only suggestions, founded on the analysis of the experience of one small group in New Guinea; when other groups are similarly re-studied these suggestions may be modified or abandoned. The great merit of *New Lives for Old* is that it opens up a whole new field for observation, experiment and speculation, a field of the greatest relevance to our present preoccupations.

V

*Cultural Community and Cultural Diversity
in The North Atlantic Nations
(1963)*

I APPROACH THE subject of your deliberations as a social anthropologist who has specialized in what has confusingly come to be called National Character. What my colleagues and I study and attempt to make coherent are the motives, the predispositions, the articulate and inarticulate values that the majority of a *society* manifest or assent to at a defined period of history; for as anthropologists our unit of study is the society, and not the nation-state. In our traditional field of study, the technologically primitive societies without literacy and without any sources of power except human and animal muscle, wind and water, the distinction between society and nation-state rarely arises. The very simplest societies have developed no state apparatus; in the somewhat more complex ones the geographical boundaries of state and society coincide. But ever since the invention of the centralized nation-state in neolithic times at either end of the Asiatic land-mass, the nation-state has tended to comprise more than one society—a dominant society and subjugated or conquered societies. In the more recent history of the last century or so the political frontiers of nation-states have been drawn arbitrarily on political or geographical lines, without regard to the social allegiance of the people inhabiting the land through which the frontier is drawn. As a consequence members of a single society may be apportioned to two or more nation-states—recent examples which have been discussed are the Somalis, the Kurds and the Armenians; but their case is by no means unique.

This distinction between society and nation-state is basic to my argument. To the extent that we are using 'culture' in its anthropological significance as the learned and shared institutions and techniques of a people, culture itself is an aspect of society, and what has been called national character is an aspect of culture. I think I can speak for all anthropologists in stating that the nation-state, as such, does not have a culture. If nation and society coincide, then the nation-state is one of the institutions of that society; if the nation-state is composed of more than one society, it will also embody more than one culture, and manifest more than one type of national character. To discuss so complex a concept as the Cultural Community of the North Atlantic Nations we must get our definitions straight; and I intend to restrict my use of the terms 'culture' or 'cultural' to the technical anthropological meaning of learned regularities of behaviour and social institutions. Culture, as I shall use the term, is an aspect of society; and a cultural community must imply a community of societies, and not—at least in the first instance—of nation-states.

I should confess that I only reached this position gradually. The earliest work on the national character of complex societies was undertaken during the last war to be of use in various aspects of psychological warfare; and the studies of the Japanese national character were studies of a nation. So too were most of the other studies of Asian societies with which I was then associated. In my book *The Americans* the title is too inclusive even though in the preface and (in the English edition) in appendices I excluded the Southern States, and, to a lesser degree, Texas, rural New England and California.

When I came to write, with the late John Rickman, *The People of Great Russia*, I emphasized even in the title that I was dealing with only one of the societies in the U.S.S.R.; and similarly with the title of *Exploring English Character*. These are the only North Atlantic societies on which I have published. I took part in a study of French culture, meaning the dominant culture of central France; and during the war I participated in some fairly superficial studies of German-speaking societies which attempted to emphasize the differences between Prussian, Bavarian and Austrian. For the other members of the North Atlantic community my information is confined to that derivable from a fairly wide reading and such observations as an alert tourist (in many of the countries) can make. I think I am aware of the gamut of the traits exhibited by the national characters of the numerous societies which make up the North Atlantic Community; but there are several societies within this community about which I have no specialized knowledge at all.

In all the studies in which I have been involved the emphasis has been placed on the uniqueness of each culture, and of the national character which is its psychological expression. Although there are few, if any, traits, customs, beliefs or values which are unique, confined to a single society, the combination and pattern of the totality of traits, customs, beliefs and values of any society is always, as far as we know, unique. I have conceived as an important task the pointing out of the differences which so frequently underlie superficial similarities. If I may quote from my study *The Americans*, the chief difficulties in Anglo-American relations arise

> because English and Americans share variants of the same language, the same religions, the same political ideas, the same laws and the same physical types [and therefore] each group expects the other to be a near replica of itself, and is continually being disillusioned and distressed when this expectation is proved to be unjustified.

This type of contrast is a constant feature of societies with a shared historical origin: for example between the Spaniards and the Portuguese, or between the Norwegians and Swedes. Indeed it could be said that for members of many societies their sense of their own identity depends essentially on a negative or a complementary definition. You know you are a Norwegian because you are *not* a Swede or a Dane, and conversely; and this sense of identity, of defining oneself as a member of a given society, would seem to be a basic necessity for the psychological well-being of peoples in advanced, technically complex societies. As far as the records can guide us, this sense of self-identity through membership of a nation-state defined geographically and politically is, comparatively speaking, very recent; earlier self-identity was defined in terms of kinship, wherever one's kin might happen to live, by religion, or, at least in the case of the Greeks of the classical period, by language. In much of Africa today the problem of identity is the cause of very much political disturbance and distress in the contest between identity as a member of a tribe, and therefore ultimately through kinship, or identity as an adherent to a supra-cultural religion, and identity as a member of a geographically defined nation-state. The opposition to the merging of nation-states into a larger community, such as the North Atlantic Community, would seem to stem in large part from a fear of the loss of identity, one of the basic fears induced by large-scale urban civilization; I would hazard that this fear of the loss of identity is a greater obstacle to the forming of a larger community for most people than are any of the overtly political complications.

The unique characteristics of each society with its culture and the resultant national character is, as far as is known, universal, an aspect of the social life of *homo sapiens*; but the discernment of the differences of culture and national character is, to a great extent, a question of perspective, of observational viewpoint. Anthropologists are professionally trained to look at every society as closely as possible, irrespective of its size and political importance, and to analyse its unique variants of the universal institutions which every society manifests; and nearly all human beings have a quasi-anthropological attitude to the customs, speech and values of those societies which are nearest to them, either physically, as neighbours, or culturally through the sharing of common history, traditions or institutions; nearly every adult can be articulate about the differences between 'us' and 'them' in the next region, canton, tribe, on the other side of the river or the frontier, and so on. But habitually this ability to discriminate only applies to the nearest neighbours; the Scots or the Welsh, for example, can be most articulate about the differences between themselves and the English and will lump all Continental Europeans together. And I wonder how many of the people here in Chicago, who could tell me with great precision the differences between the citizens of the United States on one side of the lake and the citizens of Canada on the other, nevertheless consider that the whole of America south of the Rio Grande is inhabited by one amorphous society of 'Latins'?

This question of perspective is an important one. Anthropologists group the unique cultures which are their primary object of study into 'culture areas'. To date, this concept has been most clearly elaborated in the sphere of material culture; the types of objects which are made or traded do tend to group discrete cultures into larger wholes. Since material objects are easier to study with precision than are institutions, customs and values, the most precise delineation of culture areas has been in terms of concrete traits; but underlying such expressions of aspiration as 'United Africa' or the 'North Atlantic Community' is the hope that these geographical descriptions are already, or are capable of becoming, single culture areas with sufficient shared values, customs and institutions to maintain coherence.

I myself do not believe that the North Atlantic Nations constitute a single culture area. As far as my knowledge goes, I would assume that there are three major culture areas in Europe and North America; and that these three culture areas may be conveniently, though probably not quite precisely, distinguished by the versions of Christianity which have been dominant in them in recent centuries: the Orthodox societies, the Catholic societies, and the societies influenced by the Protestant Reformation.

It is a question of the greatest complexity, which I am not competent to answer, whether the differing versions of Christianity were adopted, or prevailed, because they were congruent with the predispositions, values and character of the peoples assenting to them, or whether the preponderating influence of the churches in government and education, until very recent times, transformed the character of the peoples into congruence with the values of the dominant sect. The only clue I possess is a slight knowledge of pre-Reformation English literature; and this does tentatively suggest to me that the English had Protestant characters before they had Protestant dogma.

These three confessions emphasize three different means by which the faithful may be apprised of God's will and guide their conduct, which in turn represent three different ideal types of character. For the Orthodox, a Pentecostal illumination will show the Truth to the group, or, exceptionally, the individual earnestly seeking it. The pious Roman Catholic will keep in the Right by scrupulously following the rules laid down by his spiritual superiors who, in their turn, are bound by obedience to their superiors, and to the minutely codified laws which bind the conduct of layman and priest alike. The Protestant prayerfully searches his own heart and studies the scriptures to ascertain whether he is following the Lord's will, whether his conduct is moral.

These three approaches embody three different ideals of behaviour: the Man in the Truth, the Man in the Right, and the Moral Individual. And these three ideals not only guide the conduct of the faithful and identify the characteristics they try to elicit in their children; they also inform the climate of opinion, indicate the predominant values of lay institutions, from government to education, for the societies in which these creeds have been dominant, whether or no the majority of their members consciously subscribe to the creeds in which these values were embodied. And in many ways these three attitudes to human nature have, till now, been mutually incompatible, each convinced that they alone are correct and that the other approaches are mistaken or sinful. This mutual intolerance still persists, though the chief cause for disdain has shifted from religious to political ideology. We all claim to be democrats and to live in a democratic society, as earlier we all claimed to be Christians and to live in a Christian society; but our version of democracy, as formerly our version of Christianity, is, we maintain, the only one which really deserves that honoured name.

Because they are inarticulately held, these three different ideals of upright behaviour, and the type of society and institutions which will advance them, would seem to be a major cause for the mutual incomprehension and intolerance within the geographical area which might constitute a North Atlantic community. The Man in the Truth depends ultimately upon revelation. The Truth exists, for him, in perpetuity; it can be discovered by exceptional holiness or by exceptional historical insight, by the study of the Gospel according to St. John or of dialectical materialism according to Marx, Engels and Lenin. When the Truth has been revealed, the duty of man is to live in the Truth as completely as possible; even the slightest deviation runs the cataclysmic risk of the descent into the abyss of total Untruth, of Sin. Societies based on the revelation of Truth inevitably tend to rigidity; although different aspects of the Truth are revealed over time, at any one moment there is only one Truth and an infinity of perilous errors. Compromise on any serious point is, inevitably, a dereliction from the Truth.

The Man in the Right depends ultimately upon codified laws. Knowledge, precedent, foresight, reason, precise definitions employed with the greatest clarity and intelligence available will produce the code of laws under which the upright man should live. He may interpret the letter of the law with all the ingenuity of which he is capable; but the body of law and precedent, whether of church or state, is superior to all those who live under the law. The law will contain provisions as to how it may be modified or added to in detail; but the law, as a whole, can only be overturned by violent revolution, by temporary anarchy from which a more perfect law will subsequently be evolved. Revolution may occasionally be necessary, but it is deplorable in itself, a last resort; and, except in times of revolution, the man in the Right should live under the law, should submit himself and his interests to the regulations and interpretations made by the specialists who are by definition his intellectual or spiritual superiors.

The man in the Right has contempt for those who do not acknowledge the rule of law; they are, in the precise sense of the term, uncivilized and therefore unreliable. One can, indeed one must, negotiate with people who are not in the Right, who do not demonstrate their allegiance to the letter of the law; but one cannot rely on them and so should not get involved too deeply. They may suddenly appeal against the letter of the law in the light of a new revelation of the Truth or, what is even more unpredictable, by an appeal to natural justice against the letter of the law.

The Moral Individual, and the societies he composes, places

comparatively little reliance on revealed truth or on codified law. The source from which the Moral Individual derives the knowledge of upright conduct is from his own heart or conscience fortified by the scriptures; he believes deeply that every human being has natural capacities for discerning true justice and the proper way to forward this obviously desirable goal; if he communes with himself with sufficient earnestness and sincerity he will learn the Will of the Lord or the moral course of action more accurately than by reliance on any other source. Moral Individuals, and societies composed of Moral Individuals, believe that every individual has both the capacity and the duty to 'make up his mind for himself' on all questions of moral importance. He should take into account revealed truths, or truths held to be self-evident; he should not unwittingly flout the law, for ignorance of the law is no excuse; but the ultimate fount of authority and the individual's true guide to upright conduct is the innate sense of justice, fairness, equity which each individual possesses and can gain access to. For Moral Individuals compromise is desirable, if no principles are betrayed, if it is in accord with both parties' sense of natural justice; to refuse to compromise is to be rigid, or legalistic, both terms of opprobrium for the Moral Individual, each a term of commendation for the man in the Truth and the man in the Right respectively.

I have dwelt at some length on these three approaches to upright conduct which I think characterize the three culture areas of the North Atlantic Community because I believe that these are symptomatic of the type of difficulty and mutual incomprehension which prevents the North Atlantic community being more than a geographical expression. While the people who practise one approach to upright conduct consider that any other approach is not merely misguided, but wrong and dangerous, there can never be that delegation of authority, of sovereignty, which must precede the transformation of the North Atlantic Community into a cultural as well as a geographical expression.

Together with the differing approaches to upright conduct go differing definitions of the high abstractions which men value and wish to achieve. In the Second World War, President Roosevelt and Winston Churchill launched a slogan to subsume our war-aims: The Four Freedoms—freedom of speech, freedom of religion, freedom from want, freedom from fear. Once this neat slogan was launched it was found that it could not be neatly translated into any other language: in no other language that I know of does a single word carry the two connotations of not-being-prevented-from and being-protected-from. All agree that Freedom is a good; but there are many differences as to how this good is rightly defined. And so with all the other goods men value.

I stress the understanding of the goods, the goals men strive for in the differing cultures and culture areas which comprise the North Atlantic Nations; for a viable North Atlantic Community can only be built on the best aspirations, not the fears, of the peoples who will compose it. Fears can make, do make, a temporary alliance; but when the fears diminish the alliance disintegrates if there are not also shared aspirations. A detailed and objective study of the implications of the high value abstractions in every language would be a most useful preparatory work for all multi-cultural associations.

To the best of my knowledge, there does not exist a comprehensive map of the cultures of the North Atlantic Nations. There are linguistic maps; and where there is a difference in language, there is *prima facie* evidence for difference in culture. But the converse does not hold true. The same language may be shared by people of strongly contrasting cultures: the English-speaking peoples are a striking example of markedly differing cultures sharing the same language. The same would appear to be true of the German-speaking peoples, the Italian, Spanish and French speakers. Accent and minor turns of phrase or vocabulary will distinguish Prussians, Bavarians and Austrians; Milanese, Romans and Sicilians; North country, Midlands and Southern English; Middle West Americans, Middle West Canadians and so on; and with varying degrees of intensity these speakers of variants of the same language will identify themselves with their local culture and its geographical area rather than with the nation-state in which this culture is enclosed. Most members of regional societies have also loyalty to and a strong sense of identification with the nation-state to which they belong and, in confrontation with other nation-states will sink their regional loyalties in patriotism. When there is no such confrontation, they tend to consider themselves Bavarians or Sicilians or Scots or Southerners, and so on, in the first place; only secondarily, most of the time, will they consider themselves Germans, or Italians, or British, or citizens of the United States.

I should like to suggest to you that these local cultures are the bricks with which a North Atlantic community could be built, over time. The society with its distinctive culture is, as far as the records go, the natural, the universal unit in which *homo sapiens* has always lived his life; and for the majority of mankind over recent millennia societies have nearly all had a specific geographical location. By contrast the nation-state is a relatively recent invention in the history of the human species.

The first nation-states seem to have arisen around the great rivers of Asia and North Africa and may, as Dr. Wittfogel has suggested, have developed this form because of the need for large-scale organizations to deal with problems of flooding and irrigation; and this form of social organization extended comparatively slowly to the rest of the world. Even two centuries ago, large areas of the inhabited world were not organized into nation-states; this was true of all the sparsely inhabited portions of the globe—Australia and much of the Americas—and large sections of the more densely populated areas; over much of the world the local or tribal society was paramount. We can imagine human beings living full and adequate lives without the existence of nation-states, for we have many simple examples; we cannot imagine human beings living full lives without a local or tribal society, even though it be politically submerged within a nation-state.

The accretion and expansion of local societies has been a very gradual process, perhaps taking nearly as long a time as the history of *homo sapiens*. The very earliest men may have been organized into societies little larger than a single family and very gradually amalgamated into larger units; but in the time-scale of recent history local societies and their cultures appear much more persistent than nation-states. Examples can be found from many frequently fought-over areas of Europe or Asia; Alsatian culture, for example, or Sicilian, or Greek have persisted over centuries though the peoples have been included under a variety of national suzerainties. Nation-states change their frontiers, expand and contract, even disappear from the political scene; but, as far as the records go, the local societies and their cultures continue with a very slow natural rate of change, even though their political life be modified according to which nation-state is paramount over them at a given period.

The painful history of this century has shown that local societies and their cultures can be physically destroyed by extermination or forcible dispersal; but there are also many examples of the resilience and vitality of local cultures preserved for generations, despite the tyranny of dominant nation-states.

The resilience, vitality and persistence of local cultures are an asset which we would be unwise to neglect. As I have said, there is no cultural map of the North Atlantic area; but, did one exist, I do not think there would be very much difference between a cultural map of this area in 1800, and one made today (with the partial exception of those areas which were then very sparsely inhabited). But if one looks at a political map of 1800, showing the territories of nation-states, there are few portions of the map which are the same as those of today, apart from geographical areas with 'natural' boundaries such as sea or mountains which are also nation-states. Nation-states are unstable entities, though this fact is disguised because political history is typically written from the viewpoint of the dominant culture. We in England think that the history of Britain extends over millennia—the late Hugh Gaitskell claimed that Britain's entry into the Common Market would terminate 'a thousand years of history'; but over many centuries of this millennium England was not paramount over the territory and population of Wales or Scotland, and, for quite a few, was paramount over much of the population and territory which is now part of France.

The major reason for the instability of nation-states is that the self-definition of all nation-states includes the claim to absolute sovereignty. In the whole history of this institution there are no examples known to me of nation-states willingly abrogating their sovereignty over any considerable period. There are temporary alliances and treaties in plenty, but to date these have always been *ad hoc* arrangements, either a military alliance with a specific goal, or treaties with escape clauses or terminal dates.

This seems to me inevitable; nation-states are designed as autonomous monads. Indeed, in the early history of this invention, nation-states seem to have conceived of themselves as unique; the earliest states, Han China, Babylon, Mohenjo-daro, even Egypt did not (it would appear) need to acknowledge the existence of a rival or rivals; they were complete and absolute by themselves.

Today, a nation-state which does not retain the autonomous right to make or abstain from war and to regulate its own economic and fiscal policies is a contradiction in terms. The fact that the dominant societies of nation-states do or do not belong to the same culture area, have similar or contrasting definitions of upright behaviour and the other differences which I referred to earlier is on the whole irrelevant. If they do not share the same predispositions and values, and ignore the differences hidden under similar words and actions, this may exacerbate relations and lead to unnecessary misunderstandings; but however close the values of the dominant societies of nation-states may be—and it would seem as though, during much of Europe's monarchical history, the values of the dominant groups were very close—their relationship has always been at best an unstable equilibrium.

It follows that I agree with what I understand to be the position of General de Gaulle that one cannot build a North Atlantic community on an aggregation of nation-states. *L'Europe des patries*—a Europe of sovereign states—would seem to be one more *ad hoc* alliance. But I do not for that reason think that a North Atlantic community is impossible to achieve; I think it is essential as a preliminary to that world community which we must devise if the human race is to continue to exist. Human beings invented the nation-state; it should not be beyond human wit to devise another form of organization now that the nation-state has become too dangerous.

Although nation-states as we have known them have necessarily been incapable of long-term mutual accommodation, the submerged regional societies and their cultures have had long experience of this. In Europe I believe, though I could not demonstrate this, that the regional cultures comprise a larger proportion of the population than do the dominant cultures. This would appear not to be the case on this side of the Atlantic; but even here they are no insignificant proportion of the total population.

I should like to suggest to you that a North Atlantic Community might be able to be constructed if the units were regional societies, rather than nation-states. Regional societies have a quasi-biological permanence, compared with nation-states; the great majority have the historical experience of restricted sovereignty, of living peaceably enough under the domination of some superordinate national culture. True, a certain number of regional cultures in the past have revolted against the superordinate society which was felt as oppressive, as enjoying a national sovereignty to which the regional society felt it had an equal right; as a result we have had an ever-increasing proliferation of nation-states. Such regions had never submitted willingly to subordination by the dominant culture; typically they were dominated by conquest.

With the changed technologies of communications, production of power, and weaponry the role of nation-states could easily be diminished, and the role of regions comparably enhanced. Regional areas would need to be sociologically demarcated, for in nearly every modern nation-state the regions have been quite arbitrarily broken down into administrative units—counties, départements, states, provinces and so on—which are only casually related to the local culture of the inhabitants. It is my belief however that, with the partial exception of the metropolitan conurbations, the adult inhabitants of the countries of the North Atlantic nations are quite clear (in the vast majority of cases) about their identification with a specific regional culture; and that consequently it would not need much more work than is entailed in a national census or referendum to produce a map of the local societies and their cultures in any technologically advanced area.

Once the areas of the local societies have been determined, they should be granted the greatest amount of autonomy possible. They will not be military units, for in most cases they will not have the necessary economic base; but I presume that a North Atlantic community would aim at the disappearance of national armed forces in favour of a supra-national or multi-national force. They will not be economically self-sufficient; but here again modern technology is already evolving multi-national and supra-national industrial and power complexes. There would be a need for a common currency throughout the area, and for a minimum legal basis, for entrenched clauses which could not be repealed by a single local society. But these provisos apart, each region would be independent and encouraged to develop its own distinctive culture and view of the world and of upright conduct.

Among the rights which I should like to see assigned to every region is that of determining its adherence or relationship to a metropolis; and this right would include double adherence, of which we have a prototype in the constitution of the state of Andorra. If double adherence of a region were allowed, it would clear away most of the major causes of dispute and discontent which perpetually vex the old world. There is a very considerable number of regional cultures over which two or more nation-states claim paramountcy: I will give as examples the Tyrolese, the Saarlanders, the Transylvanians, the Kurds, the Armenians, the Kashmiri, the Somali. If regional cultures were autonomous, within the limits I have outlined, one of the major causes for dispute and war would be eliminated.

The autonomous regional societies of the North Atlantic area would constitute the units who would determine the shape and actions of the North Atlantic community. If I am right in discerning three major culture areas in the North Atlantic area, there might well be three subordinate groupings for government and religion between which the autonomous societies could choose their adherence. But I am deeply convinced that a North

Atlantic cultural community can only be solidly built by allowing for, and emphasizing, the cultural diversity which distinguishes mankind and not by wishing it away and seeking to impose a single cultural pattern. Cultural diversity is the richest of our inheritances, and the one most fraught with possibilities of human development and invention; we must preserve this with all our best efforts as earnestly as we strive to preserve the human race from annihilation.

# VI

## *The Danger of Equality*
### *(1962)*

NEARLY ALL CONTEMPORARY political writing and speaking which envisages the way our society, and related societies, can be improved for the better, contain, as an unstated dogma, the following proposition:

> The more nearly the citizens of a country resemble one another in the amount of money they spend, the goods they own, the education they acquire and the social deference they receive, the more nearly perfect will that country be.

I am using 'social deference' as a convenient term for any of those attitudes of respect or ceremony which are accorded by members of some groups in a society to any member of another group in their society solely on account of their membership in that group. The group referred to may be distinguished by any number of criteria: frequent ones are age, sex, lineage, wealth, skin-colour, holiness, or manner of speaking. What is basic in this concept of social deference is the fact that it refers primarily to groups, rather than to individual qualities or attainments. In Great Britain today, we usually think of social deference in the context of class differences; but prior to 1914 (or perhaps 1900) sex was also an important criterion for deference in a large part of British society.

I have called this proposition a dogma, because in nearly all the literature that I have read, the assumptions are treated as self-evident; what is discussed are the ways in which these aims might be implemented and over how short or long a time this implementation should take place; the aims themselves, the striving for equality in expenditure and deference, get no more discussion than, say, does the desirability of proselytising in the literature of a missionary society. The Justice of a society can, it is implied, be measured by the approximation of adult citizens to parity of expenditure and social esteem, and Justice is the paramount social good.

(I should perhaps enter a *caveat* at once that I am not discussing the desirability of a state preventing any citizen falling below a certain minimum level of expenditure, or being treated with social disrespect; but the prevention of want or of socially sanctioned contumely which affects the least advantaged sections of the population can be considered an aspect of charity, in both the religious and the common speech meaning of the term. One of the arguments advanced by some of the proponents of the dogma of equality is that it will render charity otiose.)

As far as I know, this belief that Justice is the paramount social good is a specifically modern concept which originated in nineteenth century Europe, presumably in the light of the French Revolution. Many earlier political theorists, both Utopian and practical, had considered righteousness the paramount political social good and, for these thinkers, justice was one of the components of a righteous state, though certainly not the paramount one. Other political thinkers, chiefly Utopian these, have placed individual happiness or social harmony as the paramount social goods and, in these contexts, it is the negative aspect, the absence of injustice, which is emphasized as essential to the attainment of happiness or harmony. For many other political theorists the concept of justice has played a minimal role; for these the paramount social good has been Strength, economic strength or prosperity, military strength or victory, political strength or power.

It is not however on the basis of the comparative historical study of political theory and Utopian constructs that I wish to question the current dogma, nor on an argument on ethics; I am not sufficiently competent in either subject. It is on the basis of evidence gathered by social anthropologists, sociologists and contemporary political scientists that I should like to raise the question whether equality in expenditure and deference will in fact promote a just state.

## The Danger of Equality

In every complex society which has been studied—let us say every society which uses other sources of energy besides human and animal muscles, wind and water—it has been found that certain values are unevenly distributed within the population, some people possessing a very large amount of the value, some a moderate amount, and some very little. Among these values, for which distribution has been measured either for several whole societies, or sizeable portions thereof, are wealth, education or knowledge, social deference or respect, and professional skill. Other values which are observed in many societies, but of which the distribution has not been worked out in comparable detail, are righteousness (religion or ethics), well-being (athletic or physical prowess) and popularity. Finally, and for my argument the most important value of all, there is Power; this is of course both a value on its own account, and a component of all the other recognized social values.[1]

When the distribution of any *socially recognized* value is worked out for any complex society it is found that this distribution has a characteristic pattern, which does not seem to vary from society to society nor from value to value. To the best of my knowledge, this is a regularity common to all complex societies, though I do not think this has been publicly commented on.

If you divide the value by deciles (ten per cents) or any other similar convenient proportion and place them in descending order on a graph, and make the width of each section proportional to the number of the population who have that decile of the value, you will always get a shape like a turnip standing on its base. The bottom decile is narrower than the one above; there will then be a slight increase for two or three deciles, a slightly greater decrease for the next two or three, and a very thin tail representing the top three or four deciles. It doesn't seem to matter what you measure, or in which society you measure it—this is the form in which socially recognized values are distributed in a complex society. This turnip is, I would maintain, the basic shape for the distribution of any socially recognized

[1] This list of values is derived from *Power and Society* by Lasswell and Kaplan. Yale University Press, 1950.

value within a complex society; furthermore the same turnip will be found to be characteristic of large organized groups within a complex society: for example a national church (the hierarchy of rectitude), or the armed forces or large industries of any nature.

Where societies do appear to differ is in the number of values to which they give social recognition; and, if more than one value is recognized, which value is considered of paramount importance. If more than one value is socially recognized, the position of identified individuals in each hierarchy is a question of considerable interest; from the point of view of political forms it is of importance whether or no the same individuals hold parallel positions in the different hierarchies, particularly whether the tops of the hierarchies, the tails of the turnips, are predominantly composed of the same people.

I have written 'more than one value being recognized' because, at least from the theoretical point of view, it is possible to have a single value society. That single value will always and inevitably be Power. To a considerable extent the other values are, so to speak, optional; but a complex society which does not have a hierarchy of power has never been described, nor even imagined with any sort of realistic elaboration. When anarchists descend from the level of high ethical abstractions, they generally posit some simple form of subsistence economy; to get rid of power, even in imagination, the complex society has to be abolished.

The society whose only socially recognized value is power is the theoretical paradigm of a dictatorship. No historical dictatorship has quite reached this theoretical purity—the hierarchy of skill, particularly scientific and to a lesser degree artistic skill, has been too important in international relations for skill to be completely subordinated to power; the U.S.S.R. in Stalin's last years probably came nearest to the ideal, when the Communist party revoked the Mendelian law and completely subordinated that section of the skill hierarchy which dealt with genetics to the hierarchy of power. Only if international relations can be disregarded—which today probably means a world state—would it be possible to have a single value society in which the only social difference between individuals would be in their position in the hierarchy of power; but this position is approximated to whenever power is the chief value in the society, even though there may be subsidiary value hierarchies.

In fairly recent history we can discern societies in which the dominant values have been (besides power) wealth (plutocracies). social respect (feudal societies) and rectitude (theocracies). I don't think any modern state has actually made any of the other values their chief value, though one theory of democracy, to which a good deal of lip-service is paid, would make popularity a dominant value. One can imagine, though the picture is a grizzly one, a state in which legal skill would be the dominant value; some very primitive societies with their warrior-kings have made well-being their chief value; in Plato's republic the chief value would have been knowledge. But I think that since the seventeenth century, let us say, the dominant social values of the complex societies have been power, wealth, social respect or rectitude or some combination of two or more of them.

I would maintain that the characteristic of democracies of recent centuries has been the multiplicity of hierarchies of socially recognized values, as opposed to the dominance of a single hierarchy in dictatorships or feudal or theocratic states. In feudal society power is concentrated in the hands of the people with the greatest social respect, the aristocracy; in a theocratic state power is concentrated in the hands of the specialists in rectitude, the lord bishops or sovereign pontiffs or the like; in a plutocracy —I think the Venetian Republic could perhaps be so described —power is concentrated in the hands of the specialists in wealth; and in a dictatorship power is concentrated in the hands of the specialists in power. But in a democracy?

The derivation of course does not correspond to facts in a complex society, even though it may have done so at one time in small city states; power is not in the hands of the population as a whole. At most, the population as a whole can decide at relatively infrequent intervals between rival candidates for certain positions of political power. In every democracy that I have studied the nomination of the candidates between whom the population will choose is decided upon by relatively small groups of people fairly high up in one of the socially recognized hierarchies within the society.

I should say that the characteristic of democracies as we have known them and their chief claim to being a more desirable political system than any alternative lies precisely in the fact that the locus of power cannot be precisely determined, that the specialists in power, the people who have come to the top of the power hierarchy through politics or the armed forces, do not have a monopoly of social power; their influence and their predominance are modified by those of the individuals at the top of the other socially recognized hierarchies, the rich, the socially prominent, the religious leaders, the most popular or most skilled people, and so on.

This indeterminateness of course infuriates individuals of a compulsive character for whom tidiness or clarity are absolute values, irrespective of what is tidy or clear, and disturbs people of paranoid character who feel that any source of power with which they cannot identify themselves is persecutory. It is of course the paranoid criticisms with which we are most familiar, since paranoids tend to be extremely vocal about their delusions of persecution; and it is from the paranoid vocabulary that we have received the terms to designate the centres of power which are outside the power hierarchy of democracies: Wall Street, Les Deux Cents Familles, the Grand Orient, the Elders of Zion, the Establishment, and so on. All these concepts have in common the notion of a conspiracy, the belief that individuals outside the overt power hierarchy are secretly organized to render the overt hierarchy relatively impotent. The moral that is drawn is not that the concentration of power is undesirable, but that all power should be concentrated in the overt power hierarchy with which the persecuted individuals can identify and within which they frequently hold positions of some eminence.

I, on the other hand, would be inclined to state as an axiom that the concentration of power beyond the minimum necessary for efficient functioning is undesirable; and that the value of a democracy lies precisely in the fact that power is rather vaguely diffused through the summits of the various hierarchies of recognized social values. But for power to be so diffused the other values must be socially recognized; and this brings me back to my original questioning of the egalitarian dogma; and if the foregoing arguments have any validity it would follow that by destroying the hierarchies of wealth and of social esteem you do not arrive at a more just state but at a state in which all power is concentrated within a single group.

Every society is liable to produce individuals of exceptional energy and ability and ambition to 'succeed'. How 'success' can be estimated depends on the number of socially recognized value hierarchies that society contains at that period of history. In all complex societies there are likely to be some energetic and able people who have a vocation for one of the socially recognized skills—arts or sciences—which the society has developed; but, these dedicated people apart, I think the concept of 'success' is defined almost entirely in terms of the social hierarchies existing when the young man or woman starts on his or her career; it is, so to speak, a fluid drive. If the only socially recognized hierarchy is that of power, then that is the goal which the able and ambitious will pursue; and since power consists in domination over other people, the majority of the society which is low in the power hierarchy will tend to be increasingly dominated over, controlled and regulated. By its nature power tends to increase continuously, unless or until it is checked by alternative hierarchies.

Consequently I would suggest that if one wishes to work for a society where the concentration of power is minimized—which is, to my mind, the only tolerable definition of a democratic society—one should try to multiply the socially recognized hierarchies into which ambition can be canalized. For example, I think l'Académie Française a thoroughly good invention; it occupies the energies and ambitions of a number of military and academic people who would otherwise be adding to the competition in the power hierarchy. Although I have not much sympathy with the people who strive to get into the Social Register or acquire a title or get their daughters presented at court, this seems to me a socially harmless way of using up a good deal of energy. Even the desire to demonstrate that one has succeeded by ostentatious spending seems less socially destructive than the building of a political empire to make the same point; in the latter case, instead of commanding goods in great quantity, the successful man commands people in great quantity.

There is the further implication that a democratic society has got to be a theoretically untidy society, with a considerable number of irrational features if it is analysed from the basis of any single criterion—justice, efficiency, military or economic strength, logical consistency. Since no complex state can exist without a power hierarchy, this hierarchy will always turn out to be the dominant one in a state organized to satisfy a single criterion, whatever that criterion may be. The only way by which the absoluteness of power can be modified is by granting other values equal, or approximately equal, social recognition; and this implies that in a democratic society individuals must be permitted to achieve success and social deference in hierarchies which seem unimportant, meaningless, or even slightly repugnant to people in other hierarchies. The more kinds of success that a society recognizes, the less likelihood there is of an excessive concentration of power. Democracy depends therefore to a considerable extent on a climate of opinion which will appropriately acknowledge success in as many different hierarchies as possible.

Until power is concentrated into a single hierarchy, the influence of the climate of opinion would appear to be of major importance. It appears to be in the nature of all hierarchies in a complex society to attempt to extend their own influence and power, and concurrently to diminish the influence and power of rival hierarchies. To achieve these ends, they will employ force—the law, the police, perhaps even the military—and persuasion; and in normal times the force of police, parliament, or law court can only be used if persuasion has created a climate of opinion favourable to the enhancement of the power of one hierarchy and the diminishment or destruction of its rivals. The motives mobilized are envy and resentment, which in the process are, so to speak, justified and denatured, much as hatred is in time of war. These destructive and negative vices are treated as constructive and positive virtues if they are directed at the 'right' targets; in this context this means all the hierarchies which are

## The Danger of Equality

not comprised within the hierarchy mobilizing these components of public opinion.

If mobilized public envy and resentment begrudge any social deference or conspicuous success outside the power hierarchy, then the way is being prepared for a single-value society. To the extent that the obverse of a desire for social justice is envy of, or resentment at, conspicuous success, rather than pity for conspicuous unsuccess, to that extent is the striving for a just state likely to result in a state where all power is concentrated in a single hierarchy, where all that will remain of a democracy will be a ritual whereby members at the top of the power hierarchy will exchange political positions among themselves at irregular intervals. Democracy depends on a multiplicity of values; if only a single value is emphasized democracy cannot survive.

# VII

## *A Reconsideration of the Functions of Class Distinction*
## *(1961)*

IT IS NOWADAYS a cliché to state that English society is riddled with class distinctions; and when this cliché is given an airing, as it so frequently is, the implication is almost always that this is a thoroughly undesirable state of affairs, and the sooner the distinctions are obliterated, the better for all concerned. The voicing of this sentiment gives both the speaker and any sympathetic audience the warm self-righteous glow of feeling liberal-minded, democratic, egalitarian and any other of the plus adjectives we apply to our own political and social wishes.

Since the emotional consensus is so great, the actual phenomenon, its history and functions, are seldom considered at all. It is deeply felt to be a Bad Thing; its perpetuation is a sign of our parents' and ancestors' original sin or bloody-mindedness; it is part of the same complex as workers' slums, sweated labour, imperialism, and all the other unpleasant legacies of our immediate past. It is, however, almost always unwise to accept clichés unquestioningly; and I should like to examine just what class distinctions are, the functions they perform or have performed in our society and in other societies of similar complexity, and of what might take their place were class distinctions to be destroyed.

Class distinctions consist predominantly in minor variants of speech, gesture, and social behaviour by means of which individuals claim or proclaim their position in one of the social hierarchies into which all large complex societies are inevitably divided. These variants are formally insignificant, in so far as any of the alternatives of vocabulary, phonemes (within a fairly wide range) or grammatical forms will convey the necessary information to the speaker of the same language; and any of the variants of behaviour—in much of the world outside Britain table-manners are the most indicative—will succeed in their primary purpose. The variants acquire their significance as social indicators.

In the societies which employ such social indicators the variants permeate all the social groups of which the society is composed; but they normally only acquire poignancy and emotional importance when the indicators of two adjacent social groups come into conflict. When representatives of widely-separated social groups come into contact the emotional importance of these indicators tends to be very low; neither expects to be accepted as a member of the other's group; and moreover both sides are usually unable to decode the social indicators of groups so distant from them. When the acceptance of hospitality is involved, the guest may be uncomfortable lest his behaviour fail to conform to his host's expectations; but this discomfort is not confined to members of the socially inferior group. A similar discomfort is frequent in social contacts between members of different societies; the obligation to adapt to the host's expectations of suitable behaviour is a permanent aspect of friendly contacts between members of strange societies in all stages of development.

It would appear that it is nearly universal for people to feel some unease and discomfort in social situations where they do not know the expected behaviour and when the situation is so unstructured that formal rules cannot be enunciated. This is certainly one of the besetting troubles of social anthropologists. It has been my practice, and my advice to people going into the field for the first time, to learn etiquette from the start, in a village or group other than that in which the main study will be done; in that way one can avoid giving unnecessary offence by the unwitting breach of conventions. I think that it is only social anthropologists who work so consistently and self-consciously on this analysis of etiquette; but it is of course a problem which is faced by every immigrant to a strange society, whatever may be the motive for wanting to pass unnoticed in the receiving country.

In traditional societies it is relatively uncommon for social situations to be unstructured, for people from different social groupings within the society or members of neighbouring societies to meet in social situations where the rules of behaviour for all concerned are not articulate and codified. The etiquette is fixed and clear which regulates the behaviour of noble and commoner, high caste and low caste, minister and suppliant and any other combination within the society, or of ambassadors, plenipotentiaries or merchants of different societies.

All the complex societies—societies which have developed literacy and some source of power other than human and animal muscle—have contained hierarchies of social esteem. Positions in these hierarchies may be determined by birth—much the most general arrangement—by wealth, by military or political power, by sanctity (as in some theocracies) and, more rarely, by popularity, athletic prowess, artistic skills or by learning. Societies differ in the number of hierarchies to which they accord social deference; but no complex society has been described, nor even realistically imagined, which does not possess at least one hierarchy of deference. The irreducible minimum is the hierarchy of political or military power.

The predominant pattern in England, and indeed in most of the countries of Western Europe, from the end of the Middle Ages to the end of the eighteenth century was the predominance of the hierarchy determined by birth. A man inherited his status from his father; a woman at marriage took the status of her husband, with some modification in the case of heiresses. This inherited status was never, in Europe, as completely rigid as it was and is in caste societies, such as Hindu India; wealth or outstanding ability could be rewarded by higher status conferred by the throne; extreme poverty could prevent people from being able to live in the status to which they were born. These exceptions apart, each social class, each order of society, had its own codes of proper behaviour, its own conventions, its own pride, very often its own distinctive dress; judging by the literary remains of the sixteenth, seventeenth and early eighteenth centuries, there was no or little attempt to claim a rank which one had not inherited by birth, save through the recognized channels of

## A Reconsideration of Class Distinction

marriage and ennoblement. There is a good deal of evidence that the aristocracy were disapproved of by the middle classes, the gentry looked down on by the citizens; and there was an even stronger barrier between the guilds and their apprentices and the journeyman workers.

This relatively rigid stratification started to be modified towards the end of the eighteenth century. It seems most probable that a major cause of this modification was the development of the industrial revolution, which altered the economic balance between town and country. Government was one of the gentry's prerogatives; in order to get the laws modified to discriminate less against the nascent industries, citizens and traders had to seek political power; and either as a technique of approach, or under the influence of contact, started to ape the behaviour of the gentry in an attempt to be accepted by them as equals. Simultaneously, the skilled workmen in the new trades and skills tried to claim a parity of esteem with the older established guildsmen.

The first writer I know of to comment on the attempts of people to claim a status to which they were not born is Jane Austen; she did this with great subtlety of observation, by mockery. It is worth noting that Jane Austen's mockery extends in both directions; as a daughter of the lesser gentry (her father was a country clergyman) she is quite as unmerciful to the aristocracy, and those who suck up to them, as to the daughters of traders who try to pass themselves off as ladies; the insolence of Lady Catherine de Bourgh is mocked just as pointedly as the pushingness and lack of proper decorum shown by Mrs. Elton. Jane Austen, too, is, as far as I know, the first person to have a character make a claim for the peculiar mystique attributed to the public schools. She writes in *Sense and Sensibility*:

> Why they were different, Robert explained to her himself in the course of a quarter of an hour's conversation; for, talking of his brother, and lamenting the extreme *gaucherie* which he really believed kept him from mixing in proper society, he candidly and generously attributed it much less to any natural deficiency, than to the misfortunes of a private

education; while he himself, though probably without any particular, any material superiority by nature, merely from the advantage of a public school, was as well fitted to mix in the world as any other man.[1]

Jane Austen is of course making fun of Robert Ferrars, who is a conceited coxcomb, though he did go to Westminster; the well-mannered, sensible man of the story is his privately educated brother Edward. Nevertheless, to have invented this conversation, she must have heard others of a similar tenor; and this shift from the importance of birth to the importance of education at the start of the nineteenth century marks the beginning of the class-consciousness in the English middle classes which has distinguished them from that day to this.

The expanding industrialism and the expanding empire of the nineteenth century called for far more people to take decisions, to be in command, than had the simpler economy which preceded it; it demanded a far larger ruling class than earlier times, so large that the sons of the existing gentry would not have been numerous enough to fill all the vacancies, even had they possessed the requisite ability; and the gentry were traditionally incapable of understanding commerce. At first these positions were filled by able and ambitious members of the non-gentry, driven by the motives of greed and love of power; but these motives alone produced so much exploitation and tyranny, so much human misery, that a new social invention had to be made to produce recruits for the ruling classes of such a character that they would be able to hold positions of power and responsibility without succumbing to the temptations inherent in such positions.

This social invention was a novel modification of what anthropologists call 'social mobility'. In the traditional society, some individuals could change the status into which they were born by outstanding wealth, ability or marriage. The modification which was introduced in the nineteenth century was that people of moderate wealth or ability could improve the status of their children by purchasing for them the appropriate education, pro-

[1] *Sense and Sensibility*, pp. 250-1.

vided this process was started early enough. A gentleman, it was decided, was made, not merely born. Birth by itself did not create the necessary manners and character: these were gradually evoked by the proper education from birth to adulthood. Further, this type of education could be made available to those who were not the sons of gentlemen; and by the time this long process was completed there would be little or no difference between the offspring of the two groups.

This was a very remarkable social invention; indeed, as far as I know, there is no precise parallel in any other advanced society for recruiting and training members of the ruling classes. Moreover it produced, or at least widely diffused, a new motive to impel the able and energetic to greater exertions: besides the desire for wealth and the desire for power, which are universal, it brought into play the desire to improve the status of one's children, which is probably the most altruistic motive available to the majority of human beings.

Societies which are in the process of rapid technical change depend on eliciting some sort of motive in the competent and enterprising among their citizens so that they will continue to work after their primary needs and those of their family are adequately secured. In the arts, in many of the professions, and in some aspects of experimental science societies can usually count on vocation, on finding enough people who have so much interest in their work that they find the opportunity to work an adequate reward. But it is impossible to rely on such a sense of vocation when demands for professional services—teaching, healing, and so on—are rapidly increasing; and it is doubtful whether a sense of vocation would ever supply sufficient administrators or civil servants, clerical workers or business entrepreneurs. Love of money will probably provide enough top business entrepreneurs, and love of power enough top administrators; and the hopes of achieving these goals may keep the lower ranks adequately filled, at least until society decides that the uncontrolled gratification of these lusts inflicts too much misery on other people; but how are the lower ranks of the professions, the administration, clerical and technical staff and so on to be filled?

Here again the answer was found in nineteenth-century England

(and indeed in most of Europe) by the elaboration of class distinctions. Some jobs were defined as being more 'genteel' than other jobs; the work in the more genteel jobs was perhaps cleaner and less physically arduous than those in the less genteel, but there were few other advantages: the hours were equally long, the pay never higher and often lower, and the holders of these jobs had to spend a considerably larger proportion of their wages or salaries in dressing respectably. It is difficult to see how these jobs could have been filled at that period, unless working-class parents had been convinced that it was worth foregoing their children's wages for some years and providing them with longer education or training because the children would be—not more prosperous or more secure—but more genteel if they went into these jobs. They would have got their foot on the ladder which led from the unskilled working class to the aristocracy; small niceties distinguished the upper working class from the lower middle class.

The concepts of the genteel and the gentlemanly, in the name of which both parents and children would make sacrifices, are ideas of status validated by speech, manners, and a value system. It is the value system which was socially important; the genteel and the gentlemanly both tended to develop such strong consciences that they were able to resist—and took pride in resisting—the many opportunities for financial dishonesty or social oppression which their positions of trust made possible to them. Although we take it for granted, it is remarkable how few bank tellers have ever embezzled, how few colonial administrators have been overt sadists or oppressors.

I would claim indeed that democracy in advanced societies is only possible if a sizeable portion of the population has developed such strict consciences that they will supervise their own behaviour even when it seems probable that deviations will never be discovered. Where such strict consciences are not general, you will either get corruption tempered by paternalism and tyranny, or else have to develop extremely complex systems of supervision, with overt supervisors looking out for misdeeds, covert supervisors watching the overt supervisors, plain clothes supervisors watching the covert supervisors—all the elaborations of secret police forces, 'revision' inspectorates, neighbourhood associations and the like.

Traditionally, the development of the strict conscience has been seen as the outcome of religious beliefs and practices, particularly of the puritan sects of the world's major religions. This has undoubtedly been a major source, particularly in the Protestant countries; but the concept was removed from a purely religious to a social setting when high social status was defined by character as well as by birth—the 'Christian gentleman' and his counterpart, the 'highborn blackguard'.

To my mind, it is the linking of a value system with strong emphasis on honesty and justice with certain positions in the social system which was the major contribution of the English system of class distinctions as it developed in the nineteenth century. Other social systems, of course, have made links between specified social statuses and socially desirable value systems: the knightly ethos of the late Middle Ages in Europe, the Brahmins in Hindu India and so on; but they only knew how to acquire recruits for these statuses by birth. The conscious use of education to produce a character to fit the status at which the individual, or the parents, aimed, was a development whose novelty is seldom adequately appreciated.

It is interesting to note, too, that this concept was taken over with only slight modifications by the Soviet Union in its formative years, and subsequently by other Communist governments. Although the definition of the type of family from which recruits should be sought was changed (indeed reversed) the good Communist party member was defined by his character, by his value system; and education, from infancy onwards, was designed to elicit this. In more recent years, special schools for the children of prominent party members and officers of the forces, including some boarding schools, have been developed in Soviet Russia.

In its immediate social aims the new system of class distinctions was strikingly successful. It provided the personnel for the reformed civil service, the reformed Indian and colonial administration, for the expanding mercantile and financial undertakings which were unequalled for their honesty and probity. A pretty illustration of the best values of such class-consciousness is given in the *Memoirs of a Bengal Civilian* by John Beames.[1] Beames was the son of a nearly penniless clergyman, and was actually hungry through most of his childhood; he was educated at Merchant Taylors, and was one of the last nominees of the East India Company. In his very early twenties he was put in a position of great responsibility; because he was convinced that he was a gentleman he was never tempted, by the opportunities (which many of his predecessors, raised under another system, had taken) implicit in his position for corruption, tyranny, or toadying; he was active in protecting the peasants from the exploitations of the traders and landowners, whom he looked down on; and he was not in the least awed by his superiors in rank or wealth.

These social advantages of the genteel and the gentleman were not achieved without cost. The acquisition of the desired character and the manners which validated it demanded a very considerable renunciation of immediate pleasures, compared with contemporaries who were not pursuing the same goals. This renunciation was only made tolerable by a pharisaic insistence on one's own superiority and difference to the common people, and by treating these common people, when one came into contact with them, with insolence and contempt. The not-unjustified self-righteousness was the cause of a great deal of social misery.

This misery was perhaps most poignant in the first generation of the gentlemanly and genteel, when one's own parents, and those of one's brothers and sisters who had not one's advantages, fell into the category of the 'common people'. To the extent that the neophytes had absorbed the values of the classes for which they were training, they were forced, to a greater or lesser extent, to despise their parents and their other uneducated close relations. Such an attitude to one's parents is never, I think, unaccompanied by deep unconscious guilt (in the psychoanalytic meaning of the term) and considerable conscious shame and embarrassment. I think these emotional concomitants are constant, even when the rejection of the parents is demanded by the prevailing ideology to which one may be emotionally very

---

[1] London, Chatto and Windus, 1961.

heavily committed. This rejection is a regular feature of the first generation of ideologically-tinged revolutions.

In the case of the class-mobile, who are only supported by an ethic, and not by an ideology, I think the unconscious guilt may involve the very deepest psychological processes and may be one of the reasons why today those who have been successfully mobile educationally are particularly strident in their demands that the ladder by which they have climbed away from their families of origin should be destroyed. The demands for the abolition of the public schools or the submerging of grammar schools into comprehensive schools seem to be voiced most strongly by the successful products of these favoured institutions.

It would seem that, in the nineteenth century, these unconscious feelings of guilt were masked by puritanic severity and social insolence. When we think of such social insolence and snubbing we are inclined to consider that they were only displayed by the upper middle classes and chiefly directed at the middle classes, professional people refusing to consort with people in trade, and so on; but I think that this impression is chiefly due to the fact that our knowledge of the working of class distinctions is overwhelmingly derived from literature—from novels, plays, comic papers such as *Punch* and so on; and these drew almost all their audience, and the greater number of their practitioners, from these two classes. My personal impression is that the greatest amount of social intolerance and exclusiveness occurred and occur in the two small classes between the middle class and working class proper: the superior or upper working class and the lower middle class. These two groups had much frailer supports for their consciousness of superiority than did the upper middle class, and so had to take greater precautions against being submerged and losing their identity. In the Eastern United States there were few more rigid social barriers than those between the lace-curtain and the piss-pot Irish, or between the respectable and the no-account Negroes. I shall return to this point that the frailty of other supports is likely to increase the rigidity with which class distinctions are maintained when I come down to the present day.

The breakdown of the old hierarchies based on birth or occupation, together with the increasing speed of communications, had the further result that, from the first third of the nineteenth century onwards, people could *choose* their friends and associates in a manner which was quite unprecedented in earlier periods. Outside the big cities the possible range of association was strictly limited; men from different levels of the hierarchy could mingle in such places as coffee houses, assembly rooms and the like; but intimacy was almost entirely reserved for one's equals by birth. As social intercourse shifted from groups of common birth to groups of common education, the class-indicators took on an increasing importance, particularly in denoting those acquaintances who might be seeking one's friendship for their own advantage only. This phase is admirably documented by Dickens, perhaps particularly in *Dombey and Son* and *Our Mutual Friend*.

I think it can be claimed that the first generation of conscience-ridden, conscientious, class-conscious administrators and clerks did a great deal of social good; but the sense of superiority, which made them able to resist the temptations of their offices and look down on those who had merely wealth or power started to have very deleterious effects when they in their turn became parents. The gentlemanly and the genteel characters were proclaimed by ways of speaking—by accent and vocabulary—and by social manners, etiquette. To a great extent these were taught in the appropriate schools. To an ever-increasing degree, these minor signs of class-position came to replace in importance the value system and the character strengths they were intended to indicate; the substance was to a great extent replaced by signs; until you get the ultimate absurdity of Professor Ross's and Nancy Mitford's U-indicators, where class position is validated entirely by minor variants of vocabulary. In much of the rest of the Western world—particularly those societies deriving their patterns from France or Spain—the handling of table-tools—knives, forks, spoons and so on—has the same role as vocabulary in contemporary England.

In the twentieth century the signs of class came to have considerable market value, both positively and negatively. Because so many of the first generations of gentlemen had been just and incorruptible as well as competent, it was widely assumed by employers (perhaps above all in the government) that people who possessed the superficial signs of class position would possess these moral qualities also, and that those who lacked the one would lack the other; the possession of these signs was of more use in obtaining desirable positions than almost any technical qualifications.

Largely, I believe, because of the economic value of these signs, there was a considerable exacerbation of the exclusiveness of the favoured classes and of their cruelty and insolence to those who attempted entry into their ranks without the proper qualifications. I would question whether any group, clearly not belonging to a minority, was treated with more contumely than were the new rich and the 'temporary gentlemen' (revealing phrase!) by the gentry during and after the First World War. The gentry, and to a lesser extent the genteel, were both on the defensive, trying to preserve their social and economic positions from erosion or invasion. Their attempt to exclude newcomers, at least for a generation, led to a great deal of bitterness and cruelty and towards an ossification of the social hierarchy; less than a century earlier the hierarchy based on class distinctions had been invented to destroy the ossified hierarchy based on birth.

One of the characteristics of the gentlemanly and genteel in the nineteenth century was that, compared with the members of the other social classes, they were relatively indifferent to money. John Beames, to whom I referred earlier, had far less money than the merchants whom he controlled, not to mention the Indian potentates whose revenues he helped to maintain; and he seems to have been quite content that this should be so. The genteel, those who are now called the white collar workers, accepted lower wages or salaries than their brothers and sisters in less esteemed occupations. Greed and envy were considered unworthy motives for the gentlemanly and the genteel. They did not work completely altruistically—probably only saints can be expected to do that; but they did the state and industry very considerable service in exchange for the social deference which they considered their due. In response to this deference they maintained very high ideals of conduct.

After the First War these abstemious qualities very largely disappeared from the gentry. They became both greedy and envious, taking all the good jobs they could lay hands on, and slighting all those who had money without manifesting the appropriate class-signs—foreigners such as Americans, and those who had just made their money out of manufacturing or trade. They did their best to exclude from any position of influence and power people who did not manifest the proper class-signs, people who were not 'one of us', not 'p.l.u.'. This was the period when the claims of the old school tie were pushed to their greatest extent.

The arrogance and exclusiveness with which these claims were pressed generated considerable bitterness in those who were, or thought that they had been, excluded; and as the technology of peace and war grew continuously more complicated, the right manners, even when accompanied by high ethical ideals, proved an inadequate equipment for the positions claimed. As is well known, the concept of 'officer and gentleman' did not survive the Second World War without very great modifications; and certainly one of the motives of the Labour governments and their supporters after the war has been to undermine the economic position of the gentry by their fiscal policies; and although the attempt to abolish the schools which specialize in training gentry has not yet been carried through, the idea attracts very considerable emotional support.

The genteel have not been the subject of so concerted an attack, partly because they made themselves less obnoxious, and partly, I think, because most of the egalitarians see considerable advantages in having professions and positions filled by people who will put up with less money than their brothers and sisters in return for social respect. If any politician outside the professions has claimed that teachers or bank-clerks or clerical staff should be paid as much as skilled workers in manufacturing, these claims have not met my eyes.

The attempt to abolish class distinctions by removing the economic underpinning has not, I think, been a success; I very much doubt whether class distinctions are of less social and emotional importance today than they were a generation ago. I think too that this could have been foretold, if anthropologists or sociologists had been consulted. In a hierarchical society, class position is an important part in a person's picture of himself, his ego ideal as the psycho-analysts phrase it; the fewer other reasons he has for self-esteem, the more tenaciously will he cling to those aspects of behaviour which remain within his control. I have already referred to the differentiations in two of the most disadvantaged groups in the United States—the Negroes and the immigrant Irish; another, and very telling, example can be found in the exiled or 'white' Russians who, although almost all living on the edge of poverty, yet kept up over two or three generations, all the claims to the class they, or their ancestors, had held before they fled the Soviets. Biological motives apart, one could say that this was all that made life meaningful to them.

English class-position is nothing like so rigid as that of Czarist Russia; but I think the psychological motives brought into play are very similar. I cannot see how, unless people are to be penalized for their birth or education, one can lessen the social importance of class distinctions by punitive fiscal or other legal devices. It would go against the general tenor and value system of the present day to reverse this policy; but theoretically I think it likely that fiscal and legal indulgence would diminish the emotional importance of class distinctions more quickly and efficaciously than fiscal and legal severity.

Moreover, there still remains the problem, the very urgent problem, of what to put in its place. As I said earlier, I believe that class distinctions were invented to evoke some motive, other than greed and desire for power, which would induce the able and energetic to unnecessary work (from their point of view) which would directly or indirectly benefit society. This problem is still most urgently with us. To take one simple example, why should some individuals go to the trouble of organizing an adequate export trade on which the future survival of the large population on this small island depends?

We have decided that greed will not be admitted as a motive, that people may not make a fortune by successful merchandising. Not that we have exorcised greed from our society (no complex society in the world has succeeded in doing so); but we have channelled it into areas where it will do the least social good. One can still make a fortune, and a tax-free fortune, by gambling; the success of the pools, of Bingo and other popular devices shows how very wide-spread such a desire is. With somewhat more skill, one can make a fortune by various financial manipulations and speculations; but the cleverest or the most industrious individual cannot make legitimately in a life-time what pool-winners gain every week. In contrast to most other complex societies, we will not let the greedy help us at the same time as they help themselves.

The other available motive for energy beyond the call of necessity is love of power. It would seem likely that this is a component of the motives of any energetic individual, in direct or symbolic terms; the artist and scientist enjoy exercising power over their materials, as the politician, the boss, the department head, the commanding officer enjoy exercising power over people. Most people believe that they exercise their power benevolently, for the good of those under their control. Power tends to be an insatiable appetite, for there are few or no recognized gradations of power, parallel with making one's first hundred thousand, or being presented at court, or what you will. Power is also very labile; if your power does not increase, it is likely to be taken from you.

Societies can certainly be viable with power as the chief, or the only significant, reward for the energetic; indeed, I think this would be a valid way of describing at least one aspect of communist societies. The mobilization of this lust certainly produces results, at least as effectively as the mobilization of greed in the growing phases of capitalism.

I don't think it is idiosyncratic on my part to prefer a society which has other motives for mobilizing the energetic citizens besides greed and love of power. For at least a couple of generations in England the open class system mobilized the love of parents for their children; with sufficient effort one could give one's children a higher class position than one had held oneself, and this hope was able to spur the enormous expansion of nineteenth century England; and because class was defined, at least partly, in terms of ethical behaviour, the worst results of greed and lust for power were modified largely by the efforts of ladies and gentlemen, of the genteel and the refined. This particular device has probably outlived its utility, now probably produces more stagnation than energy, more misery than it does upright behaviour; but what are we going to put in its place?

PART TWO

*Phases of Human Life*

## VIII

*Adolescence in Different Cultures*
*(1965)*

TO THE BEST of my knowledge, the rhythms and stages of physiological adolescence are identical or very similar throughout the human species. There is a vague folk mythology that peoples of different skin-colour or living in different climates reach adolescence at differing ages; probably the most widespread is the belief that, the nearer the equator the earlier the adolescence, the nearer the poles the later. It is extremely unlikely that there is any statistical basis for this belief or any variant of it, for the very simple reason that very few of the technologically primitive societies keep an accurate year-count of people's ages; in most cases it needs elaborate cross-checking and other calculations to fix the ages of members of an illiterate society within four or five years; and of course one needs far greater precision than that to make generalized statements about the age of puberty. Until we have far better records than are now available, it seems safest to assume that puberty is physiologically identical throughout the human species, with the same changes in the ductless glands and accompanying emotional modifications, and taking place at approximately the same period in the second decade of life. In other words, I assume that we are dealing with identical physiologically determined rhythms and stages of development of human beings in the second decade of their lives, and that the differing treatment that these rhythms and stages of growth receive are determined by the customs and values of a given society at a specified time.

Human societies have developed a wide gamut of attitudes towards physiological puberty and adolescence from pretending that it hasn't occurred (though this is probably only possible when the society has developed tailored clothes) to treating it as the single most significant event in an individual's life; from treating it as one phase in a series of phases or grades through which all members of the society pass to treating it as a sort of no-man's-land period, an interruption between childhood and adulthood; from treating it as the peak of life to treating it as merely one step on the road to honoured maturity.

If you count the society as a unit (rather than the number of individuals within each society) it is probable that more societies give public ritual recognition to puberty or adolescence than do not; in many of these societies, the rituals celebrating adolescence are the most elaborate of all. Such puberty rituals are very wide-spread in Africa and Oceania; but they are also reported from all the other continents of the world, with the exception of modern Western Europe.

It is perhaps not surprising that in most cases these rituals are far more elaborate for young men than they are for young women. The menarche is so striking a physiological event, the transformation of an immature girl into a potentially fertile woman is so publicly evident (before the adoption of fitted clothes) that many societies have not felt the need for much further ritual elaboration. Yesterday, the young female was a child, today she is a woman; she may need formal instruction in the behaviour appropriate to her new state; but this is often given privately by the appropriate woman of the generation above—her mother, or her father's sister, or her mother's brother's wife, for example. In a number of societies the initiation ritual for girls is as elaborate (or nearly so) as that for boys; but there are very few societies which have an elaborate initiation ritual for the girls and not for the boys. It would seem that, in the great majority of cases, girls' puberty rituals have been developed on what might be called suffragette ethics: that women should have equal or analogous privileges and ceremonies.

Male puberty, of course, has no such precise physiological start; and so a great many societies seem to have chosen a physical mutilation, accompanied by the shedding of blood, as the most important public component of the ritual which transforms a boy into a man. Circumcision is the most wide-spread of these initiation mutilations; tattooing or the production of welts is found among a number of societies; and a few societies, perhaps particularly in Australasia, have developed even more exotic alterations to the initiates' physiques. When these symbolic wounds (to use Dr Bettelheim's phrase) had healed the boy was transformed into a man.

Sometimes these mutilations are performed individually and quickly, so that the sociological adolescence only lasts over a few days; but more frequently all boys of an age are initiated together at intervals of one or more years. These ceremonies may only last for a few days; but in the areas where the initiation of male adolescents is most developed—above all Africa and Australasia—the boys are withdrawn from their families for months or even years before they are returned to their communities as men. In these societies the social adolescence of males—and occasionally of females—takes place in a different setting to that of the rest of their life.

In these initiation camps the boys are taught how to be men; specific skills are imparted by the older male initiators, both technical and (frequently) sexual; there is often quite a lot of bullying and tough endurance tests (a faint echo of these are found in the Duke of Edinburgh's awards); where men have sacred mysteries, often connected with masks or noisemaking instruments such as bull-roarers, the boys are made privy to the secrets which they must guard against all the unitiated. A very frequent part of the initiating ritual is a pantomime of rebirth, carrying the underlying, and sometimes explicit, message that while women can bear children, only men can make men. In many of the simpler societies male envy of female fertility is given overt ritual recognition. In more complex societies, including our own, this male envy is so completely repressed that it is hardly recognized by orthodox psycho-analysis; there are, however, quite a number of indications that this envy is species-wide among young males. I should be inclined to see a sign of this in the long hair now affected by many male adolescents in this country, and even more in the indignation and sense of outrage with which this long hair is reprobated by older males.

In those societies that have developed elaborate initiation rituals, two generations are involved: the adolescents and the men of their father's generation (usually but not universally) who initiate them. In these societies there are basically only two social positions for males: children or adults; and the transition from one to the other is accomplished outside the society through ritual.

There exist relatively few societies which see life as divided into three phases: childhood, adolescence, and adulthood. In these societies the children at, or near, puberty leave the parental home for 'bachelor's halls'; here they live in special buildings until they marry and found a home of their own. This arrangement is found in quite a number of societies in Oceania and in some primitive groups in Asia. Far and away the most vivid and convincing description of the way these bachelors' halls work is that given by the late Verrier Elwin in *The Muria and Their Ghotul*.[1] The Muria are an aboriginal tribe in Bastar, in Central India.

Children join the *ghotul*—the bachelors' hall—when they have achieved full physical independence and remain members until their marriage. In the great majority of cases marriages are arranged by the parents and conform to the socially approved cross-cousin type of marriage; marriage apparently usually takes place in the late teens. During the day children work with their parents, and go to the *ghotul* after their evening meal; in some villages they sleep in them every night, in others on only certain days of the week.

The *ghotul* are theocratically sanctioned, and the members have certain ritual duties to perform (I should like to emphasize this) either alone or as most important components of such ceremonies as marriages and funerals. The native arts—music, singing, dancing, wood-carving—are practised by the members of the *ghotul,* and apparently only by them. There are a number of officers, with various duties of supervision and instruction, with parallel titles in each *ghotul*; the officers are nominated from the available members on the basis of suitability of character.

The small children spend a period of 'fagging' for their

[1] Oxford University Press, 1947.

## Adolescence in Different Cultures

elders, learning habits of industry, co-operation and equality and, in the case of little girls, techniques of massage; they are subsequently admitted to the rights and duties of full membership, including heterosexual intercourse with other members. These rights are granted well before puberty.

In most of the Muria *ghotul* sexual possessiveness is forbidden, and members are fined if they sleep with the same partner more than three nights running. Sleeping partners for the night are often assigned by one of the officials. Although there are many periods of ritually enforced abstinence, all young Muria have frequent, and usually very varied, intercourse all through their later childhood and adolescence, though for girls it may not be complete before the menarche.

Mr. Elwin validated statistically two socially important facts: despite the frequency of pre-marital intercourse, there are very few illegitimate births; and marriages, subsequent to this early experimentation, are remarkably happy and stable, with very few divorces and very little adultery. For the Muria, as for quite a few other tribes with similar free sexuality in adolescence, chastity begins with marriage.

Besides the societies like the Muria who single out adolescence as a specially treated phase of human life, there is another group of societies who divide life into numerous phases through which all members of the society (or on occasion all males) must pass, adolescence being just one or two of these phases. These societies are technically known as age-grade or age-class societies. In the greater number of cases that we know about these were military, warrior societies; and as tribal war has been progressively banned in this century, so these societies have tended to disintegrate and lose their traditional patterns, without having been studied with the particularity and in the detail of contemporary standards of social anthropology. Typical of these warrior societies are the Masai of East Africa, the Pathans of Pakistan and Afghanistan, and the traditional peasant society of Albania.

In age-grade societies chronological age and biological sex are treated as the most important variables; and behaviour is considered appropriate or inappropriate, as praiseworthy or to be condemned, in relation to the age of the person manifesting the behaviour and not according to any moral absolutes. In many ways this variation of behaviour according to age is psychologically very obscure; in these societies all people, or all the people of one sex, are expected to exhibit at different times of their life characteristics which seem to us mutually contradictory. Thus Masai young warriors (probably the equivalent of adolescents) were expected to be extremely touchy and quarrelsome, and living only on milk and blood; men whose sons had become young warriors were meant to be peace-makers and near-vegetarians. The young Masai girls, of the same age-grade as the young warriors, were meant to be flirtatious and available for a restricted type of intercourse with any or all of the young warriors of their age-grade outside the bounds of incest; they were meant to be sober and faithful married women. Character traits were not classified as good or bad, but as suitable or unsuitable for a given age. There was presumably quite a lot of constraint on some temperaments: the peaceful person who had to be quarrelsome between say 15 and 24; or the touchy person who must never quarrel over the age of 45. But as far as the accounts go—unfortunately, they are not as precise as one could wish—these demands do not seem to have resulted in aberrant practice or undesirable behaviour, from the point of view of the society. All psychological impulses could be gratified; but certain types of behaviour were classified as 'no longer' or 'not yet' suitable.

In an analogous way to that in which the Masai used aggression and peace-making as appropriate for specified phases in the life-cycle, so did the Pathans and Albanians use homosexuality and heterosexuality, treating pederasty as appropriate for the early adolescent and the father of adolescent sons, and heterosexuality, including marriage, as appropriate in the intervening period and for grandfathers. Here, once again, behaviour is classified as 'no longer' or 'not yet' suitable, not as good or bad.

I am personally fascinated by the type of psychological organization which must be involved in producing the potentiality for apparently contradictory attitudes and wishes at different points of the life cycle, and regret that the interruption of the war and my health have prevented me studying one of these societies before they disintegrated. For these age-grade societies seem to be very brittle; once the function of one of the age-grades, such as tribal warfare, raiding, herding or the like, is rendered impossible by external constraints, the pattern of the whole society seems to disappear. While the societies were functioning, the behaviour and character of adolescents were prescribed in exactly the same way as the behaviour and character of the numerous other stages in life that the societies recognized, and, as far as the evidence goes, this stage was not considered in any way different from the others.

The first anthropologist to pay detailed attention to adolescence in a technologically simple society was Margaret Mead who published her study *Coming of Age in Samoa* in 1927. The dominant topic in this pioneering book is the experience of identified girls on the little island of Manu'a. Dr. Mead found that in this society adolescence was not a period of stress and revolt, of *Sturm und Drang*. Indeed, it was given no social recognition, and no special term; it was treated as just one pleasant and socially useful stage in a pleasant and socially useful life which would reach its culmination in honoured maturity. It was a period of great sexual permissiveness, of sex as fun, rather as Verrier Elwin describes the Muria; but adolescence and early adulthood were not marked by any separation from the adult community, or differences in work or skills or dress. This period of early free sexual experimentation was typically closed by an arranged marriage. The available sexual partners were people of about one's own age with whom no kin connection could be traced.

The society which Dr. Mead described was a society without emotional or artistic intensity, a society which disapproved of precocity and placed a very great emphasis on appropriate behaviour.

After Dr. Mead's pioneering work, a number of other rather similar societies have been described, societies of low intensity where the emphasis is on satisfaction rather than ecstasy, and where adolescence is seen as a period of increasing skill and strength with, almost incidentally, the capacity to enjoy sexual intercourse. The Lepchas of the Himalayas, whom I studied, were a society of this sort; they had a word for people or animals who were fully developed but had not yet borne young, somewhat analogous to our agricultural terms, such as 'heifer' or 'gilt'; but they had no word for adolescence as a period of human life; nor, save to the extent that the adolescents were not as strong or as skilled as their elders, had they any special role or disabilities in the society. In contrast to the Samoans, the Lepchas did recognize 'falling in love'; but they considered it a social disaster, which could disrupt the even tenor of life and cause all sorts of social misfortunes from jealousy or exclusivity. Like the Samoans, the Lepchas made no allowance for any intensity of emotion, religious or artistic or personal; and in both societies the children were typically raised in large conjoint households, with more than one adult in the role of father or mother, and with easy access to other households if they were temporarily unhappy or angry at home. In both societies no attempt was made to shield children from any of the 'facts of life'—birth, or copulation, or death; and so puberty does not entail making any new discoveries, but merely having the capacity to do things which one lacked before.

On the basis of these two societies, and of others more summarily described, it seems that one can specify the minimum preconditions for a society in which the physical changes of puberty and adolescence will not entail either social or psychological disturbance. The most important of these is that children shall be raised in conjoint or extended families, so that the social roles of father and mother are held by more than one adult. In such households it is possible for young children to avoid the ambivalence which is almost inevitable when children are raised in nuclear families—only one parent of each sex—which are typical of contemporary complex societies. In such nuclear families it is almost inevitable that the father or mother is the focus of both intense love and intense hate—for young children must inevitably be thwarted on occasion; but when more than one adult holds the paternal or maternal role the emotions can be, as it were, divided: the child can feel 'I hate big mummy but I love little mummy' or conversely, and the intensity of the emotion is correspondingly diminished; and when the child grows up it is much less likely to expect an intense romantic relationship with potential lovers or spouse. The relaxed quality of divided emotions render almost impossible an adolescent revolt against parents and parental standards; in a way, there is nothing to revolt against.

A second precondition for undisturbed adolescence is that children shall not be treated as though they were different sorts of creatures from adults, that there should be neither a concept of childish innocence, so that children have to be protected from the knowledge and experience common to adults, nor yet a concept of childish wickedness or animality—the child as a 'limb of Satan'—so that its conduct has to be continually watched and rectified by standards which adults do not apply to themselves or one another. Growing up must not entail either the discovery of adult secrets or the liberation from childish constraints.

A third precondition, in the case of the Samoans and the Lepchas, is that sexuality is not treated as being of much importance by anyone; it is obviously enjoyable, rather as a good meal is enjoyable, but basically not very serious. I am inclined to think, however, that it might be possible to have a society free from adolescent disturbances without the easy sexuality of the Samoans and Lepchas, though I do not know of one which has been realistically described.

All the societies so far reported in which adolescence is not a period of strain, conflict or psychological disturbance have one feature in common: there is a lack of intensity throughout the society, both in interpersonal relations and in their religion, their politics and their art (where they have any—the Lepchas have none). It seems as though intensity, passionate involvement with other people or with ideas, is an all-or-none component of human character and of the societies which human beings have evolved. Adolescence *can* be merely a phase of physical growth; but the price is emotional shallowness throughout the society.

To the best of my knowledge, these four techniques for dealing with adolescence—the public initiation into adulthood, the special role for adolescents, the treating of adolescence as one in a large series of age-grades, and the lowering of emotional intensity throughout the whole society—these four techniques are the only ones developed in recorded human societies which have no analogue with our own treatment of adolescence. In other non-European cultures, especially those which reprobate premarital sexuality in one or both sexes, adolescence is often accompanied by the psychological disturbances and conflict and anti-social behaviour which is considered typical in our own society.

There is, however, one major difference. In non-European societies, with the occasional exception of the élite, there is not the distinction between physiological and social adolescence which is so marked a feature of contemporary technologically advanced societies. In pre-industrial societies, once a young man or young woman has attained their full growth and strength they have all the rights and privileges of full adulthood and typically have all the skills they need for the degree of independence appropriate. Consequently, adolescence is a relatively brief period, measured in months rather than years.

Complex industrial societies, on the other hand, depend on prolonging social adolescence very many years beyond the end of physical adolescence. Until the industrial revolution, prolonged social adolescence was only necessary for a very small proportion of the population, the ruling and professional males. Girls were treated as adult after the menarche—may I remind you that Shakespeare's Juliet was 14,[1] and Lydia, the naughty sister in *Pride and Prejudice,* eloped with Wickham before she was sixteen; and, although Jane Austen was a strict moralist, she never commented unfavourably about her behaviour as unsuitable to her age, though her living with Wickham before they were married was deeply sinful. Boys joined the armed services very young, and took all the risks of which they were physically capable. Again calling Jane Austen in evidence, there is the history of her sailor brothers, not to mention the adventures and risks that Fanny Price's brother, William, in *Mansfield Park,* had undergone before he was eighteen.

The increasingly complex techniques of industrialization de-

[1] She was untypically precocious, according to Peter Laslett's *The World We Have Lost,* Chapter IV. (Methuen, 1965).

manded more education and/or apprenticeship from an ever increasing segment of the population; and the students or apprentices were treated as not-adult, whatever the stage of their physical development. It is the treatment of males and females in the second, and even occasionally the third, decade of their lives as not-adult that I have called social adolescence.

In Britain, and indeed in the whole of Europe, the tradition of a prolonged social adolescence for upper-class males is of very long standing; and when social adolescence was found necessary for males in the other social classes and for females, the only pattern available was that of the upper classes. I think this fact is not without influence on the style of contemporary adolescence, and the problems we think we face.

Let me recall briefly some of the features of this traditional social adolescence of the upper-class males. Britain developed the idiosyncratic pattern—I do not know of its equivalent in any society not influenced by Britain—of what might be called the double apprenticeship in leadership: the boy starting school as an insignificant new boy at nine and rising to a position of some authority at 13, and then again becoming an insignificant new boy to attain authority again at 17 or 18. But this is specifically British, perhaps specifically English; whereas the style of behaviour of university students is widely European.

University students were allowed to be quite aggressive and commit quite a lot of senseless destruction, because of their status. Some of this aggression was calendrical—boat race night in the West End of London, various rag days, founders' days and the like; some was visited on their less popular fellows—breaking up a man's rooms, debagging him, duelling, and so on; but the most serious were probably the fights between town and gown—there are a number of verbal equivalents for the other countries of Europe—which often resulted in serious injuries to the participants. This aggression was justified as 'youthful high spirits' and does not seem to have been resented by any section of the population, except perhaps the police.

Tacitly in Britain, and quite openly in most of Europe, university students were allowed quite a lot of sexual activity, with two provisos: they should not seek sexual partners in their own social class—among girls who might be the sisters of their fellow-students—and these liaisons should not develop into marriage. In British university towns, for some odd reason, the daughters of tobacconists were considered the most easily available, at the Sorbonne in Paris girls working in dressmaking establishments, the *midinettes*.

In many universities students developed their own music, typically songs sung in chorus; in some universities, such as Coimbra in Portugal, this music developed an individual style which musicians took seriously. But most of the time people with serious musical tastes thought the students' songs an abominable noise, and the words an affront to common decency.

This licence granted to students because they were not-adult was tolerable when students were a very small proportion—well under one per cent—of the population in their age-range. But as more and more of the population were classified as not-adult until they married, the adaptation of the upper-class pattern of 'youthful high spirits' became less and less acceptable. A single annual affray around Piccadilly Circus in the early spring was traditional fun; similar affrays at seaside towns on bank holidays were not looked on so indulgently.

I should like to stress the fact that this pattern of suitable behaviour for upper-class males was and is the only pattern that our culture provides for social adolescence. The rest of the population traditionally left school at the earliest legal age, went to work, and except for such minor points as voting rights were treated as adults. Today they are not treated as adults and are emphatically no longer children; a new social category has been invented—the 'teenager'—which has some imprecise chronological reference, but which is chiefly defined negatively —no longer children, not yet adults. This group is given no function which can earn it social esteem; it is rather treated as a regrettable phase which people will grow out of.

Because in the mass teenagers have more disposable money than any other section of the population, they are eagerly studied and pandered to by advertisers and manufacturers; but even this pandering and exploitation does not accord them any social respect.

On the basis of the comparative studies of many societies, I would consider that the according of social respect is essential for the integration of any sizeable group into the population. If social respect is not accorded, one of two undesirable results occur: either you get the formation of counter-mores groups, as they are technically called, groups who set up their own standards of social respect in opposition to the values of the dominant society; or you get very badly distorted characters. Examples of counter-mores groups in our own society are the criminal and the homosexual underworlds, the gangs and the layabouts. When whole sections of the population are denied social respect, as with the untouchables or 'scheduled castes' in India, the Negroes in Southern Africa or the Southern United States, you get badly distorted characters filled with resentment, and with violence never far below the surface.

Today it seems to me that the adult British population is refusing social respect to the adolescents or teenagers. A story about teenagers in the press is, almost by definition, a story of social disapproval; many magistrates feel that they can insult teenagers with the full approval of their fellow adults; their clothes, their hair-styles, their music are fit subjects for adult mockery.

This withholding of social respect seems to be driving a sizeable number of teenagers into forming counter-mores groups. I do not include in this counter-mores behaviour the experimentation with marijuana, for such evidence as is available suggests that this is a far less dangerous drug than alcohol; in particular it impairs judgement much less when in charge of an automobile; and did not the procuring of marijuana bring the young into contact with the criminal underworld, who also deal in the really dangerous drugs, it would probably be seen as a sensible adaptation to the automated age we live in. But a lot of what I read about the 'mods' and 'rockers' seems to fall into the pattern of counter-mores groups, as does some of the other conspicuous flouting of adult conventions. This is in a way a self-perpetuating situation: the more all teenagers are included in the condemnation of the conspicuous counter-mores groups, the more likely they will be to perpetuate and increase these groups. If this vicious circle is to be broken, social respect and useful social roles must be accorded to the adolescents by the adult society.

## IX

## *Dionysus and the Welfare State*
## *(1957)*

NIETZSCHE, AND AFTER him Spengler and many others, made the contrast between the Apollonian and the Dionysian as two polarities of one dimension of human behaviour which could be discerned in individual characters, in art, or in total societies. In art the contrast is much the same as that between 'classical' and 'romantic': in the classical, as in the Apollonian, reason is in paramount control and the values are order and proportion; in the romantic, as in the Dionysian, control is surrendered to intensity of emotion, and the values are sensation and self-abandonment. It was Nietzsche's contribution to show that this polarity had much wider relevance than the classification or evaluation of works of art; Spengler, and Ruth Benedict in *Patterns of Culture,* used it to characterize whole societies.

Where some confusion has arisen has been in the treating of these terms as mutually exclusive, rather than as marking the end points of a continuum. Just as there are relatively few artists or works of art which can be unequivocally classified as wholly classic or wholly romantic, so there are few personalities or societies who can be classified as completely Apollonian or completely Dionysian. In the great majority of human beings, and in the great majority of human societies, both components are present in different proportions, either overtly or potentially. People and societies will differ in which component they value and emphasize the more, whether they prefer the head or the heart, self-control or letting oneself go, order or thrills. But it is a mistake to imagine that because one of the components is emphasized or valued, the other is non-existent or can be disregarded.

By their very nature, complex industrial societies must emphasize and stress the Apollonian characteristics of their populations. Urban civilizations and machino-facture depend increasingly on the population exercising self-control, both physical and mental; the replacement of animal strength by industrial power has meant that there are increasingly fewer occasions when workers in any industry can go 'all out' physically. A few of the extractive industries which have not been, or have only partially been, modernized—as, for example, coal mining or agriculture—give regular opportunity for intense muscular effort. The vast majority of contemporary employments, if they demand physical effort at all, demand it minutely controlled and calculated. In the factory or workshop, on the roads, even in most homes with their delicate gadgets, constant watchfulness is necessary.

Contemporary psychology has paid practically no attention to the emotional effects resulting from the full use or restraint of the striped muscles. In nearly every complex society the leisured classes have employed a good deal of their leisure and money in devices which would allow them to employ their larger muscles in ways which did not derogate from their status: field sports, hunting, polo, winter sports, various organized games, and so on. All these exercises were and are considered to be self-rewarding, partly from the pleasure in using skill and especially from the 'pleasant feeling of tiredness' subsequent to these voluntary exertions. It seems probable that most people whose working lives have not been too strenuous have at some time enjoyed and even sought this pleasant feeling; but although the subjective pleasure would probably be fairly generally agreed, it is extraordinarily hard to place this pleasure within any contemporary schema of psychology or of human motivation. One of the basic hypotheses of nearly all experimental psychologies is that fatigue is unpleasure which is measured against the pleasure of the subsequent reward (food, or the like), and this is certainly a working hypothesis for experimental animals. Psycho-analysis has concentrated almost exclusively on the mucosi as a source of pleasure (a little recent work attempts to include the whole of the skin surface) and has practically nothing to say on the use of the striped muscles; and so perforce this discussion of rock 'n' roll will have to stand with very little academic or experimental support.

I should like to suggest that *as a dance-form* and as a social phenomenon rock 'n' roll (and its followers, such as the twist or the shake) represents something quite novel in this country, though it has or has had a number of analogues elsewhere. As *dance music* it seems to me (I write as a musical ignoramus) to be remarkable only for its resolute rejection of the rhythmic complications and subtleties which have generally been characteristic of jazz and ragtime; one has to go back to the gallop to find an equally insistent rhythmic beat. The antics of the orchestral performers—playing the piano standing up, the double bass lying down, and similar contortions—although far from spontaneous, carry on the Dionysiac motive which I think I discern in the dance-form.

The peculiarity of rock 'n' roll as a dance-form is the extent to which it employs large and energetic movements of the arms and legs, movements from the shoulder and hip with relatively little use of the knees or elbows. On the whole, arm movements have been used very little in ballroom dancing (at least since the gallop); and, when the feet have been raised off the ground more than in an ordinary walking step as in the charleston or polka, the movement has been from the knee rather than from the hip. Rock 'n' roll is the most strenuous form of dance which has been seen in public in England for a very long time.

Sociologically, rock 'n' roll is peculiar in the way it has entered our society. Nearly all the ballroom dances which have been successfully introduced during this century have originated in other countries—France, the United States, Latin America— and have been first presented here in a West End stage production, a number in a musical comedy or revue, sometimes performed by members of the cast, sometimes by professional ballroom dancers of whom Irene and Vernon Castle are the prototypes. The more expensive dance teachers with the distinguished clientele then adapted and codified the new dance which was first performed at fashionable private dances and hotels, and then permeated downwards as far as the palais de danse. This seems to have been the typical pattern from the bunny hug and the tango to the rumba and the samba. Rock 'n' roll, on the other hand, seems to have arrived from the United States, first in the form of fairly cheap dance records and perhaps stories in popular papers and magazines, and then spectacularly in a film which the middle-class critics considered almost beneath contempt. In Britain rock 'n' roll seems to have come in from the 'teddy boy' section of the working class, and to have permeated upwards, against quite a lot of official or semi-official opposition and criticism.

When the demand had made itself articulate, it was quickly exploited by the purveyors of entertainment to the prosperous working classes; but from all the evidence available to me it appears that the demand existed for this type of dancing before the opportunity for performing it was supplied, rather than the other way round. As Richard Hoggart has pointed out in *The Uses of Literacy*, the assiduous exploitation of the working classes by the purveyors of nationwide entertainment is one of the most marked features of contemporary English society, and makes a very marked contrast with the situation twenty-five years ago, when the sub-culture of the working class was an almost closed enclave in English society, about which the middle classes knew extremely little. I think, however, that Mr. Hoggart has exaggerated the passivity of the working classes in their acceptance of the entertainments provided for them; with rock 'n' roll the demand seems to have preceded the supply; the working classes seem to have found it particularly congenial, and insisted on it being made available.

A generation ago, the middle classes did not know how the equivalent of the teddy boys danced, or, by and large, whether they danced at all. To the extent that working-class dancing was considered, it was probably thought to be represented by the 'Lambeth Walk'. But this was in point of fact a typical West End theatre introduction, and seems to have borne about the same relationship to actual cockney dancing as the ballroom Charleston did to actual American Negro dancing. I cannot claim to know very much about purely working-class dances myself, but it seems as though most of them were highly energetic performances with no, or at most intermittent, physical contact with the partner; for Londoners 'Knees up, Mother Brown' appears to have been typical.

In urban societies this very strenuous type of dancing with large limb movements and very little physical contact with the partner seems to have occurred fairly frequently in the lower working classes: witness the 'apache' type of dancing of French bals musettes, which has frequently been elaborated into a music-hall turn, or the skilled and strenuous dances of the American Negro, such as the Lindy Hop, which only travel down from Harlem in extremely modified and genteel travesties.

If only the movements are considered, and not the social organization of the dance into independent couples of male and female, this type of dancing is nearly worldwide; in a great number of the simpler and primitive societies in every continent such dances occur, nearly always linked with religion (or in areas which have been converted to a higher religion as a syncretist or 'survival' element); and almost uniformally they are employed for inducing some type of trance. This trance may be interpreted as possession by the deity being invoked, or as releasing prophetic or supernatural powers (the witch-finding dances of West Africa, the famous Kris dances of Bali, the Maenads and Corybantes of classical Greece) or as a technique of release from the tensions and preoccupations of everyday life. It is, in short, a Dionysiac type of dancing, both, it would seem, literally as part of the ritual accompanying the worship of Dionysus, as far as this can be reconstructed, and in the figurative meaning of the term discussed earlier. It would seem that there is a human biological potentiality for inducing ecstasy or trance by violent rhythmic movements, since the technique has been observed in so many discrete societies; whether this potentiality will be exploited or ignored would seem to depend on as yet insufficiently identified stresses and demands within the society.

We know extremely little about self-induced trance, and indeed not very much about trance in general (the theory supporting the medical use of hypnotism is decidedly inadequate) since it has been one of the human potentialities which modern complex societies have almost completely ignored. In so far as trance has been used, it has chiefly been in disapproved-of religious cult groups: spiritualist mediums, and little-known revivalist and pentecostal Protestant sects; the Holy Rollers induce possession by the type of dancing we have been discussing. I have not been able to discover anything sufficiently concrete about the 'dancing mania' of the late Middle Ages; but as far as recent centuries are concerned, it would seem that rock 'n' roll is the first occasion where the type of dancing which has been used in other societies to induce trance or ecstasy has been openly performed with the knowledge, if not the consent, of the governing classes.

I am not, of course, suggesting that the majority of rock 'n' rollers put themselves into trance, or are even conscious of the possibility of doing so; I have occasionally seen dancers with the slightly glazed and unfocused eyes which, in a non-European setting, I should have considered indicative of a light trance; and the antics of many of the orchestra players do mimic 'possession'.

There are, however, many 'cultic' elements in the present rock 'n' roll craze, including an esoteric vocabulary not meant to be understandable by the profane ('squares'), quasi-compulsive dancing whenever the appropriate music is heard, however inappropriate the place (strictly analogous to the *m'deup* dancers of Senegal who have to be forcibly carried out of earshot of the drums of their special cult) and ecstatically appreciated leaders—singers or orchestral conductors. Despite the pelvic contortions of a few singers, and the double meanings in the words of some lyrics, I should consider rock 'n' roll the least sexual type of social dancing which Europe has seen in the last couple of centuries; instead of a stylization of courtship and wooing, there is practically no physical contact nor opportunity for conversation; the dance can only be performed if the pair are in good rapport before they step on to the dance floor.

It is, of course, possible that rock 'n' roll will be a purely ephemeral craze, that its implications will never be developed. But it is also possible that it represents, on an almost entirely unconscious level, a marked reaction to the moderation, the restraint, the security of the contemporary welfare states; hope

## Dionysus and the Welfare State

and fear, triumph and disaster, strenuous physical effort and orgiastic physical release have been almost completely banished by the developments of technology and the enormous elaboration of protective legislation which precludes debauchery as well as distress. It seems at least theoretically possible that the English urban working classes unconsciously, or at least inarticulately, feel that the secure and ordered life provided for them by the combination of modern technology and middle-class benevolence (of all political parties) does not provide all the gratifications they crave. Until the last hundred years life in the big English cities was notably violent in its amusements, its uproarious drunkenness, and its crimes, as well as in the precariousness of everyday working life. Relaxation was Dionysiac. It may be that for much of humanity security, control, and self-control are not supreme values; it is suggestive that in Soviet Russia the one really secure group, the children of the higher functionaries, the *stilyagi*, are the enthusiasts for dances of the rock 'n' roll type; although they are at the opposite end of the social scale they receive much the same disapproval as our teddy boys.

Modern technology, humanism, and humanitarianism all tend towards a fairly undifferentiated 'classless' middle-class welfare state under the aegis of rational planning, and it seemed as though Apollo had completely conquered; but perhaps for the younger workers, who have never known personal insecurity, Dionysus is returning in his most traditional guise, the violent dance which leads to trance and ecstasy.

## X

## *The Euro-American Way of Life*
## *(1959)*

THERE CAN BE no doubt about the facts. In their possessions, their clothes, their appearance, their taste in food and drink, their music and their entertainment, the people of Western Europe and of the United States, particularly the younger people, are more alike than they have been at any time since the American colonies threw off their allegiance to the British crown.

It is not entirely a one-way process. Traditionally the more successful people in the United States have imported from Europe the luxuries and elegances of leisured life. This custom has not stopped; and as 'leisure' has been redefined as an aspect of the life of most people instead of the way of life of a rich minority, so have these European gadgets and fashions and cooking recipes been accepted by very large numbers of younger Americans, for their holidays and their time away from work. In the European resorts popular with tourists—say Venice, or the South of France, or the Costa Brava—it is difficult as it has never been before to distinguish American students from European tourists or from the natives. It is not only the Europeans who have modified their appearance, their posture and their gestures.

For the Americans this modification may be in some part conscious and willed, an aspect of American courtesy, and a taking to heart the messages of such lay sermons as *The Ugly American*; but the result is that for holidays, for leisure, for a good time, there has really developed an 'Atlantic' style among the young; on the surface level—the way they dress, the way they act, the amusements they seek—the similarities appear to over-ride the differences in language, in available money, in the

## The Euro-American Way of Life

customs and values of their elders and of the countries from which they come.

But if the American young have been modified, the European young have been transformed. There is probably a bigger break between the generations in Europe today than there has been at any other period in Europe since the industrial revolution. The crucial year is (almost certainly) 1945, the year their countries were finally liberated, the year the buzz-bombs stopped, the year that post-war governments were installed, the year the atom bomb was dropped on Hiroshima; those who were without responsibility or awareness at that date, say roughly those who were under ten, have grown up into a world which appears quite different from that of their parents. They had to find a model for behaviour in this new-seeming world; and the model they took was America, or at least those aspects of life in the United States which were forcibly presented to their attention.

Most Western Europeans, it would seem, who were children in 1945 learned about Americans and American customs indirectly, through the more or less distorting filter of mass communications, rather than by direct contact. Although, for military reasons, more young Americans have lived in Western Europe in the last twenty years than ever before in history, they have been surprisingly inconspicuous; most of the military establishments are in isolated regions; and, except in the immediately neighbouring small towns, and the pleasure areas of the biggest cities, American service men and their families seem to have had little contact with the natives.

Mass communications on the other hand have been very pervasive; not only the obvious sources of movies and TV films, but also L.P. pop records, with occasional personal appearances of the singers, advertisements of American products, and, perhaps most influential of all, the American correspondents of mass-circulation European papers, who constantly keep their readers informed of American fashions in clothes and conduct. Although their intention may be, often is, censorious, they still give the cues to young Europeans who want to be told how to have a good time.

For most of this century the United States has represented to most Europeans the homeland of hedonism, the country where people enjoy themselves extravagantly. This, of course, was not meant as praise; for countries with a Puritan (or puritan) tradition 'hedonism' was, if not actually a dirty word, in the same relationship to one as a Latin-derived polysyllable is to an Anglo-Saxon-derived monosyllable; and in countries with a parsimonious tradition extravagance has always been looked upon as a sin. By European standards, Americans have always been extravagant; and although for Americans the insistence that people should enjoy themselves, should have a good time, carries the ethical undertones of a categorical imperative, in Europe the 'hard fun' is seen as divorced from its accompanying 'hard work', and as a rejection of the sobriety, parsimony and far-sightedness which had been considered the chief civic virtues of the respectable.

What I think has happened to the younger Europeans in the last decade or so is a radical change in their time-perspective. Typically, for all who were adult by 1939, the time-perspective was a very long one. As in all accumulative societies, present pleasures were postponed for future gains; and the future in which these gains were to be enjoyed was a long way off; when one had married, raised children and sent them out into the world; when one had retired and earned one's pension; or, for socialists, an even more distant future. The peak of life was typically late: and old age and retirement was a stage everyone should look forward to and prepare for. In the many unpensioned jobs old age had to be looked forward to with apprehension; for jobs with pensions, such as civil service jobs in many countries, retirement was the goal from the beginning of one's career, the reward for the unpleasant prelude which was the whole of one's working life.

This long time-perspective was reflected in the wage-structure. Juvenile and unskilled labour were typically very poorly paid; and the differentials for skill ensured that in most cases the highest wages and salaries were reached fairly late in life.

After 1945 this wage-structure was very considerably modified. Juvenile and unskilled labour were scarce and (comparatively speaking) highly paid; skill differentials were considerably diminished; and the fears of destitution in old age were somewhat lessened by various state pension and social security schemes. The young had more money in their pockets earlier and had somewhat less reason to dread the future than their parents had done; but I do not think that these changes would necessarily have altered their habits and their time-perspectives, if they had continued to believe in the future, and their own ability to modify it by their own exertions. But, if I read the evidence right, it is this belief which has disappeared.

This longer time-perspective was one of the major bases for the claim which so many Western Europeans made for superiority over the Americans. The claim for a greater political wisdom, experience and foresight was to a large extent based on this; so too were the reproaches of excessive American volatility, boom or bust, and the improvidence, the lack of thought for tomorrow, which resulted in such disasters as the Dust Bowl or the periodic floods. Up till twenty years ago, I think there was some basis for this claim and these reproaches. But if Americans have altered their time-perspective at all, I think they have tried to extend it, to take somewhat more account of the distant future, to pay somewhat less attention to immediate satisfactions. The Americans are, I think, making a more conscious effort to control the future; many of the people of Western Europe have abandoned the attempt.

The rational components of this change of attitude are, of course, political; the people of Western Europe are no longer masters of their own fate, decisions about war and peace have been taken out of their hands, they have no hope of surviving an atomic war. Internally, the anonymous 'they' control far more of the citizens' life than they did twenty years ago, and there is little anyone can do about it. In point of fact, there never has been very much that the majority of the citizens of Western Europe could do about their political destiny; but until 1945 they thought that they had some control; they do so no longer.

This change in time-perspective is, however, overwhelmingly unverbalized and unreasoned. The future, it is deeply but dimly felt, is not in our control, and therefore there is little point in planning for it or preparing for it; what we have is the present, and it would be foolish not to enjoy it as much as we can.

I first became conscious of this attitude in the winter after the war, talking to a lady from recently liberated Belgium. The Belgians at that time were enjoying a much more liberal and varied diet than we were in Britain; and it seemed to me that they were, so to speak, eating up the seed-corn, preparing future trouble for themselves by their want of foresight. I was, in fact, wrong in this, but the Belgian lady agreed with my arguments and ended 'Nevertheless, what we have had, we have had.' ('Néanmoins, ce que nous avons eu, nous avons eu.') She said this with a satisfaction which then very much surprised me; but her remark has returned to my mind very frequently since. I was hearing for the first time the articulate voice of non-political post-war Western Europe.

This is not an attitude of despair, except perhaps in the theological sense; indeed it could be argued that the younger people in Western Europe are more care-free than they have ever been since the start of industrialization. It could perhaps be called irresponsible, to the extent that responsibility for the future, both personal and national, has to a great extent been abandoned to others; and it certainly represents a major change, almost a mutation, in the national characters of the members of those countries who have typically worked on a long time-perspective.

When the present, and the immediate future, became of more emotional importance than the more distant future, a new model had to be found for the re-shaping of life; and this model was found in the picture they had acquired of life in the U.S.A.

As exact an imitation as was possible took place in the realm of popular entertainment. 'Pop' singers who were the rage in the U.S.A. were welcomed with an imitation of the same hysterical fervour here; and their British counterparts sang with an imitation of the American accent. American is, for the British, so much the accent of pleasure that the majority of young entertainers tried to adopt it; and, because of his accent, a Canadian has a considerable advantage in British radio and television. What are believed to be American tastes in young people's clothing, food and drink are adopted as the signs of a life of pleasure.

Much of the anti-social, mildly delinquent, behaviour would seem to stem from the same models; in Britain the naughty teenagers are trying to turn the British 'bobby' into the American 'cop', not altogether unsuccessfully.

After adolescence the imitation of America is not quite such a parody, nor, one would think, quite so distasteful to Americans. On the whole, Americans have been more successful than the people of any other country in making the leisure life of the ordinary man and woman easier and more interesting; and when the enjoyment of leisure life *now*—not in the more distant future—became the aim of a major portion of the younger people of Western Europe, American habits were an obvious model to manufacturer and consumer alike, within the more straitened limits of the Western European worker's income. Earlier visiting Europeans had frequently accused the Americans of extravagant hedonism, of materialism, of excessive addiction to creature comforts; instead of seeing this as a reproach (which it was certainly intended to be) the post-war Western Europeans have said with surprising unanimity 'Me too!'

The American model is most conspicuous and most conscious for conveniences inside the house. A well-designed kitchen is an 'American kitchen' in most of the shop-windows of Western Europe; deep-freezers, domestic air-conditioning, even for quite a lot of people domestic refrigerators, efficient central heating, automatic washing machines all have an American aura and are, to that extent, more desirable. Implements for outdoor pleasure—automobiles, small boats and the like—are usually considered indigenous. The only change in the attitude towards these is that they are now 'for the likes of us' as soon as we can make the first down-payment. It is probably symptomatic that, at least in England, current trade union demands are for more leisure—a shorter working week, longer holidays with pay—rather than for more cash.

This copying of what is believed to be an American model is a characteristic of the younger Europeans, particularly of the working classes. It is generally resented by those who were mature before 1939. Older members of the middle classes are anti-American for a variety of reasons connected with national prestige (this is very often voiced in criticism of the content of television programmes), resent more or less articulately the relative prosperity of the working classes compared with their own relative impoverishment, and genuinely deplore the diminution or disappearance of national characteristics that they prized. The older class-conscious members of the working classes are anti-American for ideological reasons; America is the citadel of capitalism and (paradoxically enough, in the light of past history) of war-mongering, and American influence is distracting the young from the politics of the class-struggle. Both groups would appear to be fighting a losing battle.

With their changed time-perspective, so many Western Europeans have adopted the gadgets and the customs which have long been general in the United States that, on a surface level, it is now possible to talk about a Euro-American way of life. But, on a deeper level, I think there is still a very great contrast. By and large, American comfort and fun have been seen as the simultaneous rewards for great industry and what can only be termed moral earnestness. Western Europe has only seen one side of the picture; and the extravagant hedonism which was the superior European's reproach to the natives of North America is now near to becoming a description of Europe instead.

It is still too early to say whether the typical Western European long time-perspective is permanently diminished or only temporarily in abeyance; it will need another decade before it can be seen whether today's young adults will later take a longer view. If they do not, the burden on the United States of maintaining the Euro-American way of life is going to be very heavy.

# XI

## *The Anatomy of a Dream Man*
*(1958)*

ONE OF THE more striking changes in the British scene since the war has been the enormous increase in number and circulation of weekly and monthly periodicals written to women, by women, and for women, almost always with the word 'Woman' in the title, with the aim of enabling its readers to function more efficiently as women. To the best of my knowledge, this development is not paralleled in any other country; in the United States the development has been in the number and circulation of magazines addressed to men, whose vaguely salacious titles and pin-up pictures should help their readers to enjoy at least a momentary sensation of manliness.

Till now, I had always regarded these publications as almost taboo—in Aldous Huxley's phrase 'like Llhasa and the ladies' lavatory', an arcana which I should never penetrate. But in the last few days I have undergone the intensive course of reading every issue of every woman's paper for a month; and I doubt if I shall ever be quite the same again.

For one thing, all the papers are completely schizophrenic. The medical and nursing features are written with a frankness which I had thought was almost entirely confined to text-books of physiology and midwifery (and with very sound and progressive ideas); and the Advice bureau prints letters from its readers which detail the most exotic dilemmas without apparently turning a hair, and giving the most reasonable advice. A typical problem might be:

> I am just eighteen and am going to have a baby in six months' time. My boy friend says he won't marry me unless I get rid

of the baby. The baby's father says he'll tell my parents if I do any such thing. What should I do?

On the other hand, the fiction, which occupies about a third of the pages, is quite incredibly chaste; if the Dream Man does kiss the girl in the final paragraphs, he is more likely to brush his lips on her hair than to kiss her mouth. Out of fifty-five stories, one was a teaser, in which through most of the tale the reader was led to believe that a woman was going to spend a week-end in Brighton in sin, only to find out that it was a reconciliation with her temporarily separated husband. Four-fifths of the stories tell how the heroine caught her Dream Man; the remaining fifth how she kept him, after marriage.

The married men in the stories are mostly quickly dealt with: they come back 'from work' or 'from the office' and are tired, but cope very well with the children if the wife is ill or away. They (and occasionally their wives) get into ruts and have to be jacked out of them. We are practically never told what they look like.

The Dream Man is another story. We are always told what his occupation is, and a few physical characteristics. Without exception, the Dream Man is Tall; since the English are a rather short people this is bad luck on the five-sixths of the girls who will not be able to get six-footers. He is usually broad-shouldered; occasionally 'big'; but otherwise no further information is given about his body. Some features of his head are, however, regularly described, in particular the eyes, the chin, the hair, and quite often the depth of his voice, but never by any chance his accent.

Brown eyes are preferred to any other colour by a margin of two to one: they can be soft, expressive, or twinkling. An occasional chin is square, but they are usually cleft; indeed a cleft chin is almost a sign of desirable virility and one of the chief distinguishing marks between the sexes: none of the heroines (and *they* are described from top to toe) has a cleft in that particular place. But it is hair which is described with the most particularity; whatever its colour—brown and black are preferred by three to one—it is always cut short or neatly trimmed.

## The Anatomy of a Dream Man

Dream Men do not go in for fancy hair-do's of any sort. 'Looking down at him,' notes a typical heroine,

> as he knelt at my feet, I could see how thick his hair was—thick and brown and springy. There was a suggestion of wave in his hair: it only needed to be damped and pinched to wave beautifully . . . but, of course, he was not the sort of young man to encourage a wave to his hair, and, of course, it was a frightfully silly idea.

The young man, incidentally, is not kneeling at her feet to propose to her; he is picking up the spilled contents of his aunt's bag and has not yet met the heroine. The hair is apparently the only feature which heroines look at closely until they know what a Dream Man's job is and what his prospects are. In a single case, the heroine notes that the man is 'smelling of some swooning essence of masculinity that he used after shaving'; but she, poor woman, was recovering from a nervous breakdown.

The forty-five dream men who are betrothed, or as good as, by the end of the story, hold the following jobs:

- 5 surgeons
- 4 reporters
- 3 general practitioners
- 2 sculptors
- 2 junior members of the managing board
- 2 architects
- 2 garage proprietors
- 2 salesmen of sports goods in a large store
- 2 university students, one taking a holiday job as courier to a conducted tour
- 1 engineer in a refrigerating firm
- 1 schoolmaster in a boys' boarding-school
- 1 vet
- 1 under-manager at a factory
- 1 apprentice electrician
- 1 salesman of agricultural machinery
- 1 artist-painter

## Phases of Human Life

1 factory owner
1 director of a printing press
1 Writer to the Signet
1 author
1 auctioneer
1 personnel manager
1 advertising agent
1 worker in a research laboratory
1 manager of a coffee plantation in Africa
1 worker in a bank
1 insurance agent
1 Portuguese Duke in Mozambique
1 wealthy Frenchman pretending to be a fisherman

One of the interesting things about this list is that the Dream Lover of an earlier generation of fiction—the romantic, well-born, wealthy, handsome aristocrat in disguise, has practically disappeared; he makes a vestigial last appearance as a foreigner. The Portuguese Duque is the hero of a serial in much the least glossy of the magazines; and (uniquely among the short stories) the narrator does not get a proposal, or even a proposition, from the wealthy Frenchman whom she thought was a fisherman. Glamour, it would seem, is out; and uniforms have lost all their allure; there is not a single member of the services in the list.

The Dream Man of today is not a Dream Lover; he is a Dream Husband, a rationally desirable *parti*. He never sweeps the heroine off her feet, and he is never bold in his approach; indeed verbal or amatory assurance is a sign of a Wolf, a bad man, who may cause the heroine trouble with the Dream Man, but will never seriously attract her. In general, both heroine and Dream Man are shy and fumbling virgins, the Dream Man shyer and more fumbling:

> She could have cried with disappointment. It had been wonderful; she had wanted him to kiss her again, and instead he had apologized.

> When Angus Frazer arrived at his office to find Miss Wilkes gone and a stranger sitting at her desk, it was a blow indeed.

## The Anatomy of a Dream Man

For one thing, the stranger was a girl, and Angus had never felt at ease with girls. An eerie, giggling race.

A few Dream Men are considerably older than the heroine—maybe over thirty—and although these Older Men are still shy and reserved, they don't fumble quite so much; they are Understanding. If not widowers, they are soured by an earlier unfortunate experience. They are grey at the temples, and have even more desirable positions than the younger Dream Men.

As can be seen, Dream Men have clean, 'white collar' jobs. Only the garage proprietors would be likely to get their hands dirty in their work, and that only till they had built up the business (with the heroine's help) and could pay somebody else for the manual labour. But they *all* have jobs; only wolves are idle.

The popularity of surgeons is a little surprising; if I had counted in the characters in episodes adapted from the TV serial 'Emergency—Ward Ten', which appear weekly in one of the magazines, the score would have been even higher. It is difficult not to see some symbolism here; however fumbling the man may be in private life, when he gets down to it with a knife. . . .

The sculptors and artist are, I think, chiefly important in giving added gratification to the heroine's overwhelming narcissism. All the heroines gaze at themselves in the looking-glass, retailing in the greatest detail the attractive sight they see there; each time they change their dress and accessories we are told what they have changed into; and if they consent to pose (fully clothed, of course) to a sculptor or painter, they can then look at themselves, and have other people looking at them, even more often.

Medicine and the plastic arts are still, it would seem, professions of glamour; but three quarters of the Dream Men just have good jobs with prospects, which will bring in enough to furnish a comfy home, and support the family adequately when the children come and the heroine has to give up her work. (Most heroines work as secretaries or shop-assistants; often the Dream Man is employed in a better position in the same firm.)

Unless they are in a hospital, or looking after children, heroines show no interest in their own work, and very little in that of the Dream Man; it's the income, and the prospects, which count.

One of the things which has puzzled me is how the Dream Men are capable of holding down their various skilled and responsible jobs; they are so uniformly chuckle-headed, gauche, credulous and irrational in their private lives that one would think them incapable of dealing sensibly with any non-mechanical problem. In their contacts with the heroine, they can be counted on to draw the wrong conclusion nine times out of ten; they continuously misinterpret the simplest statements or actions; and they invariably believe the improbable lies which the Bitches tell them.

Not all the stories have Bitches; but they occur just about as often as their opposite number, the Wolves. They are drawn with real hatred. The Bitches are usually slightly older than the heroines, more 'conventionally pretty', and more self-possessed. They are actuated almost entirely by malice; they try to separate the heroine and the Dream Man by insinuations against the character or lies about the behaviour of one or the other; occasionally because they hope to nobble the Dream Man for themselves, more often out of spite and jealousy against the heroine. It is probably not without significance that, in quite a few of the stories, the Bitch is the heroine's beautiful sister.

In none of the stories is the Dream Man seriously attracted by the Bitch; but, such is his basic stupidity, he always believes what she tells him, and acts towards her rather like the proverbial rabbit faced by a snake. Since the Dream Man, almost by definition, knows nothing about women, he believes the fluent, cold-hearted liar, and misunderstands the shy inarticulateness of sincerity. In a couple of the stories Dream Men and heroines are so inarticulate that they have to communicate and propose by letter, even though they both work in the same building.

To the extent that the authoresses of these stories are typical of their readers, it would seem as though in the last twenty years the dreams of the English woman have changed a good deal. A generation ago the dream was of Romance, of a dream lover, suave, sophisticated and masterful, who 'swept the girl off her

## The Anatomy of a Dream Man

feet' in a whirlwind of passion, taking her into the exotic settings of Arabia, or the Antarctic, or the aristocracy; marriage followed in the end, but it was the passion, the romance, which counted. Today's dream is, on the surface, far more realistic: a gentle, respectful love from a man with a good clean job, which will lead rapidly to marriage, a home of one's own and two children. It is a dream of cosy security, reflecting maybe the ever earlier marriages which are so conspicuous a feature of the United States today and, to a considerable extent, of our own country. The only trouble is that there cannot possibly be enough tall surgeons to go round; and so the numerous women who have had to make do with a short man in a routine, maybe a shirt-sleeve, job can still muse about the Dream Man who might have come along.

## XII

## *On Falling in Love*
*(1960)*

ON THE BASIS of anthropological evidence it would appear that the capacity to fall passionately in love—to feel convinced that one can only achieve bliss by the union with one unique individual—is one of those uncommon potentialities which develop spontaneously in a few individuals in all human societies that have been described.

In its distribution it seems to have the same arbitrary character as those innate potentialities which form the basis of artistic and religious creations and performances: a 'true' ear or a 'true' hand for drawing, the ability to go into deep trance and the like. It is probable that in any society which comprises more than a few hundred people there will be some man or woman with 'absolute pitch', and another with the ability to go easily into trance. Whether the people with these innate gifts will ever exercise them publicly will depend on the development and the values of their society. If there is no polyphonic music, the person endowed with absolute pitch may go to his grave without ever having been aware of, much less exercised, his gift. The person with the ability to go easily into trance will probably not escape that experience; but if the religious climate is unfavourable, he or she may well have to hide this capacity as something shameful; and, if it be discovered, he or she may well be punished or killed as a witch possessed by the devil.

The analogy between these gifts and the ability to fall deeply in love may be pushed further. The gifts in their over-powering form, so that they manifest themselves whatever the climate of opinion and the customs of the society, are statistically rare; but a large part of the population is able to develop an approximation to these abilities if the society considers them desirable and punishes their absence. Thus, there is no reason to suppose that the ability to reproduce a tune correctly, to sing in harmony, is innately more common among the Welsh than among the English or (at least in the time of Mozart) among the Czechs than among the Austrians. But because the Welsh (or the Czechs of the eighteenth century) expected every person to be able to hold a worthy part in choral singing and arranged many of their more enjoyable and respected social events around choirs, far more people developed their originally weak musical ability in these societies than they did in the neighbouring ones which had neither such expectations nor such institutions.

In most modern societies trance is a generally devalued condition, may indeed be considered to demand medical or psychiatric attention, and so it only manifests itself rarely, except among spiritualists and in ecstatic religious cults. But many other societies have demanded that every person, or every person of one sex, should experience trance at least once in their lives. Among a number of American Plains Indian tribes, a male could not become a warrior or hunter until he had found his guardian spirit in a trance vision; and in some West African societies, such as Dahomey, or among the Balinese in Indonesia, a great part of the population—perhaps half—develops the ability to go into at least light trance in the appropriate religious setting.

All the anthropological evidence suggests that the ability to fall passionately in love is completely analogous in its distribution to these other gifts. Even though a society may completely devalue romantic love, it will still occur spasmodically from time to time; and if a society puts a high valuation on this behaviour, the greater part of the population will be able to convince themselves that they have these feelings, in the same way as the American Indian youths could nearly all convince themselves that they had had visions of their guardian spirit.

Probably because the spontaneous ability to fall deeply in love is so rare a phenomenon statistically, very few human societies (apart from Western Europe and North America in the last two centuries) have incorporated the expectation of romantic love into their social institutions, or demanded that every young man and every young woman should manifest it, should feel it at some time in their lives. There are records of one or two small societies in the islands of Polynesia or among the American Indians who have considered romantic love a necessary prelude to marriage; but, these very rare exceptions apart, marriage has typically been considered a *social* union between two groups rather than a *private* union between two individuals. Many societies will pay some attention to the preferences of the man and woman most intimately concerned and will not force a marriage of mutual repugnance (other societies do not pay even that attention to the girl's sentiments); but what is looked for in these societies of social marriage is mutual compatibility, nothing stronger. Marriage is too important to too many people, and to society itself; it cannot be allowed, so it is argued, to depend on the whims of young people who do not know their own minds.

Consequently, in nearly all the societies of which we have record, romantic love is considered to be quite unconnected with marriage, and is usually envisaged as socially disruptive. This disruption may be tragic—probably the most common development in literate societies—it may be comic, it may be a social nuisance or an interesting topic of conversation; but in nearly every society and at nearly every period romantic love is a disruptive force outside of, and interfering with, marriage.

This is the case with the European tradition of romantic love. The ladies for whom the troubadours sung were never their own wives nor capable of becoming so; if the poets were not married to someone else, then the objects of their devotion were. Guinevere and Isolde and Petrarch's Laura were married women; Dante was a married man when he met Beatrice, and Paolo and Francesca were both married to other people. Moreover, never in romantic poetry was there a suggestion that marriage was the aim of these lovers. Love and marriage are treated as antithetical; if the two people who fall in love are by any chance unmarried, then it is a fixed convention that the families of the two lovers are completely opposed to the union, as in *Romeo and Juliet* and many lesser poems and plays. The tragic love of two young people thwarted by the wishes of their families, and culminating either in suicide or in holy resignation, is a constant theme of literature and drama throughout Asia and much of Europe. Romantic love was the disturber, the wrecker of cities, in Sophocles' phrase; and parents were to be commiserated with if their children developed such unfortunate propensities.

About the middle of the eighteenth century the situation changed rapidly in Western Europe and North America. Judging from the literary evidence—and there is little else to go on—being romantically in love changed from a potentially tragic to a potentially desirable condition; and when the loving couple were in a position to marry, public sympathy went to the young people and was withdrawn from the parents who tried to impose their more prudent plans. A number of social changes accompanied this change of attitude: American independence, the French revolution, the beginning of the 'industrial revolution' and the rise in influence and the increase in numbers of the middle classes.

All these changes probably had some influence; but I should be inclined to give the most weight to the last factor, the rise of the middle classes. Both the aristocracy and the peasantry were, in their different ways, attached to specific pieces of land; and the choice of daughter-in-law (or occasionally son-in-law) was very much influenced by considerations of agriculture and of inheritance; and neither group could maintain their living standards without the ownership of land. The middle classes, on the other hand, were mobile in every sense of the word; a family's prosperity was much less dependent on marriage settlements, and children were far more easily able to earn a living without parental approval or assistance. Marriages based on romantic love were at least feasible.

Furthermore, the middle classes were the major, indeed almost the only, audience for poets and novelists; and it was the poets and novelists, above all the romantic poets of England and Germany, who preached the ecstasy of romantic love and claimed the enormous superiority of a marriage founded on love to one founded on prudential parental arrangements; and their preaching made converts.

During the nineteenth century young middle-class men and women came to expect that they would fall in love romantically, and that such falling in love was the only proper prelude to, and a guarantor of, a happy marriage. This does not seem to have been the case with the other classes in Western Europe. For the aristocracies and royalty suitability seems to have remained a far more important criterion for marriage than romantic love; and the tragedies of unsuitable and disruptive love (such as *Mayerling*) continued to occur. The urban working classes during the nineteenth century were most of them so oppressed by fatigue and poverty that they lacked both leisure and energy to search for the romantically loved one. In the novels of Dickens, the middle-class characters fall in love and eventually marry; but the pictures of working-class married life are without any suggestion of romance. Some research has been done, particularly for cities in the North Eastern United States, on the places of residence of married people before their marriage; and overwhelmingly, the married couples come from either the same small urban neighbourhood or from stops on the same trolley line.

In the present century the aristocrats, the urban workers and the peasants have to a great extent abandoned their distinctive modes of life. Middle-class patterns have become increasingly widely adopted—an increase much hastened by the development of mass communications such as films, radio, and television, which offered their middle-class patterns of life to an increasingly heterogenous audience. Among these middle-class patterns none was more insistent than a demand for marriage founded on romantic love, which was the culmination of the vast majority of stories and plays offered for entertainment and as an example of proper behaviour. A marriage founded on romantic love was seen as the birthright of every man and woman from Royal Princesses to seamstresses and factory hands. As far as the records go, nothing like this has ever happened before in a complex society. We know of no other society which has expected that every young man and young woman should fall deeply in love with an unmarried member of the opposite sex and should marry their love-choice; and moreover to decree that this love should occur only once in a life-time, and should be strong enough to sustain the marriage for ever after.

This expectation that everybody should feel romantic love undoubtedly puts as much strain on some individuals as the demand that everybody should sing in tune or go into ecstatic trance does on some members of other societies. As with these other rare spontaneous talents, the majority of any population can produce a sufficient approximation to the spontaneous gift to satisfy themselves and their neighbours that they feel what they ought to feel, and so to approach marriage in what they have learned is the only appropriate frame of mind. But besides the people born with a true ear there are those who are born tone-deaf; besides the people who can fall spontaneously into trance there are those whom it is impossible to hypnotize; besides the natural lovers there are people who are temperamentally incapable of romantic love.

People of such a temperament—and we have no idea how numerous they are—are put to a grave disadvantage by the present social expectations; they feel themselves, and are often looked upon by their families and friends, as inadequate, as failures. Men and women who, in earlier centuries or in other societies, would have made the most satisfactory of spouses in marriages of suitability, may well remain unmarried and unhappy in a society which considers romantic love the only proper basis for marriage.

When romantic love is considered the supreme individual value, it can still be nearly as socially disruptive as it was in earlier periods or other societies where it was not allowed for at all. Among the most ethical people of the United States and some Western European countries between the wars it was considered profoundly immoral to stay married to a spouse who had fallen in love with somebody else; and there developed the paradox of the ethical divorce, when the self-sacrificing spouse nobly broke up his or her family life rather than thwart the partner's romantic love.

As far as my information goes, the children of these ethical divorcees tend to pay much less attention to the ecstasies of romantic love and much more attention to the companionate aspects of marriage and the pleasure of parenthood. Tender, nurturing fatherhood, which is so marked a feature of the family life of the youngest adult educated men in the United States and Britain, represents a very great change in men's emotional lives, and one for which there is no precedent in history. It seems probable that it will be incompatible with the very high valuation of romantic love which distinguished their parents' and grandparents' generations.

Many signs suggest that the pleasures of parenthood are becoming the most valued aspect of marriage in prosperous Western society; and this would imply that romantic love is again being devalued, except for those few for whom it is a temperamental necessity. If this be so, it will make for a calmer and more stable society, valuing permanent domestic happiness above the temporary ecstasies of passion. And then the universal demand for romantic love of the last two centuries will pass into history as one of the strange developments of which human beings are capable, somewhat like the dancing mania of the Middle Ages, or the glossolalia, the speaking with tongues, which falls on whole congregations in some ecstatic religious cults. As with these and the other examples earlier mentioned, a rare human potentiality will have for a short period dominated whole societies.

# XIII

## *Woman's Place*
## *(1961)*

ALL CONTEMPORARY ADVANCED societies—which may be defined as societies with some form of universal suffrage and universal compulsory education—are perplexed by a dilemma which seems to have had no counterpart at any earlier period of human history. Neither men nor women in these societies feel any certainty about what are the appropriate roles, the rights and the duties of the female halves of their populations. Before the beginning of this century this was not a problem for the majority of the population of any country, though the suffragettes were starting to bring it forcibly to people's notice; and in those traditional societies which have not been much affected by the two great proselytizing political ideologies of democracy and communism it is still not a problem today. But wherever these ideologies have penetrated, all the old certainties are questioned; we no longer know what women ought to do or ought to be, how woman's character or her place in society should be defined.

The ideologies of democracy and of communism both pose as a basic tenet the principle that women should be under no legal disadvantage because of their sex; property rights, and the rights and duties of citizens, are no longer legally determined by sex, but solely by age. Today it is only the 'teenagers' who suffer under the legal disabilities which oppressed women also until a couple of generations ago.

The formal and legal aspects apart, there is far less consensus as to how women should be treated or regarded. Should they be considered as 'the same as men' or as 'different but equal'? As weaker than men, and so needing the formal protection of law and the informal deference of courtesy? Or as potentially stronger than men, so that men need the protection of law and custom to prevent women taking their jobs and positions away from them? Should we consider that women are potentially as competent as men in every conceivable walk of life, so that their failure to achieve parity of esteem and success is due either to individual incompetence or to masculine obstruction? Or should it be held that though women are equally competent, their competence lies on different levels and employs different techniques? Is competition between men and women for the same positions and rewards desirable or undesirable, 'natural' or 'unnatural'? Is it invincibly repugnant to masculine dignity for women to occupy positions where they will regularly give orders to men? And, if we opt for the greatest measure of social, economic and political equality, is there any contemporary justification for including women in the self-sacrificing axiom of 'women and children first'?

The confusion and uncertainty underlying these questions are specific to the rapidly changing societies of the mid-twentieth century. We know of no traditional societies which have been perplexed about the temperament, aptitudes and skills appropriate to men and women, even though, as Margaret Mead documented in *Male and Female*, there is no consistency in the ascription of characteristics or abilities to one or the other sex. Once you get past the basic physiological contrast that men are hunters and fighters, women mothers and so less mobile, there is practically no skill or type of temperament which some society has not declared to be essentially masculine or essentially feminine. There are very few recorded societies which have not linked the differences in anatomy and physiology with expected differences in temperament and aptitude, and these are small, technically primitive tribes. These few exceptions apart, all recorded human societies before the twentieth century based their view of 'human nature' on the contrast between the capacities and characteristics of the two sexes.

This notion that the characters and skills of men and women are, and should be, different seems to be a permanent theme in the history of the human race. If we can speculate about the earliest phase of human history when *homo sapiens* was a rare and weak species, probably struggling for survival against other species of man as well as other mammals and natural calamities, it would seem probable that female fertility was the most highly-prized value of the community and a source of awe and envy for the males; and that very early in human history men attempted to enhance their own self-esteem and assume the life-giving magic of fertile women by various sorts of symbolic elaboration. Among these elaborations, which are practised by the most primitive of our contemporaries, are those male initiation rituals which seek to demonstrate that, though women can make children, only men can make another man (a belief which still has an echo in our own society in the qualities and effects which are ascribed to all-male boarding-schools by the proponents of this system). Another such elaboration is representative art. The creations which artists make in two or three dimensions are far more durable than the mortals born of women. We have, of course, no clue as to the sex of the palaeolithic cave artists, but, the world over, representative art has been found to be predominantly practised by men; decorative art may be practised by either sex.

The evidence suggests that men had developed the idea that symbolic elaboration in religion, art, and such primitive social prestige as was available should compensate them for their lack of real fertility, before the neolithic revolution, which really begins our modern era. When agriculture, permanent cities, and literacy were invented, men seem to have taken immediate advantage of the new opportunities offered to increase their range of symbolic elaboration and symbolic success, and to restrict women to their fundamental role of child-bearing and to the more monotonous and less rewarded tasks; the higher religions, the arts, philosophy, mathematics, social and military prestige all became predominantly or entirely male preserves.

As symbolic success became more permanent, the wives and daughters of successful men participated to a certain extent in their husbands' and fathers' prestige. As Thorstein Veblen pointed out many years ago, this participation was granted on condition that these women should be symbols of 'conspicuous leisure', that their dress should be so elaborate and their complexion so fair that everybody could see that these ladies had never had to work in their lives. Indeed they were rendered almost helpless by the elaboration or the restrictions of their fashionable dress. Such women were the only models of fashion and elegance up to the beginning of this century; it may in part be a symbolic revolt against this role of a clothes-horse and jewel-case which makes contemporary women prize a sun tan above the whitest skin and gives them a feeling of satisfaction in wearing clothes which hamper their movements as little as possible, such as slacks.

As far as we know, the larger societies after the neolithic revolution have always been male-dominated. It is possible, though unproved, that at one period the tracing of descent through the female line only was much more common than it is today; in a number of societies positions of prestige descended through the female line; sometimes (as with our Royal Family today) pedigree is more important than sex in determining the holder of an hereditary office; and many religions (apart from those deriving from the Middle East) have or had ritual roles which were reserved to women. But these seem to have been the limits of female prestige and dominance in post-neolithic times.

It is consequently most improbable that there has ever existed a 'matriarchy' as this is popularly imagined, a settled society in which the women are completely dominant and active, the men completely submissive and passive. This seems to be a nightmare of 'the turning of the tables'; and two periods when this nightmare has had some currency—among the classical Greeks with the myth of the Amazons, and among Europeans in the mid-nineteenth century—were periods when men of the ruling classes were almost completely dominant over 'their' womenfolk, and probably had unconscious fears of revenge for their tyranny. The sociological speculators of the mid-nineteenth century elaborated crude parallels of biological Darwinism; if, as was manifestly obvious, mid-Victorian England or Germany were the summit of social evolution, then they must have evolved from strongly contrasting antecedents; and so you get such fantasies as 'matriarchy', to contrast with the Victorian paterfamilias, 'group marriage', and so on.

The tyranny of the Victorian paterfamilias prompted the first articulate questionings about the innate characteristics of women and their proper place in the ideal society to which evolutionary progress must lead us. It is at least arguable that women of all classes were more exploited in the nineteenth century than they had ever been in any previous period of European history; not only did they lack political and property rights, but there was an attempt to deprive them of adult status and character; the ideal of the 'good woman' held up in the writings of such authors as Dickens and Thackeray and their imitators was practically one of arrested development; women of intelligence and initiative (the possible granddaughters of Jane Austen's Elizabeth Bennet) were at best 'adventuresses', at worst sources of moral contamination.

I think it can be argued that it was this denial of intellectual and moral capacities, at least as much as the gross financial exploitation, which was resented by potentially competent women and by those tender-minded men who felt that underdogs of any species should be protected and have their rights secured for them, and who, in the classic phrase of the foundress of the National Society for the Prevention of Cruelty to Children 'cannot draw the line' at women, and who started the process of emancipation whose development is now perplexing all of us.

Emancipation is an almost completely negative aim—not to be exploited, not to be debarred from any activity or occupation because of sex. Although this aim is by no means completely achieved in Great Britain yet, all the trends are tending towards complete legal, professional and financial equality for the two sexes. But what is a woman when she is completely emancipated? Is she the same as a man, anatomy apart? Should she compete everywhere on equal terms, without fear or favour? Should her sex be a private differentiation only, disregarded in her public life?

It would seem that this notion of sex as an unimportant private differentiation was the ideal of the suffragettes and their supporters in those countries where women were considered to be weak, such as the English-speaking or German-speaking societies. It has had remarkedly less support in those societies where women have been traditionally regarded as strong: for example, France, where women's strength and capacities were regarded as comparable to, though different from, men's; Great Russia, where men and women were regarded as equally strong; or Burma, where women were considered to be stronger and more responsible than men in most situations.

It seems very doubtful whether the suffragette ideal of a society where sex is treated as a minor variation, like hair-colour, can ever be achieved for the majority of women in any large society. It is not conceivable that a society would long be viable which paid little or no heed to female fertility and the long mothering necessary for the slow-developing human child to realize its potentialities. Even a couple of generations ago it was possible to imagine a Utopia where the infants would be raised in institutions by professionals while the mothers would return, shortly after delivery, to pursue their careers; and this has indeed been tried, and largely abandoned, in such revolutionary societies as urban Soviet Russia in its earliest years, and the pioneering Israeli *kibbutzim*. No responsible person, aware of the scientific discoveries about human infancy and growth made in the last twenty years, could advocate such a policy today. It needs the continuous love and attention from at least one identifiable human being over a number of years to bring an infant to successful maturity.

Our knowledge of the needs of infants and the indispensable functions of mothering derives from two sources: the trained observation of what happens to infants without families, as in the pioneering study of that name by Dr. Burlingham and Miss Anna Freud and the work of Dr. Réné Spitz; and the studies of animal learning from birth which have been carried out by the ethologists, under the lead of Drs. Lorentz and Tinbergen. Quite recently psychologists and physiologists have been combining the insights of psycho-analysis and of ethology to demonstrate how complex and long-enduring is the necessary role of the mother in the child's development. Although the natural mother may be replaced by a substitute, as with the traditional nannies or, in other societies, the grandmothers, it still demands the attention of one woman over years to raise a healthy and happy child. Scientifically, we are returning to the belief of our earliest ancestors concerning the irreplaceable function of motherhood.

This implies that, for the future health of the society, it is undesirable to treat women in the same way as men during their period of fertility, before the youngest child is of school-age, even if fathers do take over some of the nurturing and tender care which have been traditionally entirely women's work; and it is doubtful whether this recent development is socially or psychologically desirable. But now that the dangers of death and disease in childbirth have been so largely eliminated in advanced societies, the period of effective fertility represents a relatively short period in the average woman's expectation of life. Even if fertility is continued up to the menopause, and this is uncommon, a woman can expect to have between twenty and thirty years of life during which, physiologically, she will not be so markedly different from men.

One possible social development, which might well cause less misery and uncertainty than the present situation, would be to elaborate the different and distinctive life-patterns of men and women. Men, and those women who are physiologically or temperamentally incapable of motherhood, would have a continuous career, seeking symbolic success from the time when their education was finished. Fertile women, on the other hand, even though they may be gainfully employed for a few years before marriage, would start their serious careers in the late forties, and continue in them for some years after the men have retired, as would be reasonable with their greater expectation of life. This would of course mean an alteration in the current British pattern of national pensions, which gives women a retirement pension five years earlier than men; as Professor Richard Titmuss has pointed out, this is biologically quite indefensible. The fact that the earlier pension is less than that of a man suggests that officially we still consider both that women are weaker than men and that they have fewer physical needs.

Were late careers to become general for women, this would imply that most women would have two periods of education : a general one in childhood and adolescence, and a vocational training when the children were reared. Wartime experience demonstrated that women in their forties and fifties are perfectly capable of learning new skills with speed and precision; and it is perhaps relevant that most of the women who have been distinguished in the arts, and who have survived to the menopause, have produced their best work late in life.

Were it general for women to be educated for a career after they had raised their children, it might do much to lessen the unhappiness and aimlessness which now oppresses so many of the more intelligent women, once their children are of school age. I do not mean the discontent which is currently so common among English middle-class women who cannot act like ladies of leisure because of the absence of servants; but the much more widespread feeling of aimlessness which comes from unexercised potentialities.

The demand of the suffragettes and their supporters was that women should have the same rights and opportunities as their brothers. This demand has been in great part conceded by the men; but the unspoken proviso was added that women could only have these rights and opportunities if they adopted completely the male life-rhythms and career lines; no concession was to be made to the specifically female life-rhythms. We have had this 'sexless' one sex pattern for nearly two generations now; and it is time to ask whether this is a satisfactory solution? Are the majority of women finding their lives significantly 'fuller' than did their grandmothers? And is society adequately enriched by the contribution which women could make?

There is no research available, as far as I know, in this or any other country, which could provide convincing answers to these questions; but my impression is that the answers would be heavily qualified. I also believe that if we were to build on the differing life-rhythms of men and women, instead of forcing women, if they are to have a public life, to follow male rhythms, it would make for a far more varied society than any we know at present, and one which would use more fully the potentialities of all the population. Surely we would have a happier and more interesting society if we emphasized the fundamental difference in physiology and rhythm between men and women, instead of forcing women, if their lives are not to be private or confined to a few 'feminine' occupations, to act as though they were imitation men?

# XIV

## *Mirror, Mirror on the Wall*
## *(1959)*

MORE THAN THIRTY YEARS ago, in *Murder Must Advertise*, the late Dorothy Sayers wrote the first, the best, and, as far as I know, the most recent study of what advertisers aiming at mass markets in England actually do. They create, she wrote

> a sphere of dim platonic archetypes, the Thrifty Housewife, the Man of Discrimination, the Keen Buyer and the Good Judge, for ever young, for ever handsome, for ever virtuous, economical and inquisitive, moving to and fro upon their complicated orbits, comparing prices and values, making tests of purity, asking indiscreet questions . . . perpetually spending to save and saving to spend . . . a Cloud Cuckooland, peopled by pitiful ghosts. . . .

Miss Sayers wrote her masterpice in the depression and when the only media for advertising were the press and posters; she had worked in an advertising agency herself, and it was with inside knowledge that she discussed some of the psychological implications of the work that advertisers do to persuade the public to buy one product rather than another. What the advertisers are trying to do is to create an image of such a sort that the man or woman exposed to it feels, however inarticulately 'The person in the advertisement is in some respects like me, or rather like I would wish to be; if the goods in the advertisement please them, their family etc., then they should please me and my family, make me, them, nearer to that quite attainable ideal.' The advertisement strives to be a mirror to its public, a somewhat flattering mirror of course, but with the main features sufficiently recognizable. If the picture is too distorted, the products do not sell and the advertising campaign stops; and consequently the contents of advertisements would seem capable of telling the inquiring investigator quite a lot about the public to whom they are addressed.

As far as I know, social scientists have almost completely neglected this potential source of information. In a few studies I and other social anthropologists have paid passing attention to the type of goods which are frequently advertised, as this gives some indication of widespread areas of anxiety; if the press is filled with specifics against lost virility or for disguises of any sign that the male face grows a beard, for example, you have some clues to the preoccupations of the public these advertisements are directed at; but the actual content of advertisements, advertisements as a mirror or a portrait, have been almost completely neglected. A student of Dr. Margaret Mead's wrote an unpublished thesis on the contrast between United States and British press advertising, particularly the different image of the family in the papers of the two countries; and that is the only study on the subject that I have heard of. Consequently it seemed to me it might be interesting to investigate what picture of ourselves the advertisers on television throw into our living rooms night after night.

Because of the enormous size of the public, television advertisers face problems of a different nature to advertisers in the press or even on posters. The readers of even the most widely circulated newspapers represent only a relatively small section of the population, and quite a number of facts have been accumulated about the interests, prejudices and habits of the readers of different papers; posters are placed in definite localities, and the population of that locality, in contrast to other localities in the same area, and of the different regions of England can, if necessary, be estimated. But with television, all these sectional calculations disappear; the advertiser is reaching practically the whole population within range of the transmitter. He may well ignore the poorest people, because they are not likely to have a set, and the richest and best educated because (as Dorothy Sayers shrewdly pointed out) they 'buy what they want when they want it' and are not likely to be influenced by mass advertisements; but between those two extremes he has to try to please and portray Everyman and Everywoman and, above all, must try to offend none of them.

This task is rendered much harder in England than it would be in some other countries, such as the United States, because the English are still a pretty strongly segmented population, where the different social classes and the different regions have each their own pattern of life, their own preferences and taboos and, worst trap of all, their own manner of speaking, their own accent. Bernard Shaw used Professor Higgins to point out that English people's accents place them socially and geographically; and, without any articulate sophistication, most English people place other English people as soon as they open their mouths. So what sort of accent can you use when you wish to speak to or for Everyman? How can you avoid appearing condescending or mocking to some part of the potential audience?

The most popular way of getting round this problem seems to be to avoid using the natural voice. Filters, and other electronic devices, are used to produce comic (at least in intention) sounds which might emerge from puppets or animated cartoons; or alternatively what might be described as a 'demonstration' voice is used by an invisible speaker while the screen shows actors impersonating 'ordinary' people. By a 'demonstration' voice I mean the kind of clear impersonal articulation which is taught to people who have to make public announcements, telephone operators, station or airport announcers, demonstrators in large stores. This type of voice is nobody's natural speaking voice, but a great number of English people seem capable of learning it; nobody is placed by it. Finally, you can avoid speech altogether, and sing instead; either having singers on the screen, or the heavenly choir mooing in the background.

So the first component in the picture of the English is of people who don't speak in their natural voices when other people are listening for fear that the audience may either look down on them as uneducated, or be put off by their la-di-da intonations. Although this has been brought about by the fears of the advertisers in the present instance, it is probably a not unimportant component in the well-known English shyness, and the general silence in public places.

As far as the advertisers are concerned, the most important section of the English population are married couples with young children; next come the young men and women who will shortly be married and have young children; the remainder hardly count.

Although growing families are treated as so important, it is relatively uncommon for a complete English family, mother and father and young children, to be pictured together on the television advertisement; this is one of the biggest contrasts with similar advertisements in the United States. The father is the rarest member; he is absent much of the time; but when he is present either the children are likely to be asleep, or he himself is unwell and is being tended by his wife or his daughter, but not often by both together. One of the few complete families is pictured by the makers of a brand of packaged soups; these apparently come in six flavours, so you have a husband, a wife, two boys and two girls seated round a dinner table each claiming one of the flavours as his or her favourite. This is a rarity.

English parents demonstrate their love for their children by feeding them; and English children show their love for their parents by demonstrating their enjoyment of what they eat. This is perhaps the most constant theme in English television advertising: the active person shows love by putting something into the loved one's mouth; the loved one responds by showing enjoyment of the insertion.

I have stated this in this rather generalized way because other objects are used as well as food in these one-sided transactions: cigarettes or cigars, which will turn aside a husband's irritation or capture the notice of an attractive young person; confected drinks which will do away with loneliness, build up strength, add vitamins or indeed do almost anything except quench thirst; various medicaments; and, of course, sweets. Apparently English wooing is carried on to a large extent by putting sweets into girls' mouths; this of course stops them talking (which we have seen is always desirable); but they may unglue their lips long enough to make a remark about how much they love those centres.

This feeding theme perhaps reaches its apogee with the feeding of pets: dogs, cats, budgerigars are made for ever young, for ever healthy and happy, by providing them with the right brand of food; and there is certainly some resemblance in English life between the treatment of pets and the treatment of children. But we don't actually watch pets eating to anything like the extent that we watch children doing so.

I doubt if you could turn on I.T.V. for half an hour at any time while it is operating without seeing some child stuff its face. This is apparently an endlessly gratifying sight; an English woman feels herself to have been a good mother to the extent that her children guzzle with gusto the food she has provided or, occasionally, prepared. When her husband is at home, she will provide him with the food, sauces or gravy that he relishes; but she has fewer opportunities for this. We very seldom see the English mother eating herself; she apparently got her nourishment while she was being courted.

I'm not sure if there is any conscious connection between the fact that Mum (apparently) gets so little to eat and her liability to fly into a nervous rage with her children or, occasionally, with other people; her temper is explained by the fact that she sleeps badly, or is in a state of 'nerves' or 'wound up'; and these conditions can be brought on by under-nourishment. In the mirror of the television advertisements, it is apparently only English women who get into these nervous states; men get 'run down' but don't fly off the handle like women do.

It is perhaps on account of Mother's nervous condition that English couples are so rarely shown entertaining friends. In one household, husband rings up at the last minute to say he is bringing guests home (how lucky she keeps lots of tinned food in the cupboard); in another two couples are shown seated round an empty table admiring the whiteness of the tablecloth. But entertainment in the home is not shown as an English custom after marriage. Men go to the pub (the 'demonstration' voice puts on a truly rural Loamshire accent for beer); mother consoles herself by making her children's clothes whiter and brighter than those of their playmates.

I have an impression that this obsession with whiteness is not congenial to the English character, that it is an import from the U.S.A. I have found that, when talking to people about television advertisements, it is the advertisements for detergents which they are most likely to pick out for condemnation. I don't think that they are in fact more numerous than the advertisements for other commodities; but if they do not fit in with the English viewers' picture of themselves, they will, in recollection, be far more irritating than the numerous more congenial advertisements which surround them.

An American import which irritates me personally derives from Dr. Dichter, of motivation research fame. He apparently found that American women felt some scruples about eating sweets, and he calmed these scruples by the slogan 'You deserve a candy'. English advertisers have jumped on to this simple formula, and we viewers are constantly being told we deserve food, drink, house-paint, even a garage. What I think we most deserve is a rest from this slogan.

How do English girls become housewives? or, for that matter, how do English boys become househusbands? Apparently by making their hair shiny and glossy and, in the case of girls, wavy too. The uniquely aphrodisiac attraction of hair in the proper condition is constantly being emphasized; it is, to the best of my recollection, the only condition which will get a boy and girl alone together and embracing. It is, I think, subsequent to this embrace that they pop sweets and cigarettes into each other's mouths.

Except with shiny hair, presumably unmarried couples are not shown together. Either people will be shown alone—the way people behave by themselves will be dealt with shortly—or else in trios or a large group; not, as far as I know, in foursomes. The prevalence of trios I find a little difficult to explain; I have no evidence to suggest that it is, in fact, a common feature of English life, as it is in Portugal or in parts of Southern Italy. But young people are very frequently shown in threes, with the pair of the same sex paying attention to the indifferent third: a situation which is dramatized on the 'Amplex' posters.

Young people attend mixed gatherings, at which everybody is on their feet, either standing about or dancing. No older people are present and it is quite unclear who is the host or hostess; what we are asked to concentrate on, to identify with, is the shyness or diffidence of the late arrival, who only finds reassurance by offering or receiving something to put in the mouth. Unless, of course, the hair is shining like a heliograph, in which case the new arrival will become the centre of attraction.

Men and women—but seldom, as far as I have noticed, young people—are frequently shown alone in a variety of situations; but these situations have one thing in common: the men and women appear to be having a much more enjoyable time by themselves than they do in the company of their family or their friends. By themselves, men munch and chew, smoke and drink with the patent signs of satisfaction which, in mixed groups, are only manifested by school-children. Women hardly ever feed themselves, even when they are alone; but instead they have an apparently rapturous time looking at themselves in the mirror and stroking their skin.

Mirror-gazing would appear to be a very widespread feminine trait, and not a special trait of English women only; but, as I discovered when I was doing the research for *Exploring English Character,* English women tend to expect a very great deal from the looking-glass: not only information about their appearance, but also information about their character and their motives; many women, when they wanted to be honest about themselves or understand where they had made mistakes, would take a long look in the mirror in search of the answer. In the television advertisements, the mirror's reply is apparently always a satisfactory one, if not at the beginning of the gaze then certainly at the end of it.

This pleasant self-inspection is very often accompanied by a most enjoyable stroking of the skin, gentle yet firm and rhythmic, nearly always upwards on the face and neck. The eyes are half-closed, like a cat purring; the exercise may be intended to add future glamour, but it is also obviously an end in itself. Even when away from a looking-glass women will caress their own skin; a soft fabric held against the face is apparently almost as nice as one's own hands. Watching the kiddies eat with gusto gives moral self-satisfaction; but sensual pleasure comes from the caresses a woman gives herself.

I have not dealt in this article with those very numerous advertisements which merely recommend or demonstrate goods for sale; nor have I raised the question of the desirability of advertising on television, nor where the advertisements should appear in relation to the programme. The advertisements are there, whatever our views about them; and I have tried to pick out the main features of the reflections of ourselves which are implied in the pictures which the advertisers project on to our living-room mirrors, night after night. It is of course only a partial picture; but would you say that its implications are altogether false?

## XV

## *An Anthropologist Considers Retirement*
*(1961)*

SOCIAL anthropologists study the various ways that human beings living in society organize or have organized their lives. Ideally, the social anthropologist deals with all human societies, past or present, simple or complex, of which any coherent record is available; but of course in practice no single individual can control all the literature. But apart from his own experience of different societies, any social anthropologist is aware of a good deal of the work of his colleagues, to the extent that he can make *comparative* statements of the ways in which different societies have solved the problems which are common to all human beings everywhere. All human societies, for example, must have rules for educating children, for dealing with adolescence, for deciding who may or may not marry and for regulating sex outside marriage, for preserving law and order, for exchanging goods and services, for dealing with death and the supernatural, and the other problems which are inherent in being human. The social anthropologist can point out in most such situations what is the gamut of solutions which human beings have devised, how little, in many cases, can be ascribed to 'human nature' and how much to social custom; can correct the assumptions so generally made that the values or customs of one society at one time are necessarily true of other societies or other periods. Because of his systematic knowledge of many societies he can often put problems peculiar to one society at one time into a new and wider perspective.

Anthropologists tend to group societies together according to the complexity of their culture, and have made the presence or absence of certain skills or techniques the criteria by which the societies are grouped. The simplest of contemporary societies depend entirely on hunting and food-gathering for their food; the next simplest are those who have systematic agriculture and/or herding. It is these societies which are usually described as primitive; the most usual criterion for separating the primitive from the complex is the possession of literacy. Within the complex, literate societies differentiation is made on the sources and amount of power available for work: societies entirely dependent on human muscle, those using a combination of human and animal muscle, those using wind or water power, and those using the assorted mechanical devices which have increasingly distinguished the Western world for the last three centuries.

Each increase in the level of complexity produces additional problems which the society has to solve, without, customarily, doing away with the problems inherent in the simpler forms of society. Literacy and advanced technology produce problems of education, of organization and institutions which have no or only very faint analogues in primitive society; but the basic human problems, those founded on biological processes and the direct relations of man with his fellow human beings, are common to societies at all stages of development.

Because of this, I thought, when I was first invited to discuss retirement, that I should be able to find a number of parallels from societies in other parts of the world or other stages of development, and should be able to describe how other peoples have dealt with this problem. But as I went over the records in my mind and in my library, I found that this first thought was inaccurate. Of course all societies have had some old people, and have devised various ways of treating the elderly, a point which I shall come back to later; but retirement, in the sense that a great part of the society can expect to live some years after giving up the work of their maturity, is something completely novel in human history.

In a way, this is the most important thing that I have got to say. Retirement, as a normal expectation, is an unparalleled development in human life and human history; it poses problems which no society before the twentieth century has had to try to solve. Apart from the problems inherent in novel technology, this is, I believe, unique in the vicissitudes of human existence; I know of no other situation which has no analogues either in the past or in the less developed areas of the contemporary world.

There are a number of contributory causes to this novel development. The most immediately obvious is the change in the expectation of life. Far more people of the present generation in Western societies can expect to live beyond the age of, say, 70, than has ever been the case at any previous time or in any other areas of the world.

But this is only a change in quantity. Old men and women have been recorded in nearly all human societies (there are a few where life is so strenuous or so precarious that grandparents are very uncommon); the fact that they are more numerous today than a few generations ago need not, by itself, have involved any change in the way old people were treated by their juniors, nor in the expectations that an individual in middle age might hold about the closing years of his life, should he live so long.

In most of the world throughout most of its history old age has been chiefly defined physiologically. People were treated as old when their physical strength was obviously waning, when they could no longer do a full day's work. But we define old age by the calendar, quite arbitrarily; people are treated as 'old' when they have reached a certain age, quite irrespective of their physical or intellectual capacities. It is this calendrical arbitrariness which is one of the cruellest aspects of retirement, and which has so greatly increased our social category of 'the old'.

As old age has become commoner, it has become progressively devalued. Formerly experience was a highly esteemed quality, most highly esteemed in societies which had no or little literacy, and for crafts and skills which were not completely, or not at all, verbalized. In nearly all situations which did not involve physical skill or prowess, the accumulated experience of the old was of value to the community. Because he or she has seen and experienced more than we have, it was felt, he or she must be wiser; the old know more.

Today we feel that the old know less and that what they do know is irrelevant. In very many spheres this is quite true. Because technology has developed at a geometric rate in the last half-century, only a modicum of skills acquired 50 years ago are of any relevance today. On very many levels, children are growing up at ease in a world their parents never knew; from household gadgets to industrial processes or means of transport, the young are more at home than their parents. Only in skills involving people without the interposition of technology or in traditional learning do we sometimes still accord respect to experience as such.

A revealing side-light on the common attitude to the old was shed by a research I did by questionnaire some few years ago. I asked people what they considered their best qualities; and a number of the younger adults replied: 'Fondness for children, old people and animals'. This triad could be summed up as 'fondness for the weak, who cannot look after themselves'; and this generous attitude does, I think, illumine the way the old are commonly regarded.

Coupled with this attitude to the old is a change in the general attitude to work. Work is no longer seen as an inevitable aspect of the life of most human beings—'if you don't work, you won't eat'—which it has been for all but a fraction of humanity through all of recorded history; nor is work generally seen as good and useful or interesting in itself. Work is now a means to an end, not an end; one works in order to gain the money which one will enjoy when one is not working. Work and pleasure are treated as antithetical; the reward of work is pleasure in the future; the cost of pleasure is work in the past.

But if work is considered a means, and not an end, and unenjoyable, and if old people and children are considered weak and to be protected, then you get the concepts of legal minimum and maximum ages for working, of compulsory schooling and compulsory retirement. The two notions are joined together on many levels; among the compensations of high social and financial position are longer education and earlier retirement. These compensations were the rule in nearly all complex societies up to 1900, in most up to 1939; recent social arrangements have made them available to a much wider section of the population.

The concept of retirement as a desirable phase in everybody's life can only be interpreted as a benevolent rule in the light of these underlying assumptions about the nature of work. If these assumptions are not correct, do not generally correspond to the emotional facts, then compulsory retirement is not a benevolent rule; on the contrary, it could be seen as a deprivation imposed on the old and weak by the younger and stronger to get them out of the way.

I think that, in point of fact, our attitude to work is much more ambivalent than the concepts that I have outlined. Hard manual labour and purely repetitive work are probably generally felt to be unpleasant and a means to an end which people believe that they would willingly abandon when they can afford to do so; at the other end of the gamut, vocational work and work in the arts and sciences is usually felt to be so rewarding in itself that the practitioners will not desist while they retain their strength and faculties, though they may be moved out of an institutional setting. But work for most of the population in contemporary complex societies does not fall into either of these categories; it is neither physically nor intellectually exhausting, nor is it predominantly self-chosen, as are the vocations. Most people do not work as they will, but as they must.

It is this lack of freedom, in the way that one's time is organized and in the fact that during working hours one is mostly implementing decisions which one has had little or no part in determining, which is frequently seen as the most unpleasant feature of work: 'when I retire I shall be my own master'. But the recompense for this surrender of freedom is the status which is accorded to people in virtue of their position in the work hierarchy; and this status is inevitably surrendered when freedom is reclaimed.

I had perhaps better enter a *caveat* that I am using 'status' as a sociological term. It is a very useful general term to describe the formal aspects of the relations between people within an institution. All the people within an institution have a status: to take the example of an army, there is the status of a private as well as the status of a general. Either position determines the way the holder of that status behaves towards other members of the institution and is formally treated by them. Unfortunately this term, like so many other terms from sociology and psychology, has been taken into common journalistic use in a distorted sense; and 'status' is now used with a sort of sneer as a pseudo-scientific way of describing social climbing, as in 'The Status-Seekers' or describing a Jaguar as a 'status-symbol'. The word, however, is too useful to abandon to journalists and politicians. It is a neutral word, describing the representative character of an individual within an institution, and the rights and duties inherent in any position. Since all institutions within complex societies tend to be hierarchical, there are higher and lower statuses within each institution, measured by the deference given and received at each position.

Status is a very important component of man's view of himself, of his self-esteem. Geniuses and idiots apart, we tend to judge ourselves as others judge us; if our status gives us respect from others, we respect ourselves; if this respect is withdrawn, we fall in our own self-esteem, sometimes disastrously.

Because of the complex character of modern industrial and institutional life, status within an institution is seldom recognized outside. There are a few techniques for informing strangers about one's status—titles, decorations, honorary ranks used by retired service officers; but these are only available to a few; and for most people their status is only confirmed within their occupation.

It consequently follows that when people are retired, they are immediately and completely stripped of the status which was inherent in their employment; and no alternative status is offered by society to replace that which is taken away. The size of the pension, when this is public knowledge, may give a faint shadow of former status. Individuals may have achieved status outside their occupation—in their neighbourhood, through leisure interests and the like—and these of course will remain; but the more devoted and emotionally involved people have been in their career, the less likely they are to have these subsidiary statuses, or to accord them much importance if they do possess them.

It is the sudden loss of status which is the cruellest aspect of compulsory retirement as it is practised today. I must emphasize again that by status I do not mean the minor symbols of high position—the carpet on the floor, the key to the directors' lavatory, or whatever else may be current; but the self-respect which comes from being respected by others for filling a role, doing a job, adequately. Self-respect is of the greatest emotional importance to most people; if this self-respect is destroyed, the result may well be despair.

Despair implies that the future is envisaged as without hope, as hopeless, and that one sees oneself as having become worthless and valueless. There are many well-authenticated cases of primitive people, suddenly reduced to despair, lying down and, as it is said, 'willing themselves to death'. I think very much the same thing happens in contemporary society. Even in my sheltered life, I am frequently hearing of business men suddenly dying, usually of a coronary, a few weeks before they are due for retirement or a few weeks after. The inter-relations of body and mind are a complex enough problem; but I am inclined to interpret deaths in these few months as symptoms of despair at least as much as the result of excessive cholesterol following years of too much delicious food.

If I am correct in considering loss of status the biggest deprivation of compulsory retirement, then the problem can be considered somewhat more clearly. It is a problem for society acting as a whole, rather than for individuals or members of a single existing institution: it is to devise situations in which retired people can achieve a new positive status, instead of, as now, being in the negative position of no-longer-working, no-longer-useful.

By this roundabout way we come to the lessons which an anthropologist can derive from other societies. Though, as I have said, retirement as such is a novel problem, old age is age-old; the devices which other societies have developed for giving self-respect to the old—and in most societies the loss of physical strength is much more serious than it is with us—may give some guidance on possible lines of development.

Outside the contemporary world few societies have paid much attention to the actual number of years people have lived; in much of the world it is uncommon—or at least has been uncommon until this century with its censuses and birth certificates —for people to be able to state their own age in years. In societies which pay attention to horoscopes—that is most of the non-

## An Anthropologist Considers Retirement

Muslim societies of Asia—people will know their birth-year in one or two of the recurring cycles on which horoscopes are calculated; but it needs quite elaborate calculations to transform this into a year-count. There are, too, a small number of warrior societies which arrange their male population in what are called age-grades; these group people into classes of four or five years interval, and all the people, or at least all the men, of one class change their roles and functions together. The Masai of Kenya and Tanganyika, or the Pathans of Pakistan and Afghanistan, are tribes which were organized in this manner. They will be warriors for so many stages, then they will leave the army, marry and become cultivators; in both of these roles they are meant to be touchy, ready to take offence and to give cause for argument, grasping and self-assertive. But when some point is reached —when the youngest son has joined his warrior-class, or when the eldest son has finished his service and is to be set up as a land-owner and cultivator—the old man becomes a peace-maker, no longer touchy himself, and a composer of the quarrels of his juniors, a sort of combination of magistrate, duel referee and counsellor. As such he holds an indispensable role; these societies put so much value on the masculine qualities of courage and honour and aggressiveness in their younger men, that there would be a danger of relapsing into complete anarchy were it not for the peace-making role of the old men who hold the society together. Although these old men are acting in quite a different way from what they had done before their 'retirement' as warriors and land-owners, they still have value in their own eyes and those of their juniors. These societies which are founded on fighting have invented a status for the man too old to fight.

Apart from these age-grade societies, old age is usually defined in relationship to becoming grandparents—either when the first grandchild is born, or when the youngest child is married and a parent, or some other combination. A point is marked by some public event by which the neighbours know that people should now be considered 'old' and will act in a different way to what they had done previously and in which their juniors still act. If they are Hindus or Buddhists they may devote themselves to religious duties and pilgrimages, giving up their business or agricultural interests and spending their time seeking salvation or a better re-incarnation. If they are traditional Japanese, particularly from the smaller villages, they can start to flout all the constraining rules of etiquette and good manners which have restricted their early life. For traditionally-reared Japanese women this gives old age considerable attraction: they can wear bright colours, talk loudly, get drunk in public and make risqué jokes, in short let themselves go and do, with full public tolerance and approval, all the things which no respectable Japanese girl or younger woman dare do, lest she cover herself and her family with shame and disgrace.

This idea of old age as a time of licence seems to me one which might be worth exploring. At the moment we only give licence to the young, to teenagers as the current jargon dubs them; and it is clear that society as a whole does give this licence, however much disapproval may be voiced by a censorious minority. It is amusing to contemplate our society developing two licentious groups—the unmarried young (as at present) and the retired old, both scandalizing the sober and hard-working middle-aged—the old developing their own conspicuous fashions, monopolizing some public places of entertainment, disturbing some staid neighbourhoods by the lateness and noise which mark their return from a night out. This is not too far from the traditional Japanese picture (except that the young, particularly the girls, had much less fun). We had traces of this in our traditional lower-class urban slums, when grandmothers could go alone to the pub (which no other respectable working-class women could do) and get merry together on port-and-lemon. This could be extended, I think.

More general than these special roles for the old is the system which anthropologists call the system of alternate generations. In this society, and societies which have kinship systems like ours (including those I have just been discussing), generations are arranged in linear order—great-grandparents, grandparents, parents, children, grandchildren, and so on—so that they make, as it were, a stepladder, each generation one rung higher (or lower, according to your viewpoint) than the next. All our terms of address, all our conventional behaviour within the family, are determined by this stepladder.

In very many societies this is not the rule. Alternate generations are treated as though they resembled one another far more than they do the intervening generation. In the simple three-generation family this means that grandparents and grandchildren are in many ways treated alike, in contrast to the intervening generation of parents. Very often they use the same terms of address to one another—a thing which we only do within the same generation (and even that not very often now)—'cousin', 'sister', etc.; if the language has intimate and formal terms, like *tu* and *vous* in French, the grandparents and grandchildren use the intimate terms to one another, and the formal terms to their children and parents. Grandparents and grandchildren are treated as natural intimates, in a way which parents and children can never be expected to be. Grandparents have a major role in the education and amusement of their grandchildren, grandchildren in the care and entertainment of their grandparents.

This is not at all the same sort of thing as the employment of a grandparent as an occasional sitter-in or substitute when the parents want to leave their children for a short period. Every child learns, as it learns the world, that grandparents are companions and fun, parents more severe, more distant, and more occupied. Parents know that they must be strict with their own children, but can indulge their grandchildren, and be indulged by them, to their heart's content. The tender and playful aspects of parenthood are postponed a generation, in effect to retirement age.

This system of alternate generations can only work unthinkingly in a society where the techniques of child-rearing and education are unquestioned, traditional, and stable. In societies which are changing rapidly, such as ours, the notions of the proper way to treat and teach children changes with each generation, sometimes even more rapidly; old people have, almost by definition, old-fashioned and unsuitable notions.

If we were to develop the idea that one way of giving the retired status, emotional interests and occupation, would be to develop this concept of alternate generations, and greatly enrich the present rather empty bond between grandparents and grandchildren, both literally and figuratively (such as apprentices), between people in their seventh and eighth decades and those in their first and second, then it would be necessary to establish schools or similar institutions, where those who are about to retire, the literal or figurative grandparents, could learn the accepted contemporary techniques of treating the young. It would be necessary for both men and women to attend such schools, and they would both have to bring to them a certain amount of humility. Men who have been successful in their careers would have to admit that there were areas in life about which they were ignorant; women who have raised their own children to successful adulthood would have to admit that in many cases the techniques and practices which they employed were no longer completely acceptable today—the refusal to admit this is one of the most fruitful sources of disagreement between mothers and their married daughters in this country. In such schools it might be possible for grandparents and grandchildren, or their equivalents, to attend together. Both could learn through teaching. The young can give their elders a new view of the world. The people who are now nearing retirement age have experienced more change in their lifetimes than any other generation in the known history of the world. If they can recall and explain this experience of change, they can greatly enrich the youngest generation's ability to face a world in which change is likely to be continuous. In the year or years before retirement, men and women would be released from work for schooling, in a similar way to that in which apprentices are released now. This process has already started in some firms and localities.

I see nothing impractical in this notion. If, after a lifetime of regular work, people can expect some years of compulsory leisure, it seems quite reasonable to train for this. It implies, of course, that society as a whole must be prepared to recast its ideas of the proper relationship of parents and children, and of grandparents and grandchildren. But if we are not going to have an ever-increasing section of the population without status, without function, without occupation other than hobbies, then society has got to recast its ideas and institutions over a very wide field.

## An Anthropologist Considers Retirement

You cannot alter the status of the old without to some degree modifying the status of all the other members of the community; and this system of alternate generations is one that has worked in a number of societies in different stages of development.

I have not mentioned the economic aspects of retirement, either in this or other societies, because that seems to me to be outside my terms of reference. The ideas which I should like to leave with you are (i) that universal retirement is a quite novel development in human society; (ii) that apart from the loss of income, which is in the process of being dealt with, the greatest deprivation of retirement is the loss of the status which has been associated with employment; and (iii) that it is up to society as a whole to make such social inventions and adjustments as will give status to the compulsorily retired, and significance to their remaining years. I have outlined some of the social inventions which other societies have made to give significance and enjoyment to old age. None of them are applicable, as they stand, to our much more complicated and much older society; but they suggest possible approaches which we shall have to develop if we are not to condemn an ever-increasing segment of our population to apathy, triviality or despair.

# PART THREE

*Questions of Sex*

## XVI

*Justification by Numbers*
A Commentary on the Kinsey Report
*(1948)*

FOR THE SOCIAL scientist, a best-seller is always an interesting and provocative phenomenon: what is it, he asks himself, that has made this book or play so much more acceptable to the reading public in this society at this period than the other books or plays produced at the same time? If this question can be satisfactorily answered, it invariably gives insight into the hidden wishes and fantasies of the book-reading public, and so throws light on the psychological dynamics of the society which has accepted the best-seller. Even though the conscious promotion of best-sellers has been very highly developed in recent years in the United States, a best-seller cannot be established unless there is some congruence between its underlying material and the underlying wishes and fantasies of the purchasing public.

This year (1948) has witnessed an unparalleled phenomenon in publishing history: a dull and turgid scientific book, full of figures and tables, and published at a relatively very high price, has been selling at a rate paralleling such simple fantasies as *Gone With The Wind* or *Forever Amber*. The miscalled *Sexual Behavior in The Human Male*, by Kinsey, Pomeroy and Martin, is firmly established in the best-seller lists. It has been the subject of numerous articles and innumerable conversations; to parallel the immediate impact of a scientific book, one would probably have to go back to 1859, and the publication of Darwin's *Origin of Species*; and even then the sales were not comparable. Of course the social penetration of this book, and indeed of any book, should not be exaggerated; even if it sells a million copies, and each copy is looked at by five people—a generous estimate—it will have reached only three per cent of the American population; but even this is remarkable diffusion, and calls for comment and an attempt at explanation.

The pre-publication publicity campaign, with vetted articles strategically placed, was one of the most ingenious and carefully executed in recent publishing history; and undoubtedly a certain number of purchasers bought the book in the hope of pornographic titillation. But if this had been its main drawing power, its sales would have quickly dropped, for few texts dealing with such a subject could be less stimulating. Nor, in such a case, would it have received the long and solemn digests, in lieu of reviews or criticisms, which appeared in most of the public press.

I do not intend here to criticize the book from a scientific point of view. Competent specialists have pointed out, or will point out, the unsatisfactory nature of the sample on which Dr. Kinsey bases his generalizations; the dubious practice of treating memories of sexual behaviour many years ago as absolutely veridic, when no law court will accept unsupported testimony of any event in the distant past; the ignoring of the accumulated psychiatric knowledge of the last fifty years on sexual behaviour, and the (surely wilful) distortion of the theories and viewpoints of psychiatry. If this book had only been bought by specialists competent to criticize it, its impact as a social phenomenon would have been minute; but the vast mass of the readers, like the reviewers, accept the material uncritically, so that it is true for them. On this basis, what can one deduce about the attitudes and expectations of college-educated urban Americans (far and away the largest component in Dr. Kinsey's sample, and almost certainly also in his customers) from the contents of the book, its reception in the popular press, and its echoes in conversation?

The chief novelty in the material, and the aspect which has been most consistently stressed, is the demonstration that certain types of sexual behaviour are more widely practised than had hitherto been supposed. That is all. No moderately sophisticated person can have been unaware that such practices existed; Dr. Kinsey has provided figures of distribution.

Why then has such a pother been made about these figures of distribution? Why have reviewers stated, in various synonyms, that the book contains 'potential dynamite'? Why have there been numerous suggestions that, in the light of these 'disclosures', the laws meant to regulate sexual behaviour and the instructions and admonitions given to young people will all have to be changed?

I suggest that this springs from what is in some ways the fundamental democratic fallacy, which may be called Justification by Numbers. If a few people do or think something, it may be wrong; but if a lot of people do or think it, then it is obviously right. This argument underlies a great deal of American advertising: to state that the brand you are marketing is the 'most popular brand' or 'sells more than double its nearest competitor' is to suggest forcibly that it is therefore better. On the political level the votes of the majority should undoubtedly be decisive on those issues on which they are called upon to vote (and these are remarkably few); but to extend this principle to moral, psychological or physiological activities is completely illogical.

An illustration may make this clearer. A colleague of Dr. Kinsey conducts a survey in India entitled *Eating Behavior in the Human Male* and finds that, say, eighty per cent of the sample has a calorie 'intake' of 1,500 units daily, that seventy-three per cent only have two dietetic 'intakes' daily, and so on and so forth; in the light of his 'disclosures' it will become clear that 1,500 calories daily divided into two meals is 'normal' eating behaviour, and that all our views on dietetics and nourishment have to be revised.

Most people would reject this as obvious nonsense, for we have scientifically determined standards of adequate nourishment, which have nothing to do with temporary and local practices; but the arguments are as valid in the one case as the other. The scientific determination of adequate and satisfying sexual behaviour is by no means so well established or agreed upon (for, despite Dr. Kinsey, the implications of sex are much more complicated), but they will not be determined by a study of distribution. Dr. Kinsey's figures *can* be interpreted to mean that neurotic disturbances in sexual life in the contemporary United States are as widespread as malnutrition in contemporary India.

I do not mean to suggest by this that it would not be highly desirable to change or modify the laws of the various states which are meant to control sexual behaviour; but an unjust law does not change in injustice if it potentially affects thirty per cent of the population instead of three per cent. At most it makes the savage punishment of those who are convicted even more arbitrary than it had appeared before.

A second important aspect of this book is what might be called the 'atomization' of sex. Until Dr. Kinsey came along, sex had generally been viewed as one of the most complex of all human activities, involving not merely the genital organs, but all the psychological and emotional components of the personality, both conscious and unconscious. But with Dr. Kinsey, everything except overt genital behaviour has been omitted; sex has been reduced to statistics.

This atomization is in congruence with one of the major trends in contemporary American culture. The triumphs of mass production have been produced by the calculated atomization of the manufacturing process and of the worker's movements. The atomization of knowledge into a series of discrete and equal facts can be seen from the intelligence tests administered to pre-school moppets to the check lists which in many colleges constitute the chief examination before proceeding to graduate studies; from the 'quiz' shows to the crossword puzzle; from teaching temporary officers new techniques to public opinion polls. Now sex has been added to the list.

By thus oversimplifying or atomizing sex, it is possible to indulge in this domain too in the popular and widespread American habit of rating oneself. One of the chief recurring motives throughout American life from infancy to old age is the striving for relative success with one's equals and near-equals: precocity, marks or grades at school, athletic success, relative income, popularity—the list could be indefinitely prolonged. This 'self-rating' has become so emotionally important for so many Americans that the greater number of popular papers have scoring cards by which one can rate oneself for knowledge or for the possession of certain qualities (20 to 16, excellent; 15 to 11, good; 10 to 6, average; under 6, poor). Now Dr. Kinsey

## Justification by Numbers

has supplied a great number of tables by which one can rate oneself; and, in an appendix, has thoughtfully broken them down by age, education, marital status, etc. With a little trouble one can find out how one stacks up in frequency of 'outlet', variety of 'outlet', and even more intimate anatomical details, with one's peers. 'Keeping up with the Joneses' acquires a new, and perhaps slightly ribald, significance.

As in all such 'self-rating' tables, admiration goes to the high scores. Behind the mask of dispassionateness, one can easily discern Dr. Kinsey's astonished admiration for the people with the larger rates of 'outlet', and his contemptuous pity for those making poor scores. A little anthropological knowledge might have rectified this attitude. We have enough information from enough primitive societies to suggest that there is an (apparently) direct correlation between high rates of intercourse and lack of emotional interest in sex or belief in love; the Lepchas from the borders of Tibet, whom I studied, had rates of outlet in their early adult life which would make Dr. Kinsey's high scorers look like pikers. For the Lepchas, sex was a satisfaction no more important than food; they did not believe in love, made no allowances for it, and the exclusive possession of a spouse was legally impossible. As a matter of fact, Dr. Kinsey probably already had the evidence to confirm this; among his highest scorers are his ubiquitous male prostitutes (p. 216)—a group which surely figures rather more importantly in Dr. Kinsey's sample than in the population at large. To equal the performances of such people is perhaps not wholly enviable.

It may be remarked that these 'self-rating' tables are liable to produce more disquietude than satisfaction in the people who consult them. Forty-nine per cent of the population is always below the median. People so unsure of themselves as to need support from 'self-rating' are not too likely to get it. On the other hand, judging by previous experience, people who are disturbed about their 'deviance' will not get psychological comfort for more than a very few days from the tabular demonstration that their deviations are more widespread than they had suspected.

A probable by-product of these rating scales may well be

further ammunition for the anti-intellectualism which is already widespread. In comic books and cartoons, professors are always 'long-haired', and scientists are always 'mad'; now Dr. Kinsey brings evidence to show that, compared with the less educated, they are less 'manly', 'make' fewer girls, and sleep less often with their wives than do the men who leave school as soon as it is legally possible. The implications are obvious.

To parody a phrase of Marxist dialectics, Dr. Kinsey's tables result in the devaluation of all values. An involuntary nocturnal emission, a little boy sliding down a rope, a murderous rape, or Romeo spending the night with Juliet, Damon with Pythias, Paolo with Francesca, are all equated as one 'outlet'; physiological itch, lust and love are reduced to their lowest common denominator, and it couldn't well be lower. Just as the dollar which may save oneself or one's family from starvation is no different from the dollar added to the billionaire's bank deposit, so in Dr. Kinsey's treatment all sexual 'outlets' are reduced to a dead level of physiological spasm. Like dollars, the more you have the better. Chastity, even though it be Abelard's, results in a low score; and who wants to rate low?

Inspection of the tables suggests a couple of further generalizations about the men whom Dr. Kinsey interviewed. They do not easily tolerate physiological discomfort, and will get rid of it some way or other. Just as there is in the United States very low tolerance of even mild hunger or thirst or cold—as witnessed by the corner drugstore, the numerous drinking fountains, the central heating—so relatively mild gonadal pressure will be relieved somehow, almost as a health measure.

Secondly, despite the devaluation of all values, people are seeking for a greater level of satisfaction in sex than can generally be achieved. This I think is the explanation for much of the pre-marital, extra-marital and occasional homosexual behaviour which Dr. Kinsey demonstrates. Some of these excursions may be due to the search for a 'good time' under the influence of alcohol, some to adolescent experimentation; but much would seem to be due to the seeking for an unattainable ideal.

I should be unhappy if it were deduced from this article that I am opposed to the scientific investigation of sexual behaviour;

on the contrary, I think it is one of the most important gaps in our knowledge of contemporary society which, when filled, may do much to remedy the disquietudes and restlessness of this Age of Anxiety. But it needs a more integrated approach than that of an entomologist; an act which can consummate love and produce children cannot be measured with the calipers that determine the variation in the wingspan of wasps. For a society which believes in love, be it sacred or profane, the physiological aspect of sex cannot be separated from its emotional and psychological concomitants without reducing it to meaninglessness. We need statistical studies of human sexual behaviour, but they should be studies of the behaviour of human beings, not of genital organs.

To revert to the original query of why the Kinsey report has had so widespread and ready an acceptance in the United States today, I think the answer can be found on two levels. It does not contain a single novel or disturbing idea, no new insight into human behaviour, such as caused the initial rejection of such pioneers as Havelock Ellis or Sigmund Freud; and its underlying attitudes are in complete congruence with some of the predominant, though not necessarily the most valuable, attitudes and ideas of contemporary, educated, urban Americans. To the extent that Justification by Numbers is a valid concept, the phenomenal sales of Dr. Kinsey's book demonstrate that he has provided what his public wanted.

# XVII

## Nature, Science, and Dr. Kinsey
*(1954)*

IT IS GRATIFYING to be able to report that the second volume of the Kinsey Reports, *Sexual Behavior in the Human Female*[1], omits many of the more objectionable features of the first volume. There is no longer the ludicrous attempt to extrapolate from a sample which is overwhelmingly college-educated, and confined to small urban areas of the North-Eastern United States, to the whole population of that country and by implication to the world; tables are analysed into means as well as medians, so that the 'averages' are less misleadingly high; professional purveyors of sex (prostitutes and the like) are not lumped together with the amateurs, as they were with the males, so that in this way also the totals are less inflated; and cultural differences are given some acknowledgement by reference to some anthropological studies. Dr. Kinsey has obviously profited by the minority criticisms levelled at some aspects of the first volume; and for a man who has received such adulation and uncritical acclaim to do so should count very greatly to his credit.

Although there is considerably less inflation of the reported incidence of sexual activity among American women than there was among American men, it is still not entirely absent; but, except in one instance, it does not appear particularly gross. Unless the chapter, with the relevant tables, on the pre-marital intercourse of American women is read with extreme care, a very distorted picture of American sexual morals is likely to be formed. Nearly half (48 per cent) of Dr. Kinsey's sample are reported as having intercourse before marriage, which suggests a remarkable degree of licentiousness in a mainly Protestant population; but one finds in a small paragraph on p. 292 that

[1] W. B. Saunders, London, 1953.

## Nature, Science, and Dr. Kinsey

just on half this number had only had intercourse with their fiancé, anticipating by a few days or weeks the legal ceremony. Certainly such behaviour can only be technically described as pre-marital intercourse; but this fact considerably alters the picture of sexual promiscuity which the gross figures give. Instead of the sensational statement that nearly half the female population engages in intercourse before marriage, we could have the much more sober statement that over three-quarters of the women in the sample were technical virgins until they slept with their husbands (legal or anticipatory). Apart from criticisms of this nature, Dr. Kinsey's presentation of his data in this volume is relatively unexceptionable, and occasionally informative.

Nevertheless, although the manifest content calls for less detailed criticism than did that of the first volume, the assumptions underlying the collection and presentation of the data are even more objectionable and unsatisfactory in the case of women than they were in the case of men; and much of the propaganda, masked as the *obiter dicta* of 'science', calls for comment and analysis.

The fundamental criticism which, to my mind, invalidates a remarkable amount of industry and perseverance, is that, by Dr. Kinsey's implicit standards, sex becomes a quite meaningless activity, save as a device for physical relaxation, something like a good sneeze but involving the lower rather than the higher portions of the body. If 'tensions' build up, one either takes a pinch of snuff or a mistress; it doesn't matter which, and both are equally efficacious.

The concept of love is completely omitted from the analysis of sexual behaviour; the word does not even figure in the admirably full thirty-one page index. All 'outlets', all orgasms, are treated as equal and interchangeable; no qualitative difference is considered or discussed. But surely, even on the grossest physiological level, there is considerable difference between an involuntary nocturnal dream and the consummation of love, between a few minutes' casual encounter and the nights of a honeymoon. Dr. Kinsey resolutely ignores all such distinctions; in the long (and interesting) chapters on the anatomy and physiology of sexual response and orgasm, orgasm is treated as though it were invariant, as though all orgasms were identical and total.

In the chapter on masturbation he writes:

> We have already noted that a variety of physiologic disturbances, including a considerable development of neuromuscular tensions, are involved whenever there is sexual arousal. When the sexual responses lead to orgasm, these tensions are suddenly released and the individual thereupon returns to a physiologically normal or subnormal state. . . . Then she may function more efficiently in her everyday affairs. . . . Most persons live more happily with themselves and with other persons if their sexual arousal, whenever it is of any magnitude, may be carried through to the point of orgasm.
>
> . . . we may assert that we have recognized exceedingly few cases, if indeed there have been any outside of a few psychotics, in which either physical or mental damage has resulted from masturbatory activity. We have, on the other hand, recognized a tremendous amount of damage which has been the result of worry over masturbation, and of attempts to abstain from such activity (pp. 166–8).

I do not, at the present moment, wish to dwell on the propaganda implicit in this quotation, but rather on the explicit assumption that masturbation is a completely adequate technique for relieving 'tensions'. Surely this is contrary to the experience of nearly any person of either sex who has had a moderately satisfactory love life.

The argument, presumably, for ignoring all questions of intensity in sexual experience, is that such chiefly subjective variables are difficult to elicit in fairly short, single, quick-fire interviews and too complicated to manipulate statistically. If such arguments are advanced, it seems to me rather a criticism of a method of research which cannot deal with the most highly valued aspects of the activity being investigated. The English-speaking peoples place a very high value on love, and reprobate a marriage based on any other considerations. Though many people do engage in sexual activities without love, to assume that the presence or absence of love is irrelevant is surely a grave departure from common sense.

Not only is sex, in Dr. Kinsey's presentation, as meaningless as a sneeze, it is also equally unproductive; after the equivalent of blowing the nose, that is the end of the matter. It seems almost incredible, but is nevertheless true, that gestation, birth and nursing of children are completely ignored. Motherhood, for Dr. Kinsey, has no sort of connection with sex. In the tables on the behaviour of married women, we are told on all occasions the amount of their education, their age, and their relative religious devoutness; but not in a single table are we informed whether they be sterile or fertile, whether they have living children or no. Even from the sociological point of view, one would expect interesting and consistent differences in adultery and other postmarital carryings-on between the mothers and the childless. This variable is consistently ignored.

Quite a few of Dr. Kinsey's interviewees were more realistic than their interviewer:

> Something between 1 and 3 per cent of the females had dreamed that they were pregnant or that they were giving birth to a child. It is notable that these were reported as 'sex dreams'. . . . Such dreams need further consideration, because the connection between the reproductive function and erotic arousal is probably not as well established as biologists and psychologists ordinarily assume. By association, many males and apparently some females may become erotically aroused when they contemplate any reproductive or excretory function, probably because it depends at least in part on genital anatomy, and this may explain why some females consider dreams of pregnancy as sexual. It is more likely they consider their pregnancy dreams as sexual simply because they know, intellectually, that there is a relationship between sexual behaviour and reproduction (p. 213).

Consider the implications of this passage! The link between intercourse and procreation is either purely intellectual, or else excretory! As they say in the disclaimers before some American novels: 'any connection is purely coincidental'. None of Dr.

## Questions of Sex

Kinsey's interviewers or senior assistants are women (technically, a major error in the research set-up: one would have liked cross-sex and simili-sex interviews as a check on the type of material elicited in different interview situations); and although he is always having recourse to the animal kingdom to demonstrate that disapproved-of behaviour is 'natural', it would seem that he has never observed the reproductive cycle of the larger mammals.

With domestic animals, such as kine, pigs or dogs (not perhaps with the anthropoids) the behaviour of the males is fairly analogous to that of human beings; as far as one can judge from facial expressions and muscular movements, etc., particularly the rather fatuous slavering grin, their physical pleasure in intercourse is 'almost human'. But the same cannot be said of the oestrous female. She acts as if she were possessed of a devil, an intolerable itch, which drives her to almost any behaviour which might provide relief. Intercourse provides this relief, but not, judging by the same criteria, any sort of positive pleasure; she looks passive and bored, and would almost certainly eat an apple or read a newspaper if there were such a thing handy. The sow's or bitch's pleasure comes from suckling her young; in that situation you can observe the same rather fatuous but completely contented grin that the boar or dog wore during intercourse. 'I have given suck and know How tender 'tis to love the babe that milks me.' In other contexts Dr. Kinsey stresses the diffuseness of the female's sexual response, the fact that the genitalia are often only indirectly involved; but nothing connected with bearing children can be sexual, for then sex might be serious.

Incidentally, it seems at least hypothetically possible that there is some connection between the increase of non-marital sexuality (which Dr. Kinsey documents) in the 'flaming twenties' and the very strong propaganda in the United States at that period against breast-feeding, or any considerable display of maternal affection. This was the great period of 'formulae' in bottles administered on strict 'schedules', and of banning the kissing and fondling of babies as 'unhygienic' and undesirable, the hey-day of Watsonian behaviourism. Motherhood must have been almost a more unsatisfactory experience among the better educated

Americans of that period than at any other place or time in human history; and this may have driven the unfortunate victims of 'science' to search for substitute satisfactions. Dr. Kinsey's notions of psychology obviously stem from this period; he attempts to account for all sexual deviations by direct adolescent or adult 'conditioning' (p. 645); and his philosophy is summed up in the simplest anti-religious materialism : 'The same sort of misinterpretation has led to the dualistic distinction of mind and body to which many persons have been inclined. But form and function are co-ordinate qualities of any living cell, and of any more complex assemblage of living cells' (p. 642). It can be a matter of little surprise that the holder of such views quite consistently distorts, when he does not ignore, the views of psychiatrists and psycho-analysts.

As has been said, Dr. Kinsey is a great one for invoking the practice of 'nature' to justify any type of behaviour not permitted by the States' legal codes in America, on the ground that they are part of man's 'mammalian heritage'. This leads to some quite comic passages, notably the pages (410–412) finding mammalian analogues to adultery (!) which is as 'natural' as all get-out. In the earlier pages he writes :

> We shall find that a great many of the aspects of human sexual behaviour, including many which various religious and cultural codes have considered the most abnormal, are, in actuality, basic to the whole mammalian stock (p. 137).

And when he has covered most of the detailed data, he sums up :

> Psychologists and psychiatrists reflecting the mores of the culture in which they have been raised, have spent a good deal of time trying to explain the origins of homosexual activity; but considering the physiology of sexual response and the mammalian backgrounds of human behaviour, it is not so difficult to explain why a human animal does a particular thing sexually. It is more difficult to explain why each and every individual is not involved in every type of sexual activity (p. 451).

It is difficult to deal with this appeal to 'nature' seriously; from the moment man invented tools, preserved fire, and used language he was presumably acting 'unnaturally', for he was doing things no other mammal had ever done; and the attempted regulation of sexual behaviour by laws, sanctions or religion is certainly completely 'unnatural', as 'unnatural' as engaging in scientific research or publishing best-sellers. Dr. Kinsey apparently thinks it would be a Good Thing if everybody had lots and lots of sexual 'outlets' (one of his rare evaluative adjectives occurs in the sentence: 'As with the male, the [erotic] dreams often had a distressing way of stopping just short of the climax of the activity') and that is a perfectly tenable position; but to make propaganda for this viewpoint on the ground that 'birds do it, bees do it, little squirrels in the trees do it' does not seem to show very great respect for what is a presumably educated audience.

In one respect, this appeal to the animals appears to be seriously misleading.

> The wide distribution of non-coital sex play among all of the mammalian species on which there are sufficient data is evidence of the ancient origins of the anatomic and physiologic bases of such behaviour some millions of years ago in the ancestral stocks of the class Mammalia. . . . In a biologic sense, petting is a normal or natural sort of behaviour, and not the intellectually contrived perversion which it has sometimes been considered. In a biologic sense, the real perversion is the inhibition and suppression of such activities on the supposition that they represent 'acts contrary to nature' (pp. 230, 231).

If this means that infra-human mammals capable of coitus engage in sexual activities from which coitus is intentionally and completely excluded, I think it is simply nonsense. Adolescent male animals may engage in mounting rehearsals, often with inappropriate partners, until they have learned the proper techniques, and oestrous females will engage in all sorts of random behaviour to ease their intolerable itch; but I can find no evidence that adult animals in partial or complete freedom indulge in heterosexual non-coital sexual play, though bored specimens in zoos or laboratories who are provided with food may perhaps do so to eke out the monotony of an existence from which the food-quest, the major preoccupation of all wild mammals, is completely excluded. For the rest, I think much of Dr. Kinsey's interpretation of mammalian behaviour springs from the pathetic or anthropomorphic fallacy. Most mammals are very highly dependent on olfactory and gustatory cues as guides to behaviour; and much activity, which would have sexual implications if engaged in by humans, should almost certainly be regarded as research and analysis. Parenthetically, it is curious that in his discussion of psychological sexual stimuli Dr. Kinsey should have completely disregarded the sense of smell; there is a little laboratory, and quite a lot of anecdotal, evidence to show that men and women respond differentially to certain smells, and that for many women some smells are sexually stimulating. The numerous and costly advertisements of the perfume industry, especially in the U.S.A., harp on the suggestion that scent is aphrodisiac; it is likely that the chief purchasers of perfume are women, and they must presumably consider the advertisement claims as not improbable.

'Petting' would seem to be one of the rarest types of human sexual behaviour. For it to occur with any regularity a number of pre-conditions are necessary: the society must (i) postpone marriage for several years after the girls are nubile and (ii) at the same time place a high valuation on virginity at marriage, so that pre-marital intercourse has to be intermittent and furtive, and (iii) allow young men and women of marriageable age to associate without supervision. I know of no societies, other than those facing the Atlantic during the last fifty years or so, in which all these conditions operate simultaneously. It is of course perfectly legitimate for anybody to argue that 'petting' is not harmful or is positively desirable; but if the chief arguments are derived from alleging that such behaviour is widespread among mammals or general in most human societies, one can only conclude that there is very little to be said for the practice.

As can be seen, Dr. Kinsey is not really either dispassionate or neutral (probably nobody dealing with human emotions and values could be); behind the 'scientific' smoke-screen of statistical tables, graphs, codes and rebarbative language there is a continuous propaganda for more, and more varied, sexual 'outlets' as physiologically good in themselves. There is even the stupendous claim that taxonomic studies of behaviour should be the basis for laws:

> There cannot be sound clinical practice, or sound planning of sex laws, until we understand more adequately the mammalian origins of human sexual behaviour, the anatomy and physiology of response, the sexual patterns of human cultures outside of our own, and the factors which shape the behavioural patterns of children and of adolescent youth. We cannot reach ultimate solutions for our problems until legislators and public opinion allow the investigator sufficient time to discover the bases of those problems (p. 8).

Note the arrogance of the phrase 'ultimate solutions'! To show just how indefensible such pretensions are, let us for a moment consider another widespread mammalian instinct with many of the same physiological components as sex, aggression. Murder, the killing of members of one's own species, is common in some situations among many groups of mammals, is enjoined by many (head-hunting) cultures outside our own, and is found in nearly all societies. Similarly, robbery is a most widespread mammalian and human characteristic; cannot we have 'sound planning of criminal laws' until the investigator has had sufficient time to present us with 'ultimate solutions' of the desirability or undesirability of regulating murder or robbery?

All societies attempt to regulate the sexual behaviour of their members in the light of their over-riding values. Few societies (except perhaps our own) have such cruel, foolish and unenforcible laws as those current in the forty-eight States of the American Union; it would be highly desirable that such laws should be modified or repealed; but the only motives which are likely to make this happen are an increase in charity, courage, and understanding among the legislators and those who influence them; the demonstration that disapproved-of practices are more widespread than had been thought may well provoke savage panic rather than greater tolerance.

It would be ungrateful to close this article without some reference to the new information I have gathered about women in general and American women in particular from *Sexual Behavior in the Human Female*. As far as American women are concerned, Dr. Kinsey demonstrates impressively that the active practice of religion is the greatest safeguard of female virtue, a fact which my own investigations confirm for England. He also gives support to the folk belief that those women who are chaste before marriage will be likely to be faithful thereafter, and conversely; or, if this statement sound too moralistic for some readers, here is the same information in scientificese:

> Among the 514 females in the sample who had had extra-marital coitus up to the date on which they had contributed their histories, over 68 per cent had also had coitus before marriage. Since only 50 per cent of all the married females in the sample had had pre-marital coitus, it would appear that the pre-maritally experienced females were somewhat more inclined to accept coitus with males other than their husbands after marriage.
>
> To put it in another way, 29 per cent of the females with histories of pre-marital coitus had had extra-marital coitus by the time they contributed their histories to this study, but only 13 per cent of those who had not had pre-marital coital experience (p. 427).

It is interesting to note that among the college-educated American women who contributed their histories to Dr. Kinsey and his associates, the pattern of adultery is not a long-lasting liaison, but a short 'romance' during a holiday or sea voyage or similar brief encounter—just one of those things. For both sexes Dr. Kinsey's sample of the respectable working and lower-middle classes is woefully inadequate; but it is interesting to note that the great differences in practice and toleration of aberrant practices which he reported between low-educated and much-educated men seems to find no echo at all in his analysis of women's sexual behaviour; with the possible exception of the practice of female homosexuality, education (which is Dr. Kinsey's criterion for class differences, and, by and large, a fairly acceptable one for the U.S.A.) seems to make no difference to the sexual behaviour and attitudes of American women. There is an odd lack of 'fit' here between the reports in the male and female volumes; and there is also a lack of 'fit' between the amount of heterosexual experience both in quantity and number of partners claimed by men and admitted by women; observation suggests that male recourse to prostitutes does not account for the marked difference.

Of Dr. Kinsey's generalizations on the sexual nature of women two seem to me of particular interest. Firstly, there is the demonstration that, as opposed to the sudden early peak and then continuous decline in the sexual capacities of males, women tend to rise slowly to a plateau round the age of thirty and then maintain a fairly even level for a considerable number of years, well past the menopause in most cases. This suggests that the pattern which was traditional among the French bourgeoisie (to what extent it was practised is another question) was the one which most completely fitted the physiological capacities of both sexes. In this pattern the young man, at the height of his sexual powers, has his early liaisons with women a generation older than himself (*'la femme de quarante ans'*) also at the height of their powers; and when he becomes older, with lowered capacities, he takes as wife or mistress a young girl who has not nearly reached her maximum. Needless to say, such complementary relationships receive little approval in the United States.

Secondly, his chapter on Psychological Factors in Sexual Response shows that very few women respond in the way most men do to partial or symbolical references to sexual activity or potentialities. Women are rarely *voyeuses* or exhibitionists, get little or no pleasure or stimulation from the observation of nakedness or from erotic, pornographic or obscene literature, art or conversation; 'showing one's etchings' is an inefficient technique of seduction. Even in directly sexual situations any interruption may destroy a woman's interest while the man's will be maintained. The differences elaborated in this chapter are of considerable interest.

I am too ignorant of anatomy and physiology to be able to comment on Dr. Kinsey's assertion that, with the exception of the ovaries and testes, male and female genitalia are exact homologues, and that orgasm is physiologically identical for both sexes. Dr. Kinsey shows that among women orgasm is certainly a learned response, requiring in most cases quite an amount of practice; some ninety per cent of his sample eventually claim to achieve it. He has loosed the cat among the chickens with a vengeance by flatly denying that there are two types of female orgasm, which is one of the basic tenets of all psycho-analysts and most psychiatrists; it is up to these specialists to produce their counter-evidence. This does not seem the place to take up the question whether Dr. Kinsey is justified in treating orgasm as the sole criterion for satisfactory sexual experience in women; but it can be stated that there is quite a lot of evidence, chiefly from cultures other than Britain and the U.S.A., to the contrary.

Since Dr. Kinsey allows the minimal anatomic and physiological differences between men and women, he has to find some other source for the contrasts in sexual capacities and psychological responsiveness referred to above. In two chapters on neural mechanisms and hormonal factors in sexual response he suggests, somewhat tentatively, that the differences between the sexes may reside in the cortex and the pituitary gland; these are provocative suggestions, though I am unable to criticize them. Taken in all, the 200 pages of 'Part III. Comparisons of Female and Male' are a useful and scholarly addition to our limited knowledge of sex; had they been published as scientific studies normally are published, without the ballyhoo worthy of the late Mr. Barnum, they would have merited, and doubtless received, considerable judicial praise. But by his practice of maximum publicity, Dr. Kinsey has moved his reports from the scientific to the propagandistic level; and it is on that lower level that I have thought it useful to analyse them.

# XVIII

## Man to Man
*(1961)*

*A Minority* by Gordon Westwood (published by Longmans) consists of the analysis of interviews with 127 male homosexuals, most of them from London, and is a most detailed and careful piece of research, within its limits superior to anything else which has appeared on this subject.

It is superior in two respects: first, the informants (or contacts, to use Mr. Westwood's phrase) were drawn from the population at large, instead of, as in nearly all previous studies, from prisoners or from psychiatric patients. Mr. Westwood achieved this by persuading his original contacts to introduce friends to be interviewed; over two-thirds of the sample were found in this way, though only three secondary contacts were taken from each original contact, to prevent concentration on a single clique (as seems to have been the case with G. W. Henry's *Sex Variants*); in this way a good scatter in age, education, social class, and occupation was achieved.

Secondly, a consistent attempt has been made to see the homosexuals in the setting of English society; their family background is explored to attempt (on a rather superficial level) to give some statistical backing to various theories of the 'origin' of homosexuality, and a lot of attention is paid to their occupations, their religious life, their attempts to get help and advice, their meeting-places, and their relationship with the law, both the offences they commit against public decency and their sufferings at the hands of the police and magistrates, of blackmailers and assailants. This is a great advance on the taxonomic approach, as used from Krafft-Ebing to Kinsey, which concentrated on overt sexual behaviour. If I now proceed to criticize some aspects of Mr.

Westwood's study, these criticisms should not be understood to modify my commendation.

Despite its considerable merits, I think Mr. Westwood's study suffers from his psychological and anthropological naivety; and this naivety, which is by no means peculiar to Mr. Westwood, ultimately rests on a semantic confusion. 'Homosexuality' is a false isolate, a term covering a number of conditions whose only common bond is that some sort of sexual relationship takes place between two people of the same sex. It is a false isolate in much the same way as 'cancer' or 'schizophrenia' are false isolates. Little progress was made while cancer or schizophrenia were looked on as entities, with one 'cause' and one potential 'cure'; advances occurred when these false isolates were treated as clusters, when researchers acted (even if their vocabulary did not entirely reflect their practice) on the assumption that they were dealing with an indefinite number of cancerous or schizophrenic syndromes and studied one at a time 'the cancers' or 'the schizophrenias'.

In a very analogous fashion, I feel sure that one should think about 'the homosexualities'. On the present evidence, there would seem to be three major forms, and one minor one; they probably have different aetiologies, and certainly have different social consequences. To discuss them it is necessary to introduce a vocabulary; and I propose to use the terms *pederast* (pederasty) *homophile* (homophilia), and *pathic* (pathicism). Paedophiliac (paedophilia) is already in the vocabulary for the minor form, the child-molesters; this would appear to be considered a grossly pathological condition in all societies of which we have record and does not call for discussion. (Mr. Westwood probably has three among his contacts.)

According to present evidence, all the homosexualities are socially produced or induced; and societies have been described in which they do not occur. All these societies (such as the Arapesh, the Lepcha, the Mundugumor, the Siriono) are on a very simple level of technical elaboration; and they all share the common characteristic that they make little contrast between the concepts of masculinity and femininity, between the ideals of manhood and womanhood. Boys are not brought up with the instructions: 'All real men do . . .' or 'No proper man does . . .'; and there is no possibility of confused sexual identification. Male and female are defined by their primary sexual characteristics only, not by temperament, interests, or aptitudes which may be considered incongruous in one sex or the other. Although there may be habitual division of labour between the sexes, a man does not derogate from his masculinity by performing women's tasks.

When on the other hand the roles of the sexes are very strongly contrasted, and particularly when women are secluded, there is a high probability of institutionalized pederasty. This is not a universal; and when there is a very strong contrast between the roles of the sexes and no institutionalized pederasty, a certain number of pathics would seem to occur.

The characteristic feature of pederasty is that there is an age differential (typically a generation, but in some age grade societies an age-group) between the partners, the older being the lover and the younger the beloved; and in many societies only the lover is meant to achieve genital gratification. Behaviour should be governed by age rather than temperament. Typically the adolescent boy is chosen as a beloved by an older man; after the passage of some years whose termination is defined in various ways (shaving of the first beard, moving into the next class of warriors, and the like) the young man marries and produces children; when his own children are reared, he becomes the lover of adolescents.

This pattern is socially viable, and has been found in a considerable number of societies all over the world, typically warrior societies with harems or the equivalent, from feudal Japan to classical Greece and very nearly contemporary Pathans and Albanians. By socially viable, I mean that it can be followed by all or most of the men of the society without psychological discomfort or the production of obvious neurosis, and without interfering with the genital competence and fertility necessary to maintain the population. In many of these societies pederasty has been the main subject of the arts, particularly lyrical poetry, and the main source of tender and elevated emotions. Of all the homosexualities, it is probably the most alien to our society and on some levels the most shocking. We tend to feel disapproval, if not disgust, at heterosexual couples when there is a considerable disparity of age between the partners; and we are disturbed at the notion of adolescents having strong emotional attachments to adults, even where there is no overt sexuality.

It is probable that the full sequence is temperamentally congenial to some men in most societies; but it also seems unlikely that the full sequence is often followed in societies where it is not socially approved (an abbreviated version of the sequence, without the heterosexual period, has not been uncommon in all-male boarding-schools and similar institutions). It is impossible to tell whether any of Mr. Westwood's contacts should be described as pederasts; he has not used the concept himself; and owing to the over-riding necessity of protecting his contacts' anonymity, neither quotations nor tabulated experience are connected with identified individuals. Some nineteen of his contacts had their first sexual experience with an adult when they were under seventeen; the same number (but there is nothing to show whether they are the same people) as adults are willing or would like to have sexual relations with boys under seventeen; ten were married at the time of the interview, and seventeen hoped to marry. If these figures refer to the same people in any instances then, it would seem, they could properly be described as pederasts.

I have chosen the term *homophilia* (which, according to Mr. Westwood, is current in high-minded homosexual circles in Switzerland and Scandinavia) to describe the situation where the object of the homosexual's desires is another homosexual, to a greater or lesser extent a mirror image of himself. The relationships between homophiles seem to approximate very closely to the relationships between adult heterosexual men and women (with the obvious difference that both partners have male genitals) running the gamut between settled and prolonged monogamous cohabitation and complete promiscuity. One of Mr. Westwood's contacts said: 'Most of my friends are in what might be called the young married set of the homosexual world'; and some two-thirds of his contacts have had, or are enjoying, affairs, which are defined as 'a strong emotional relationship between two men which has lasted over a year'. It is probably a pair of homophiles whom most people think of when they refer to 'consenting adults'; and it is the same picture which Brigadier Terence Clark, M.P., of Portsmouth West, boisterously depicted in the House of Commons on June 29, 1961, as 'a couple of hairy old males sitting on each other's knees and liking it...' Homophiles certainly make up the major portion of Mr. Westwood's sample, at least a half (from the table on page 157), and probably over three-quarters. On this evidence, homophilia is the most prevalent of the homosexualities in England today; and may well be so in other Western countries. The homophile contacts come from a wide scatter of social classes, professions, and occupations; apart from their sexual tastes they seem to represent a good cross-section of adult English males.

In contrast to the pederast and the pathic, it is very hard to find examples or analogues of homophilia in societies outside the Judeo-Christian tradition; and there do not seem to be many examples within it before the last century, as far as the literary evidence goes. There are accounts of some courts where the kings had 'favourites'—James the First of England, Henry the Third of France, and so on; in 19th-century novels there are occasional pairs of men 'chumming' together (for example, Mortimer Lightwood and Eugene Wrayburn in *Our Mutual Friend*) and emotionally attached to one another; and that, as far as I know, is about all. It is possible, of course, that the subject was surrounded with so much mystery and unholy horror that outsiders knew nothing about it and insiders left no records; but even in the erotic or pornographic books that I know of there are no characters who could be considered homophiles, though sodomites and pathics are relatively frequent. I think it may be a genuinely modern phenomenon.

Although the aetiology of any of the homosexualities is obscure, it seems likely that among the antecedent conditions of homophilia are castration anxiety (in the psycho-analytic sense of the term) and the absence of a model of appropriate male behaviour at significant periods of the young boy's development. Castration anxiety may be induced directly by threats against infantile masturbation and possibly analogically, following operations or other attacks on the body during early childhood.

Adult interference with infantile masturbation does not seem to be widespread in most non-European societies; and the survival of sickly children, through medical or surgical intervention, has very greatly increased in the last century. It may be significant that two-fifths of Mr. Westwood's contacts reported that they had bad health in childhood.

The absence of an appropriate male model becomes much more likely when the typical household is reduced to the nuclear family of a man and wife living alone with their children. This again is a relatively uncommon phenomenon outside the advanced industrial societies in the last hundred years. Although the middle and upper classes lived in isolated dwellings, adult men were numerous as indoor or outdoor servants in these richer households; the poor lived either in composite households or so closely on top of one another that male models were always present. The isolated nuclear family household is not common in non-European societies. In about a fifth of Mr. Westwood's cases there was no man in the home; and over half of his contacts were an only child or an only son.

Pederasts (in the active phase) and homophiles resemble heterosexual men in that the goal of their sexual strivings is a genital orgasm; the objects which produce these orgasms are different but the physiological concomitants are similar. With pathics this is not the case; their pleasure comes from the orgasms they provoke in other men, and they have either abandoned more or less completely the pleasurable employment of their own genitals ('I hate anything to do with my own penis and I hate anyone to touch it' says one of Mr. Westwood's contacts); or else, possibly, use them for heterosexual intercourse only. It seems likely that pathics are more frequently married men than are homophiles.

England is uncommon among modern nations, or languages, in not recognizing the pathic in common speech or insult. If we wish to impugn the masculinity of another man, either seriously or metaphorically, we call him a 'bugger', which suggests a type of genital activity; in similar circumstances an American calls him a 'cocksucker', a Frenchman *espèce d'enculé*. (It is a curious point, not without significance, that in common speech none of these words have reciprocals, to designate the insulted man's partner.) For a vocabulary we have to go to Latin; imperial Rome appears to have been much preoccupied with the activities of pathics, which are detailed with (surely sanctimonious) disapproval; Juvenal, Martial, and Petronius cannot let the subject alone.

Rather surprisingly, the pathic has been socially recognized and integrated in some societies, as priests in some of the middle-eastern cults (for example, that of Cybele; see Apuleius) and also in some of the Siberian tribes, as shamans. The most remarkable integration was the institution of berdache in some of the warrior tribes among the American Plains Indians. A youth who felt temperamentally incapable of attaining to the highly aggressive ideal of masculinity demanded in these societies could opt for the alternative of becoming a 'social' woman, wearing women's clothes and learning women's crafts, following their taboos and even going through a simulacrum of child-birth. It is said that, while the parents of the berdache were very distressed at such a choice, the berdache himself was socially accepted, but some contempt was felt for his 'husband', chiefly because he had so much easier a life than the men married to weak women who had to support real children. The same point comes up in Mr. Westwood's book (quoting F. J. G. Jefferiss) in the discussion of what he calls 'facultative homosexuals' : 'the male consort is less clinging and cheaper, not requiring so much courting and money spent on him . . . and . . . there is no risk of making the partner pregnant or being trapped into matrimony'.

The 'facultative homosexuals', in Mr. Westwood's vocabulary, are those men who consider themselves heterosexually 'normal' but engage on occasion in some form of homosexual intercourse. None of Mr. Westwood's contacts can probably be so considered (it is surprising that, in the discussion of this group, Mr. Westwood has not considered narcissism as a major motive for allowing homage from anybody of any sex willing to give it); but they are relevant in this context as the probable partners of the pathic. Almost by definition the pathic does not desire partners who are themselves homophile.

A fifth of Mr. Westwood's sample are 'very interested in non-homosexuals, would prefer them as sexual partners'; and for just on the same number (though apparently not predominantly the same people) passive anal intercourse was the most usual and preferred technique. Unfortunately, in his short paragraph on oral-genital techniques (preferred and practised by less than ten per cent of his sample: other cultures would probably produce very different figures) Mr. Westwood does not distinguish between those who perform and those who submit to this; but it seems likely that something more than a tenth of his contacts were wholly or predominantly pathic.

Pathicism is for most people *uncanny*, since it seeks a sexual pleasure which is not immediately involved with the primary sexual apparatus. It is in a way symbolic magic; the pathics are taking 'goodness' or 'strength' from their 'normal' partners. And it is, I think, this uncanny, magical aspect which accounts for some of the holy horror which people feel for the whole subject of homosexuality. In the House of Commons debate on the Wolfenden report on June 29th, 1961 (already referred to), Mr. Godfrey Lagden, M.P., of Hornchurch, voiced an almost clinically perfect expression of this magical fear:

> Especially should people be punished if their actions, which I contend are evil, have physical and mental danger to those with whom they come in contact. . . .
> In my opinion, in the general run the homosexual is a dirty-minded danger to the virile manhood of this country. The Right Hon. Lady the Member for Warrington (Dr. Summerskill) laughs, but it is important for any country to have a virile manhood and to see that it is not corrupted by such men as these. . . .
> I am sure that if many Hon. Members had seen the mental and the physical state to which some young men have been reduced by being corrupted by these homosexuals they would know what was their duty tonight.[1]

This plea would scarcely need the alteration of a word to re-

[1] In the House of Commons debate on the same topic on February 12th, 1966, Mr. William Shepherd of Cheadle, arguing against reform of the law, said: 'The proper way to look at homosexuality is to regard it not as something separate but as something to which any of us can succumb if the circumstances of our lives or the weakness of our outlook make us susceptible.'

present the fear which is felt in so many cultures (and in our own a few centuries ago) of the effect of malicious witchcraft, of sorcery. Mr. Westwood experienced the prevalence of this fear in the difficulties, which he recounts in the first paragraph of his acknowledgements, in getting funds, co-operation, or facilities for his research.

In this outline of some of the major forms of the homosexualities, I am not suggesting that every man who engages in homosexual activities falls neatly and unambiguously into one of the categories. What I do suggest is that these syndromes form clusters, and that if Mr. Westwood had been aware of them and had tabulated them separately, his analysis of family constellations, work records, community integration and the like might have given more consistent and revealing tables. When all the homosexualities are lumped together the results (if my contention is correct, inevitably) become so blurred that there remain practically no generalizations one can make about the group except for the sex of their preferred partners and their unhappy position in relation to the law and (though to a lesser extent) to society at large. On these latter aspects Mr. Westwood is admirably humane and level-headed; *A Minority* is the best book for the non-specialized reader which has yet appeared on the subject.

# XIX

## *The Marquis de Sade: Sado-Masochism and Theatricality*
### *(1962)*

I ORIGINALLY made a study of the life and writings of the Marquis de Sade twenty-nine years ago, very shortly after Hitler came into power; my object at that time was overtly political, journalists were constantly referring to the sadistic character or behaviour of the Nazi regime, and I thought I should be able to gain—and to communicate—understanding of the contemporary world by exploring the views and activities of the man who had given his name to the perversion of sadism. In his writings and, for a short period, in his life de Sade was much occupied with politics and political themes; and it was this aspect of his work and personality which I stressed in my original study.

Once the book was written, I paid very little attention to de Sade for about twenty years; but shortly after World War Two an enormous amount of new material became available. The Marquis de Sade's descendant—the Marquis Xavier de Sade—made available to Gilbert Lely all the unpublished manuscripts and correspondence which remained in the family possession—a good deal had been lost when the château was sacked by the Nazis in 1941; and this material was scrupulously edited and most of it published by Lely in the ensuing decade and summarized in a masterly two-volume *Life*. Our knowledge of de Sade as a man was completely transformed by this work, and our knowledge of his writings very considerably increased; and this new material has prompted me to a reconsideration of the character of de Sade and of the relationship between his sexual perversions and his literary, above all his theatrical, creations and activities. I hope, of course, that he is a paradigm.

The de Sades were a very old noble family from Provence—Laure de Sade inspired Petrarch's famous sonnets—; the Count, de Sade's father, was a very self-conscious grand seigneur, who represented France as Ambassador in various European capitals. His wife, de Sade's mother, was a member of the princely house of Condé, and so closely related to the French Royal family. Donatien-Aldonze-François, the only son, and the only surviving child of the marriage, was born in the Condé palace in 1740. To the best of my knowledge, no other European writer was so highly born.

It seems as though his parents had very little contact indeed with their son; there is no evidence to show that, after the first few weeks, parents and child ever lived in the same house. The father was abroad on his ambassadorial duties, his wife either with him or living in a convent; the little marquis spent four years or so in the Condé palace, brought up with the young prince, four years his senior, who, it was planned, would thereby be his life-long friend and patron; but, according to the unique childhood memory which de Sade has recorded, this relationship was broken up by de Sade attacking him furiously because Prince Louis-Joseph de Bourbon would not give up a toy de Sade considered to belong to him; he described his own childish character as 'haughty, despotic and quick to anger'.

He was removed from Paris and may have spent a year or so with his paternal grandmother at Avignon; he was then put in the charge of his paternal uncle, the abbé François de Sade, a scholarly but notoriously libertine ecclesiastic; at the age of ten he was removed from the abbé's care and put to school in Paris in the charge of another ecclesiastic—this one unrelated and probably a hired tutor; at the age of 14 a commission was purchased for him and he was sent into the army, then engaged in the Seven Years war; he served all through the campaign with distinction, rising continuously in rank. He was demobilized at the age of 21.

It seems difficult to imagine a bleaker childhood and adolescence for a boy who was not an orphan; with the possible exception of his infancy, his life seems to have lacked any constant maternal figure, any woman on whom he could count for affection and succour. It would seem that de Sade was consciously and continuously resentful of this neglect; in his fictions all the mothers, all the pregnant women, are subjected to constant ill-treatment and torture; he argues, on the basis of the current physiological theories, that there is no consanguinal link, and consequently no 'natural' affection, between mother and child; the mother is merely the repository of the homunculus from the father. At the same time, de Sade's ideal woman, as displayed in his fictions, is the cold, beautiful, lustful woman who abandons and, usually, destroys all the men with whom she has anything to do. The woman without tenderness, without pity, is portrayed as irresistibly attractive. Her most important incarnations are Juliette and Isabelle de Bavière, the titles and heroines of two of his novels.

One other deduction can, I think, be made with relative assurance about his infancy; his toilet training was early, severe, and decisive in its influence on his character. If anyone could be so described, he was polymorphously perverse; but the anal theme is dominant in his writings, and, as far as the evidence goes, in his life.

We know very little about de Sade's life in the army. There survive a couple of letters to his father, promising to be less extravagant, to gamble less, to behave more circumspectly in future; and a letter from a brother-officer talking about his 'little head being inflamed once again'. De Sade seems to have been very attractive to women, as he was constantly attracted by them; there are no surviving portraits of him, but a miniature which survived in the de Sade family till 1941 is said to have shown a very good-looking young man. Passport descriptions from the revolutionary years, when he was past 50, describe him as short —5 foot 4 inches—fair-haired and blue eyed with a rounded chin and a small mouth. By that time he was very fat, the result of thirteen years solitary confinement on a rich diet; as a young man he must have been a handsome little bantam.

After his retirement from active service de Sade spent two years in Paris as a young aristocrat on the town. All we know definitely of this period is that he had as mistress a well-born young lady, who incidentally infected him with gonorrhea, to whom he was very attached and to whom he considered himself betrothed at the very time when his father, without it would seem consulting him in any way, arranged his marriage to a Mademoiselle René de Montreuil.

The motives of the Comte de Sade in arranging this marriage are obscure. It was a mésalliance, for the de Sades were of the highest nobility, whereas the de Montreuils were nobodies, their estates and titles newly purchased, their very recent wealth derived from the practice of law—they were outstanding examples of the *robinocracie,* as it was called, the pre-eminence of lawyers and judges which characterized the last decades of the old régime. They were very rich, but correspondingly grasping; though the dowry was not very large, there were great expectations. It was probably this consideration which influenced the Comte de Sade, the extravagant father of an even more spendthrift son; and he may well have been glad to get rid of, or share, the responsibility for his son. Madame de Montreuil, who completely dominated her husband, the Président, had enormous influence at the Court. De Sade claimed she had the devil's own charm.

Even though such arranged marriages were customary among the nobility of France at that time, this was carried through in a particularly heartless fashion; without apparently any liking, much less affection, the marriage was celebrated with the greatest pomp in 1763. The new Madame de Sade seems to have been a dutiful and well-meaning young woman, but without many personal attractions and at that period 'too cold and too puritanical' for de Sade's tastes. There may have been a short honeymoon on the Montreuils' estate in Normandy; but within weeks de Sade was back in Paris engaged in the reckless pursuit of pleasure which was already making his name notorious. Simultaneously he was indulging his taste for the theatre; most of his identified mistresses of this period were small-part actresses or dancers. He was also engaged in amateur acting himself; and his earliest surviving writings, which date from this period, consist of prologues composed for theatrical evenings and short plays. Since I am trying to establish the links between sado-masochism and theatricality, it seems worth while documenting the nearly simultaneous appearance of both interests in de Sade's early adult life.

We have of course no evidence when de Sade discovered that he could derive intense pleasure from flagellation, whether active or passive; but he was arrested for 'scandalous debauchery' within six months of his marriage; and the probability is that flagellation was involved here, as in the two subsequent notorious law-suits. In the several attempts which he made in his writings to analyse the reasons for pleasure in submitting to or inflicting pain, he invariably gives priority to the passive experience; because one has got pleasure from being beaten, therefore one will give pleasure by beating, on the principle of reciprocity by which one wishes to gratify one's partner in the same way as one is gratified.

It is possible that his relish for flagellation and the search for increasingly complicated varieties of sexual stimulation may have had a physiological as well as psychological determinants. In a strange agonized letter which he wrote to his wife from prison when he was just over forty, he complains of the enormous difficulty he has in achieving physical orgasm, the great pain which accompanies it, and ends by asking for medical help. He wrote: 'It's truly an epileptic attack—and without boring precautions I am sure that people would have suspicions in the Boulevard St. Antoine [the street outside the prison]—convulsions, spasms, agony—you saw some samples at La Coste [the Sades' château in Provence]—it has simply doubled so you can judge what it's like. . . . Imagine a rifle charged with a bullet, a bullet with the quality of growing larger the longer it remains in the rifle; if you shoot after two days, the explosion is a light one, if you let the bullet get big, it will break the rifle when it does come out . . . the crisis is very long with movements and unimaginable convulsions the whole time it is going on.' This painfulness of the orgasm, and the difficulty of achieving it, may well have had a basis in a physiological malformation; and this immediate experience of pleasurable pain or painful pleasure may well have been the direct cause of de Sade's sexual perversions; more indirectly, it may have laid the basis for the moral masochism which seems to underlie so much of his reckless behaviour.

His conduct in the first five years after his marriage was extremely reckless. Other libertines of the period hired a small house in the Paris suburbs for their debaucheries; de Sade hired five, in his own name; and the way he treated the girls he took there was such that one of the police inspectors in charge of morals gave a warning to one of the fashionable bawds not to provide him with girls, though without giving reasons for his advice. His most notorious mistress was the well-known courtesan La Beauvoisin; he took her with him to his ancestral home at La Coste, introduced her to the neighbourhood as his wife, with her help started spending his wife's dowry in transforming one of the large rooms in La Coste into a fully equipped theatre room, and gave performances with her.

In 1768 there occurred the first of the two scandals which blackened de Sade's name with his contemporaries—the case of the widow Keller. On Easter morning de Sade was accosted in Paris by a 37-year-old Alsatian widow who was begging. He told her she could earn some money by coming with him to his little house in Arcueil. She consented, and after a short delay he took her out in a carriage, brought her into the house by a side door, took her upstairs to a bedroom, got her to strip, beat her with a *martinet*, a whip made of knotted cords which was in common household use for beating dust out of furniture, culminating in a very noisy climax; he then took her into an adjoining room, gave her an ointment which he said would take away the sting of the whipping, and went to fetch her a cold lunch. Madame Keller was terrified, escaped through the window by knotting the bedsheets together, climbed over the garden wall, and went to the neighbours for help and protection. De Sade's confidential valet ran after her with money, but she refused to listen to him. She took refuge with the wife of one of the village notables, who spread about with considerable exaggerations the pathetic story which Rose Keller told her. One of the incidents she recounted may have been based on fact: the widow Keller said that she begged de Sade not to kill her since she had not made her Easter confession; whereupon de Sade sat down and said she could confess herself to him. But the more gory details—that de Sade cut her with a penknife and dropped hot Spanish wax on the wounds, and so on—were flatly contradicted by the medical evidence.

The scandal was enormous. De Sade was apprehended and imprisoned in Lyons; his mother-in-law, Madame de Montreuil, despatched his old tutor to buy off the widow Keller, and she eventually withdrew her complaint for the enormous sum—for the period—of 2,000 livres. Nevertheless the criminal prosecution continued with the utmost publicity, even to the extent of the Paris town-criers calling for de Sade's apprehension while he was known to all the authorities to be in gaol in Lyons.

There are two explanations for this enormous and unwarranted publicity. First, de Sade was a pawn in the rivalry between his father-in-law and a legal rival, the Président de Maupéou, in whose jurisdiction the offence occurred; and secondly, de Sade may have been chosen as a scapegoat for the popular anger against much more blood-thirsty sadists, such as the notorious Comte de Charolais, whose nearness to the throne gave them complete immunity. However de Sade escaped any legal penalty on this occasion; through the help of his mother-in-law he got from the king a 'letter of abolition' which freed a man of proved nobility from the penalties of his acts. He spent six months in prison at Lyons under a *lettre de cachet*—a form of preventive imprisonment granted to a private person; he was joined by his wife there, and on his release they both went to La Coste.

This is not the occasion to develop the very complex relations between de Sade and his wife. From this period onwards for the next twenty years, Madame de Sade appears to have been completely devoted to her husband, forgiving him everything, aiding and abetting him in his debaucheries, resolutely taking his part against her own mother and society at large, a very devoted helpmeet; de Sade seems to have learned to place almost complete reliance on her, though the relationship was never a tranquil one. The extraordinary series of letters which de Sade wrote to her in his subsequent long imprisonment run the whole gamut of emotions from furious rage through tender and licentious teasing to the most profound trust.

During the next four years at La Coste de Sade's two younger children were born. The de Sades lived extravagantly, apparently entertaining a good deal with private theatricals; de Sade was having his own plays acted. In 1771 they were joined by Madame de Sade's younger sister, Mademoiselle de Launay; and the three of them gave theatrical performances together, not only at La Coste but also in the châteaux of the neighbours. This agreeable life was broken in 1772 by the second great scandal in de Sade's life, the case of the so-called poisoned sweets.

De Sade went to Marseilles on business accompanied by one of his valets, and there arranged an elaborate orgy with four young prostitutes, hired from a bawd, but taken to a more discreet part of the town. This involved flagellation, chiefly passive —de Sade kept a score with his penknife on the wall and according to this received 800 strokes from a besom broom, since the girls would not use the parchment whip studded with nails which he produced—sodomizing of the girls by de Sade, and—according to one of the girls—sodomizing of de Sade by his valet. In voluntary self-abasement he called the valet 'Monsieur le Marquis' and was himself addressed as 'la Fleur'—a stage name for a valet. In addition he had provided himself with homemade sweets containing cantharides and aniseed. The intention was that the cantharides should act as an aphrodisiac and the aniseed as a carminative, to produce copious flatus; but he had obviously miscalculated the amount of cantharides, and the two girls who had swallowed the sweets—another accepted but threw hers away, whence they were recovered and analysed—became severely unwell with continuous painful vomiting for a few days, particularly the girl who was treated by an unqualified man. The police were called in, and once again de Maupéou, the rival of de Sade's father-in-law, was in charge of the court; de Sade and his valet were accused of poisoning, even though the girls were completely recovered within a very few days and formally withdrew their complaints, and for sodomy, for which the death penalty was no longer exacted, and for which the evidence was dubious though the charge was probably true; they were found guilty, condemned to death and, since their persons could not be secured, were executed in effigy.

De Sade had somehow been warned of his peril, and had escaped to Italy, accompanied by two valets and by his sister-in-law, Mademoiselle de Launay. It seems as though he was passionately in love with this girl, on the evidence of the semi-autobiographical novel *Aline et Valcour*; but the elopement was the most imprudent action of his rash life. It transformed his powerful mother-in-law from an unwilling protectress into a most virulent enemy. Her motive in arranging the match between her daughter and de Sade was probably the social advancement of her children and grandchildren; and she certainly had equally ambitious views for her other children. The public elopement made it difficult to arrange a suitable marriage for Mademoiselle de Launay, even with the most impoverished peer, while de Sade was at liberty; at the same time the conviction against de Sade must be quashed, or her grandchildren would be stigmatized. To attain these ends she used her wealth and her influence with complete unscrupulousness and lack of pity for her elder daughter.

De Sade and Mademoiselle de Launay travelled for six months in Italy, where de Sade, using one of his secondary titles, met many of the reigning groups as well as some savants with whom he established correspondence. In the autumn they settled in Chambéry, then in the kingdom of Sardinia, and hired a house; Mademoiselle de Launay left for France, presumably to see her sister and to get further funds, accompanied by one of the valets. She and de Sade probably never met again; her mother arranged a match with a Flemish nobleman, but it never actually took place and she died unmarried a few years later. Either from her, or from his agent and business man whom she had suborned, or from intercepting letters to her elder daughter, Madame de Montreuil learned de Sade's address; she appealed to the ambassador of the King of Sardinia; and, to oblige so influential a lady, His Sardinian Majesty was delighted to arrest her son-in-law and have him incarcerated in a fortress.

Apart from the loss of liberty, this imprisonment was neither unpleasant nor degrading; de Sade was treated as a gentleman, allowed to have a valet with him, order his food from outside, and pass his time with the other gentlemen detained. But for de Sade liberty was the first of all goods; he tried everything from furious rages, fake suicide attempts, menaces and pamphlets to solemn attestations that he would do nothing to interfere with the proposed marriage and willingness to accept exile in vain attempts to mollify his mother-in-law. Madame de Sade courageously set out in male dress with a single male companion in a fruitless attempt to help him. Eventually, after seven months, he made his escape from the fortress in the best tradition of the romantic novel: a lamp left burning, an ironical note of apology to the governor, a midnight evasion through a lavatory window. He was joined by Madame de Sade, perhaps in Switzerland; and they travelled about for some months before returning surreptitiously to La Coste. They used what money was remaining to turn the château into a fortified place with a drawbridge which was kept up; and secret hiding places were constructed, in which de Sade effectively hid from the police and the soldiery when they were sent on the instructions of his mother-in-law; however they wrecked the furniture and abstracted 'damaging' papers, which de Sade was still trying to recover fifteen years later; it is highly probable that they were notes on the varieties of sexual behaviour which had come to his attention or about which he had been told; it is possible that there was also subversive political or anti-religious material—two other themes with which he was subsequently much occupied.

The general pattern of the next four years was that in the summer months de Sade would travel, either in France, in Italy or the Low Countries, while Madame de Sade would pass the time in Paris, trying to get the verdict against her husband reversed (the death of Louis XV and also the disgrace of Président de Maupéou made this a realistic hope) and to raise money; her mother had no difficulty in thwarting all her efforts. In the autumn they would meet somewhere in France, typically Lyons, and proceed carefully to La Coste. But they did not travel alone. Madame de Sade engaged a series of young girls as 'housemaids', de Sade 16-year-old youths as 'secretaries'; and a dancer of dubious character was hired as 'housekeeper'. De Sade was still quite reckless; he got the dancer to buy and bring with her a human skeleton, which he used to decorate a small room completely hung with black; when this setting had produced the desired theatrical effects, the bones were buried in the garden. But this 'joke—or rather stupidity', as de Sade called it was, naturally enough, the source of the most alarming rumours, probably fanned by Madame de Montreuil, although she claimed she was trying to hush them up; in the spring the parents of the various young persons turned up in alarm, to reclaim their offspring; they were all returned safe, if not sound.

In January 1777 de Sade set out for Paris to attend the deathbed of his dying mother. She was actually dead before he set out, and it seems not impossible that he was inveigled by a false message. Madame de Sade travelled at the same time by another route; her mother was easily able to get de Sade's address out of her, and had him arrested within three days of his arrival. He was taken to the old prison of Vincennes, under a *lettre de cachet* granted to Madame de Montreuil.

This first imprisonment in Vincennes lasted 15 months. De Sade was in solitary confinement, seeing nobody except the man who brought his food once a day, and almost completely denied exercise. His health deteriorated very badly: he suffered from headaches, haemorrhoids, insomnia. His mental distress was even stronger than his physical sufferings; 'neither my temperament nor my character can stand close restraint' he wrote in a plea to Madame de Montreuil to allow him to go into permanent exile. But this did not suit her plans. The Flemish suitor of Mademoiselle de Launay would not feel secure, if de Sade were at liberty; she wanted to regain control of the remainder of her daughter's dowry; and she wanted her grandchildren to be of unimpeached nobility. Her first plan was to have de Sade declared legally insane; but he refused to co-operate in this. She then decided to have the Aix condemnation annulled—Président de Maupéou had been disgraced—which would achieve the third aim; to accomplish this she had to make use of her daughter who was always fooled by a show of kindness. There was not much difficulty about this; the poisoned girls were alive and well, and were perfectly willing for a consideration to withdraw the charge of sodomy, to which they were the sole witnesses; the judgement was quashed, de Sade admonished from the bench, ordered to pay a small sum to charity and to keep away from

Marseilles for three years. No other legal charge was ever brought against him; nevertheless he spent all but ten of the 37 years which remained to him in close confinement.

From 1778 to 1790 he was held in preventive detention under a *lettre de cachet* granted to Madame de Montreuil; he was literally held under that lady's pleasure. This indeterminate sentence added greatly to de Sade's mental distress.

In the first months his physical treatment was appalling. His room in the old fortress of Vincennes was very dark, very high, very cold, swarming with rats and mice; when the corrupt governor was angry with him he was fed through a grill in the door, like a wild animal. The total or almost total deprivation of exercise added very greatly to his torments; as he wrote in one appeal 'the loss of freedom is the greatest torture possible for a man with the sort of physique I have received from nature.' During his imprisonment he grew enormously fat, suffered severely from bronchial troubles, and had nose bleeds when he lay flat; and some eye affection racked him with pain and, when he was finally allowed visits from opthalmologists, left him permanently blind in one eye.

Under this murderous régime he started elaborate delusions of persecution—he was of course being persecuted—and very complicated delusions of reference. These took the form of a crazy numerology; anything from which he could extract numbers—the number of lines in a letter, the number of words in a line, the number of candles sent in a parcel—were all encoded into 'signals'; most of these signals referred to the date of his release or the restoration of his exercise; others disclosed plans to send him to the Islands, or to have him made ambassador; the 'signals' in his wife's letters showed she was being physically unfaithful to him, and produced a crisis of violent and quite unjustified jealousy which continued for five months. For when his calculations were proved false, de Sade did not deduce that the system of 'signals' was incorrect; people were purposely giving him false information through the signals, to torment him even more.

This period of delusions seems to have lasted about three years; gradually he resigned himself to what seemed as though it would be a life-time of solitary confinement, turned his back on the world, and devoted himself with the greatest seriousness and application to becoming a professional writer. He was able to have sent to him all the books and periodicals he requested, and all the writing materials; and he could send manuscripts out of the prison to have fair copies made. He read omnivorously—I doubt if there is a major writer available in French to whom he did not refer either by quotation or indirectly—and he copied out numerous extracts; he wrote very rapidly, though he had an elaborate routine of expansion and revision. The great bulk of his writings in prison is dated after 1784, when the fortress of Vincennes was closed down, and he was transferred to the Bastille, with much better accommodation and a more humane governor.

His earliest writing was predominantly concerned with the theatre; he wrote fifteen plays, as well as a long discourse (now lost) on the art of writing comedy. One of his plays was acted during his life-time, with indifferent success, and also published; the remainder still exist in manuscript in the possession of the Marquis de Sade; but even so passionate an advocate of de Sade as Gilbert Lely cannot bring himself to publish even one of them. For what is remarkable about these plays is that they are almost completely without merit, dull, wooden, conventional, written mostly in laboured alexandrines, without an original, much less a shocking, idea. As a novelist, de Sade was a writer of the greatest originality and daring, and of very considerable skill; none of these qualities appear in his plays, of which he thought so highly.

This seems to me an interesting paradox; and, in one of the earliest pieces of writing of his which has survived, the plot of a play *Zélonide*, I think he gives a clue to his motives in playwriting, and the reason why he could not admit their emptiness. The plot is a fantastic imbroglio of children changed in their cradle, and making apparently incestuous advances to their supposed parents: the silence of the one character who knows

> will put the audience in a terrible state, trembling as they should in seeing taking place under their eyes this double

intrigue that they will believe to be criminal; the public will share the dilemma of the young people who know nothing, of the two friends who can say nothing, will be always ready to cry out to the young people 'Unhappy people, what are you doing?' and will wait for the dénouement with the greatest impatience . . . will be very moved and very surprised at the end.

I would suggest that this attempt to manipulate the feelings of the audience is a socially acceptable equivalent to the manipulation of the feelings of his victim and partner by the sadist, that de Sade expected analogous satisfactions from the audience of *Zélonide* as from the young chambermaids shown the black room hung with a human skeleton.

At the same time as he was writing his lamentable plays, de Sade was composing at least the first draft—all that survives, and that by a series of accidents—of his masterpiece, **Les 120 Journées de Sodome.** The core of this extraordinary book—the most impure ever written, de Sade says at the end of the introduction when he calls on the reader to harden his heart—is the cumulative description of six hundred sexual perversions. The number is of course excessive, the outcome probably of de Sade's obsessions with number and symmetry, swelled to its total by dividing bestiality, for example, among all the available farmyard animals or elaborating all the possible sources of material for coprophagy; but it is by a century the first *psychopathia sexualis,* and none of the subsequent researches have demonstrated omissions. On the contrary, de Sade listed many symbolic actions, as substitute sexual gratifications, which were ignored by the sexologists of the nineteenth century, only to be discovered by the psycho-analysts in the twentieth. As an example, he described 'motiveless' theft as a substitute for rape, and dealt with a number of fetishisms.

In his years of freedom, de Sade had conscientiously explored the available sexual pleasures within very wide limits—as he wrote to his wife from Vincennes

> I'm a libertine, I admit it; I've imagined everything that could be imagined on that subject, but I certainly have not done,

and certainly will never do, all that I have imagined. I am a libertine, but not a criminal or a murderer.

Somehow, he had such easy access to his unconscious that he could put on paper not only every recorded perversion, mutually contradictory though they often are, but nearly every sexual and/or aggressive fantasy which psycho-analysts have painfully elicited from themselves or their patients. De Sade was quite conscious that he was adding to scientific knowledge by recording the varieties of human sexual behaviour. He also tried to account for them inductively, explanations which are now unacceptable because of their reliance on an outmoded physiology based on 'animal spirits'; and he tried to moralize them. These tastes were innate, in 'nature', and therefore right, because all that nature does must be right; therefore the human political problem was to devise a society which would impede the expression of 'natural' desires as little as possible. The political implications are chiefly explored in the books subsequent to *Les 120 Journées*.

For the perversions are only the core of an elaborate fiction. They are recounted at the rate of five an evening by four wicked old prostitutes, who place them in the history of their lives. Their audience consists of four war profiteers—a duke, a bishop, a judge and financier—their wives, and a harem of 28 subjects of all ages and both sexes; the four chief characters discuss and analyse the perversions described, as well as trying out most of them. The setting of this four-month-long orgy is a desolate Gothic castle in the Black Forest; all the settings are described like stage sets, intended to produce emotional responses from the viewer or reader; fancy dress and assorted *tableaux vivants* play an important part in the description of the orgies.

This is the only clandestine work of de Sade's which has survived from his imprisonment; besides the plays, he wrote a collection of 30 short stories, alternating sombre melodrama with more humorous invention; a lost miscellany called *La Portefeuille d'un Homme de Lettres*; the first two versions of his most notorious book, *Justine*; and a four-volume novel entitled *Aline et Valcour.* This work is a curious combination of Richardson and Swift; the first and last volumes consist of an extremely well-told tragic love story in letters with clear autobiographical passages; one of the middle volumes is an adventure story; the other consists of a nightmare version of civilization placed in Africa, and de Sade's Utopia, placed in the South Seas. This volume is overtly political and in many places clearly foreshadows the coming French revolution.

It is, indeed, tempting to say that de Sade did not merely foretell the Revolution, but precipitated it. In July 1789, de Sade was one of the seven prisoners left in the Bastille, which was being reconverted to its ancient role of a fortress. As a result of the work being undertaken, de Sade was refused his customary exercise on the roof of one of the towers; furious, he improvised a loud-speaker out of a metal tube and a funnel which were used for emptying slops, and called out of the window to the populace in the street to come and rescue the prisoners whose throats were being cut. A crowd was gathered by this device and the governor of the prison was sufficiently alarmed to request the removal of 'this person whom nobody can subdue'. 'If Monsieur de Sade,' he wrote urgently, 'is not removed from the Bastille tonight I cannot be answerable to the King for the safety of the building.' On July 3rd de Sade was duly removed to the hospital at Charenton; eleven days later the nearly empty fortress of the Bastille was stormed by the crowd, whose anger against it has never seemed to have adequate grounds. Three quarters of de Sade's manuscripts 'whose loss he wept for in tears of blood' were pillaged. De Sade himself was released six months later, in April 1790, when the constituent assembly released all prisoners held by *lettre de cachet*; he had been in virtual solitary confinement for 13 years.

He was fifty when he was released, and he found re-entry into the world very difficult. In his own words:

> In prison my sight and my lungs have been ruined; being deprived of all exercise I have become so enormously fat that I can hardly move; all my feelings are extinguished. I have no taste for anything any more. . . . I have never been more

misanthropic than I am now that I have returned among men.

At first he was emotionally quite alone. Madame de Sade, who had supported him so valiantly against her mother for so many years, had finally surrendered; either the influence of her mother or, as de Sade suspected, the confessors at the Convent where she had lived, had prevailed; and they only met again in the presence of lawyers, in arguments about property. His two sons saw him, but de Sade felt that the Sades' provençal warmth had been cooled by Montreuil calculation; they subsequently emigrated, and put their father in peril as the result. But a few months after he was released, de Sade met the second great love of his life, the actress Constance Quesnet; she was under 30, the separated wife of a commercial traveller in the United States, with a young son. After a few weeks they set up house together; and thereafter they were never voluntarily separated. In the 24 years of life that remained to him, he stayed completely devoted to her, and engaged in many devices to assure her future. In 1793 he made an affidavit that she was his 'natural and adopted daughter', to legitimize a pension he wished to settle on her out of his sequestered income; there is no reason to suppose there is any truth in the assertion.

He probably met her professionally, for his first visits on his release were to actors, and he did all he could to get his plays produced and to set up as a professional playwright. In the next three years five plays were actually accepted, though only one was produced, and that with little success. He had more success with his novel, *Justine,* though that was produced anonymously. This version is not obscene in its language, though it is very bold in its theme. Its subtitle is 'The Misfortunes of Virtue'; and it stands in the same relation to Christianity as Don Quixote does to the concept of chivalry. It is the lamentable story of the misfortunes of a pious penniless young girl and the assorted perils which her exercise of pity, charity, piety and other virtues involve her in. She encounters a series of eccentric criminals and vicious characters and is always their victim. It is a very well-written, but extremely depressing book.

De Sade's long novel, *Aline et Valcour*, was also accepted; but owing to the difficulties of the publishers, its appearance was delayed for a couple of years.

Besides working as an author, de Sade was active in his local revolutionary committee, the Section des Piques. As their representative he inspected the Paris hospitals, and apparently made humane recommendations for ameliorating the treatment of patients; he also wrote a number of pamphlets in their name —some of them of considerable political interest and insight— and delivered orations for them. I see no reason to suppose that this activity was prudential or insincere. As chairman of his section he was called upon to judge various 'enemies of the state'. Among the accused were his parents-in-law, Président and Madame de Montreuil, the immediate cause of most of the misery of his adult life; he had them put on a *liste épuratioire* for pardon. He wrote immediately after 'If I had said a word they were lost. I kept my peace. I have had my revenge'.

This clemency to his greatest enemies is a striking example of de Sade's consistency. He was deeply opposed to the death penalty, for only passion can legitimize murder and the State is passionless; he would not sully himself by using legal power for private revenge, as Madame de Montreuil had so consistently done. His magnanimity was worthy of his heroine Justine; and like Justine he found that virtue is always unfortunate; four months later he was imprisoned for moderantism.

During the next ten months he passed through four different Republican prisons. He was condemned to the guillotine as an aristocrat, but was sought in the wrong prison; the Thermidor reaction just saved his neck. In his last prison the guillotine was almost under the windows, and 1800 victims of the mob's rage were executed there and buried in the prison gardens. A year later, he was still haunted by nightmares of this: 'my national detention, with the guillotine under my eyes, did me a hundred times more harm than all the Bastilles imaginable' de Sade wrote. This experience is obviously relevant in judging de Sade's subsequent writings; and his moderation, one might almost say his squeamishness, during the Terror gives evidence about his character.

Although his life was saved by Thermidor, he was still in prison; but thanks to the efforts of Madame Quesnet, he was fairly soon released with certificates of being a good citizen. He was however nearly penniless; owing to a confusion in Christian names, he could not get his name removed from a Provençal list of émigrés, indeed never succeeded in doing so; and consequently his land revenues were sequestered. His appeals for employment were fruitless; he sold his property at La Coste and bought two small farms near Paris; but to earn money for food he turned to writing pornography. This short work is entitled *La Philosophie dans le Boudoir* and is written in dialogue form. The theme is the sexual education of a young girl, a very common erotic theme; but de Sade's treatment is as much intellectual as physical. The heroine's prejudices are destroyed as completely as all her virginities; in the course of the action she is transformed from a lively schoolgirl into an orgiastic bacchante.

An unusual feature of this book is that a third of it is taken up with de Sade's most important political pamphlet—*Frenchmen, a further effort if you wish to be Republicans*—in which he outlines his views on the minimum of laws and the maximum of licence in the fields of religion and morals suitable for a free society. The concept of a free society, where the passions and the intellects of its members could receive the utmost extension, continually occupied him; and the contrast between this ideal and contemporary society and other societies he had visited or read about is a constant theme in his work.

This was certainly one of the dominant themes in his most notorious work which was published two years later: *La Nouvelle Justine, ou les Malheurs ae la Vertu*, followed by the story of her sister *Juliette, ou les Prospérités du Vice*—ten volumes in all, four devoted to Justine and six to Juliette. The new *Justine* is a reworking of the older novel, using the crudest and most precise language, and swollen by the inclusion of the life histories of two minor characters. Juliette is the success story of a cruel, pitiless lustful woman whose career brings her into intimate relationship with representatives of most of the governing classes and a majority of the crowned heads in Europe. It is on the basis of these books that Krafft-Ebing took de Sade's name to identify the sexual perversion (Sacher Masoch incidentally was an Austrian novelist, of little interest); and it is probably on a back-formation from these works that the various horrific legends were built round the life of de Sade.

Besides the analysis of the mechanisms of tyranny and the pleasures of tyrants, de Sade was also trying in these books to reconstitute the lost 120 *Journées de Sodome* by presenting an enormous collection of sexual monomaniacs and perverts, with explanations of their deviations; and he was also furthering his life-long attack on Christianity, culminating in the half-volume-long interview between Juliette and the Pope. The books, however, are too diffuse and episodic to compare with the concentrated and symmetrical misanthropy of his lost masterpiece.

All his life long de Sade publicly denied the authorship, but the books were very quickly ascribed to him. They may have temporarily alleviated his poverty, but his condition was growing continuously more precarious; letters of supplication to various officials of the Directoire exist, still rather humiliating, as well as poignant, to read; he begs for employment, begs to have his name taken off the list of émigrés, begs to have his plays performed, particularly a patriotic tragedy called *Jeanne Laisné, or the Siege of Beauvais*. He received no help. He lived for a time as boarder with one of his tenants; later he had a menial job in the theatre at Versailles, where his play *Oxtiern* was revived, he playing the role of the inn-keeper. Even this refuge failed; his sight got so bad that he could no longer see to write, and he greeted the nineteenth century from the Versailles public hospital or poor house, utterly dependent on charity, and 'dying of hunger and cold'. Madame Quesnet worked for both of them, even pawning her clothes; and in the spring of 1800 circumstances improved somewhat and they were together again.

In 1800 de Sade published his play *Oxtiern* and eleven of his long short stories, written in the Bastille, together with an Essay on the Novel as a preface, under the title *Les Crimes de l'Amour*. He must have been busy with his writing, for when he was arrested at his publishers in the following year four manuscripts of his were seized, only one of which—a collection of his lighter tales—had certainly been written earlier. Of the remainder, which were destroyed by the police, two were most probably obscene or blasphemous; the fourth, about which nothing else is known, is subtitled a political work.

De Sade and his publisher were arrested for planning to publish *Juliette* 'an immoral and revolutionary work' and it seems likely that the publisher led de Sade into a police trap, for he himself was released three days later. Until Gilbert Lely published his definitive researches, it was always believed that the real reason for de Sade's arrest was a lampoon mocking Napoleon and his immediate entourage; but there is no evidence for de Sade's authorship of this ill-written pamphlet. The 'political work' may well have been anti-Napoleonic; but no prospering tyrant could allow the exposures of the mechanisms of despotism in *Juliette* to be circulated. Napoleon's police tracked down and destroyed every copy that could be found.

De Sade was confined in an ex-convent where Madame Quesnet could visit him three times in every ten days. His case never came up for hearing, although legally he should have been charged within ten days. His appeals to the Ministry of Justice went unanswered. After two years he provoked a minor scandal, was moved for a month to another gaol, and then, for the last time in his life, to the lunatic asylum of Charenton. Officially this move was made at the request of his family; but there are no documents to substantiate this. A number of people whom Napoleon thought dangerous were declared mad and shut up in asylums.

The asylum of Charenton housed the insane of both sexes; and de Sade was extremely fortunate in the director, the ex-abbé Coulmier. He seems to have understood and sympathized with de Sade, made his life as agreeable as possible, allowed frequent visits from Madame Quesnet—she even spent some time there as a voluntary boarder—and other friends; and, probably even more important for de Sade's happiness, he allowed him to institute a theatre for the madmen. Occasionally, it appears, actors and actresses came from Paris; but more frequently the casts were found among the less disturbed of the inmates. De Sade was producer, elocution teacher, master of ceremonies, stage manager; he was even able to have the happiness of seeing some of his own plays acted. The performances became quite important social events; distinguished local dignitaries came for the evening, and were ceremoniously received by de Sade.

Coulmier also protected de Sade from police and official persecution. There seems to have been great fear in some quarters of his publishing further writings, and regular searches were made for manuscripts which were confiscated. In 1804 he listed four books of his which have not survived—two historical novels, his Confessions and, it appears, a treatise on atheism. In 1807 an enormous manuscript, 117 notebooks which would fill ten volumes, to be called *Les Journées de Florbelle,* was confiscated; it was destroyed by the police at his son's request some years after de Sade's death. We only know a brief outline of this work; it involved characters whom de Sade may well have known—Louis XV, Cardinal Fleury, the Comte de Charolais and so on—and was principally in dialogue. In the very last years of his life he wrote three more historical novels, one of which was published anonymously in his life-time, probably thanks to Coulmier's benevolence; the other two remained in manuscript until the last few years. In the development of the historical novel, using contemporary documents for verisimilitude, de Sade seems to have been a technical innovator; Scott's *Waverley* was published the year of his death.

There are two vivid descriptions of de Sade in his old age; they depict him as quick-tempered, extremely courteous, very fat and white-haired, with the remnants of grace in his movements, and occasional flashes from his dying eyes. He died at the age of seventy-four, the cause of his death being given as 'pulmonary congestion'.

In this very summary account of the life and works of the Marquis de Sade, I have not been able to indicate the strange qualities of his most characteristic writing, the odd combination of completely uninhibited fantasy, logical argument and pre-scientific analysis which make his books quite unlike anything else in recorded literature; they are still by far the most shocking productions of the human imagination. Although this century has seen far greater horrors than de Sade imagined, the motives for engaging in them on the part of the perpetrators have not been subjected to the calculus of pleasure.

The themes I have tried to emphasize are, firstly, the incidence of active algolagnia in his sexual life, and the theatrical or quasi-theatrical mise-en-scène of some of these incidents; and secondly de Sade's life-long preoccupation with the theatre, his constant desire to win public acclamation as a dramatist, his gross over-estimation of his minimal dramatic talents, which apparently he always rated far above his narrative fictions. If de Sade were merely an aberrant individual, the combination of these two themes would be merely anecdotal; but I think he may be considered a paradigm, not merely because his name was taken for a perversion, but because he was so remarkably in constant contact with his deepest unconscious, with all the nightmares of the primary processes. Consequently, I wish to suggest that this linking of sado-masochism with theatricality is relevant on a number of levels.

First of all, there is very great similarity in aim between the playwright and actor on the one hand and the sado-masochist on the other. Both wish to control the emotions of their audience or partner, to make them laugh and rejoice, shudder and weep by their actions and skills; audience or partner is essentially passive, without independent volition except their willingness (either voluntary or enforced) to respond to the stimulus of the actor's behaviour—'actor' to be understood in the most general sense of the word. The playwright and theatrical actor achieve their aims by symbolic and socially-approved techniques, the sado-masochist chiefly by concrete and socially disapproved techniques; but as de Sade illustrated copiously in his works, sadistic satisfactions can also be achieved in symbolic and socially tolerated forms. What is basic is that the emotions of the victim should depend on the will of the sadist.

Secondly, it has frequently been reported by sexologists that many of the sado-masochistic clients of prostitutes demand the re-enacting of some chosen scene, even providing suitable costumes and other props for the client and the prostitute to wear. This can surely be considered a special type of theatrical performance, with an audience of one. Negative evidence must always be treated with the utmost caution, but, for what the observation is worth, I do not know of any reports of overt sado-masochistic perversion from a society which has not theatrical performances, as a form of public amusement.

If it be granted that there are links of some complexity between overt sado-masochism and theatricality in the lives of many adults, it may be permissible to speculate on the psychological origins of these two types of behaviour. Classical psychoanalytic theory tends to interpret artistic creativity, of which playwriting and acting are two manifestations, as sublimation of unacceptable instinctual urges or wishes, almost as a type of defence mechanism. It is, I think always interpreted as secondary, a derivative from unacceptable primary sources.

I should like to suggest that this may not be the case, in every person. The urge to artistic creativity is very mysterious, and we really know very little about it. There are, however, a number of well-authenticated cases of musical prodigies, from Mozart to Yehudi Menuhin, who when infants in arms have responded to their first experience of music in a fashion which suggests that this is an innate response, and not a reaction formation. It seems to me at least feasible that this urge to creativity may be primary in certain individuals for all types of artistic expression and not merely for music.

If this be granted as a possibility, what occurs when the urge for creativity is not matched by the technical talents necessary for the urge to be adequately fulfilled? Then, I would suggest, you may get a back-formation to sexual perversion; the failure to move or fascinate an audience by artistic means may produce the desire to move or fascinate a partner or accomplice or victim by the most direct physical means. In short I am suggesting that the Marquis de Sade was an active sado-masochist at least in part because, despite his best endeavours, he was incapable of being an adequate tragedian or playwright; and also that this sequence of perverse sexual behaviour as a substitute for creative artistic satisfactions may well have wider application than this single case.

## XX

## *The Uses of Pornography*
## *(1961)*

i

PORNOGRAPHY—IF FOR the moment we stick to the etymological implication of writing—is an aspect of literacy. To the best of my knowledge, there is no record of a society which has used literacy for profane and imaginative purposes and which has not produced books dealing with sexual topics; of these books some have been considered unsuitable for general reading, their circulation has been more or less clandestine, and where laws have been concerned with private morals, have been interdicted by the law. As far as I know, there is no surviving pornography from Mesopotamia, Pharaonic Egypt or Crete; but there is so little written matter surviving from these civilizations which is not concerned with religion, law or business transactions that no argument can be based on these omissions. Further, we know nothing about the literatures of the high pre-Columbian civilizations of Central and South America; Peru had a copious industry of pots decorated with realistic portrayals of perverse and complex sexual activities. But all the literate societies of Europe and Asia from the time of the ancient Greeks have had pornography as one aspect of their literature. In very many cases the texts have not survived; but references to them occur in more seemly authors, usually in a context of reprobation.

Since pornography is an aspect of literacy, it is confined to the higher civilizations; it is not a human universal, found in societies of every stage of development, as is obscenity. All recorded societies, however simple their technology and unelaborated their social organization, have rules of seemliness;

certain actions must only be performed, certain words only be uttered, in defined contexts; if the actions be performed, or the words uttered, in unsuitable contexts or before unsuitable audiences, then the rules of seemliness have been broken, and these infractions are obscenities. In the etymological meaning of the word actions have been performed, or words spoken, on the stage which should only have been performed or spoken off the stage (that is in a suitable context); and this metaphor is valid for all definitions of obscenity in all societies, if any situation where two or three are gathered together in one place is considered to have some of the components of a theatrical scene.

Obscenity is a human universal, and I do not think that one can imagine a society without rules of seemliness and obscenity. Furthermore the responses to obscenity witnessed or recounted seem to vary very little from society to society. When witnessed, there is shocked silence and embarrassment on the part of the audience, confusion and shame on the part of the perpetrator, either openly manifested by such physical responses as blushing or giggling, or masked by bluster and defiance. When, however, obscenities are recounted in a suitable group, typically a one-sex group more or less of an age, the topic is enthralling and the climax of an anecdote is greeted with a peculiar, and easily recognizable, type of laughter. In different societies, laughter has a varying number of forms and functions; and until one knows quite a lot about a society one cannot interpret the significance that laughter has within it. But laughter at obscene jokes has (it would appear) the same sound nearly the whole world over. You may know nothing at all about a society; but you cannot fail to recognize this specific type of hilarity.

Obscenity impinges on pornography because in many societies (including of course our own) some aspects or actions of sexuality are regarded as obscene. This is, however, not universal; societies with phallic or fertility cults may place sexuality very literally on the stage, as part of a sacred mime. Nor do I know of any society in which obscenity is exclusively sexual. Defecation, by one or both sexes, is frequently treated as obscene; at least in the Trobriands (according to Malinowski) the public eating of solid food is an obscenity. Other societies surround death, either

## The Uses of Pornography

natural or violent or both, with the aura and circumspection of obscenity;[1] and in many societies the use of personal names, either in public or before specified kinfolk, has all the horror of an obscene utterance.

In societies with elevated ideas of the sacred, obscenity and blasphemy shade off into one another. The misuse of sacred words, the abuse of sacred figures, have all the overtones and responses customary to obscenity, except that blasphemy is much more rarely a subject for hilarity. In swearing and abuse both the obscene and the blasphemous vocabularies are frequently combined as forms of aggression against God and man; this is typically horrifying to the believer, amusing to the sceptic.

These digressions have seemed necessary because, despite the title of the Obscene Publications Bill, the connections between obscenity and pornography are both tenuous and intermittent. In Latin literature such writers as Juvenal and Martial used the complete obscene vocabulary without apparently being considered pornographic; we do not know what vocabulary Elephantis and her colleagues employed, but for contemporaries it was the subject matter, not the language, which made her books reprehensible. Conversely, to the best of my recollection, *The Memoirs of Fanny Hill* (one of the few masterpieces of English pornography) does not use a single obscene term. When obscene words are used in pornography, it is customarily due to the poverty of the writer's vocabulary; occasionally, as in some of the Victorian works, it is to enhance the law-breaking, blasphemous aspects of the actions or conversations described. But pornography is in no way dependent on obscene language; and, as it is customarily defined, it does not deal with more than a small portion of the subjects and situations considered obscene by the society at the time it was written.

ii

Pornography is defined by its subject matter and its attitude thereto. The subject matter is sexual activity of any overt kind,

[1] It is said that the *Christian Science Monitor* avoids the word 'death' with as much circumspection as it does more customary terms.

which is depicted as inherently desirable and exciting. In its original meaning—writings of or about prostitutes—pornography consisted either in manuals of sexual technique (*The Ananga-Ranga, I Ragionamenti* of Aretino) or in the extolling of the charms and skills of identified prostitutes (*The Ladies' Directory* and its very numerous predecessors); but in its most usual form it is a fiction, in prose or verse, narrative or dialogue, mainly or entirely concerned with the sexual activities of the imagined characters. As far as my knowledge goes, Asian pornography, from Arabia to China and Japan, has sexual interludes embedded in narratives of which they only form a small section. The Chinese, and those who were influenced by Chinese culture and ideas, apparently considered all fiction reprehensible, frivolous, and subject to censorship. A writer engaging in a work of fiction was already going beyond the bounds of seemliness; once this step was taken, there were, it would seem, no conventions limiting the situations which could be depicted; and as a consequence you have a masterpiece like *Chin P'ing Mei* (*The Golden Lotus*) with numerous sections which, in 1939, Colonel Egerton had to veil in the decent obscurity of dog-latin, and which, by themselves, would certainly be considered pornographic in any literate society. They, however, become valid as literature because they serve to illumine the characters who are also described in a great number of other situations.

With very few exceptions, European pornography does not have any characters. The drama and novel are respected literary forms in which characters can be portrayed in nearly all situations except the overtly sexual; all that was left for pornography was genital activity. And even that has become more and more circumscribed. The manuals of sexual technique, as far as heterosexual coitus is concerned, have been taken away from the pornographers by high minded writers of books on marriage guidance; the existence of sexual perversions, whose naming fifty years ago would have made a book suspect, is now common currency, thanks to the diffusion of various diluted versions of psycho-analysis; pornography is left with little but the description of the activities of various sets of genitals. As such it apparently commands a steady sale.

## The Uses of Pornography

The graphic equivalent of pornographic writing—the depiction of single figures ready for sexual activity or of pairs or groups of figures engaged in sexual activity—has likewise been an aspect of the painting, drawing or sculpture of every society in which these arts have been developed for aesthetic pleasure; in Hinduism they have on occasion been incorporated into sacred architecture. When mechanical means of reproducing works of art have been developed—woodcuts, engravings, etchings, pottery moulds—they have reproduced these works as well as the more conventional. Such pornographic art ranges all the way from masterpieces produced by the greatest artists of the period (for example, many Japanese woodcuts) to the most summary and feeble daubs. Except for the medium, they do not seem to be different in intention or effect from the literature; and I shall not further refer to them separately in this essay.

During the last century mechanical means of reproducing pictures and sounds—photographs, films, gramophone records and the like—have also been put to pornographic ends, 'feelthy' pictures, 'blue' films and so on. Some of those few I have had occasion to see have struck me as unintentionally fairly comic; but their intention is serious enough. They are not able to achieve the idealization—perfect beauty, health, vigour—which is so general a feature of pornographic art and literature. Otherwise, they do not seem to me different in intention or effect from pornography in other media; and I have not heard of any which have non-pornographic merits. These too—it would appear—command a ready sale, probably today from a bigger public than the literature.

The greatest amount of pornography in all media is produced by hacks with no pretension to aesthetic skill or competence. Some, however, has been produced by writers and painters of repute; and it is likely that, in such cases, the greater amount has been destroyed either immediately or after very limited circulation among friends. Some however has survived. There have also been a few European artists and writers whose main talent or output has been pornographic: Giulio Romano, Fuseli, Rowlandson among painters, Andréa de Nerciat, John Cleland, Pierre Louys among writers. When pornography is produced by writers or artists of talent it is usually dubbed 'erotica'; but I see no value in maintaining that distinction when the aesthetic qualities are not the major consideration.

I know of no study of the reasons which impel writers or artists to produce pornographic works; it is obviously an extremely difficult *genre,* and the technical problems of maintaining interest or variety with such an extremely limited subject matter may have been an attraction for some. In the mid-nineteenth and earlier twentieth century realistic and lyrical writers almost certainly felt thwarted by the strict conventions (to a great extent imposed by Mudie's lending library in Britain) limiting the subjects and situations with which they were allowed to treat; and the production of pornography may have been a sign of private revolt. Some of the nineteenth-century English works are ascribed to the most austere Victorian characters, though with what justice I would not be prepared to say. It is possible also that willing creators of pornography get much the same satisfaction out of their activity as do willing consumers of it.

### iii

The object of pornography is hallucination. The reader is meant to identify either with the narrator (the 'I' character) or with the general situation to a sufficient extent to produce at least the physical concomitants of sexual excitement; if the work is successful, it should produce orgasm. The reader should have the emotional and physical sensations, at least in a diminished form, that he would have were he taking part in the activities described.

The literature of hallucination is a vast one, perhaps particularly in English, and deals with a considerable number of emotions and situations besides the sexual. Perhaps the nearest analogy is the literature of fear, the ghost story, the horror story, the thriller. In these the reader is meant to identify either with the narrator (the 'I' character) or with the general situation to a sufficient extent to produce at least the physical concomitants of panic, increased heart-beat, clammy hands, stirring hair and the rest; if the work is successful, the reader should feel some anxiety about looking behind him, or of turning out the light. Why people should want to scare themselves with imaginary dangers is obscure on any rational level; but from Catherine Morland to the choir-school audiences of Dr. M. R. James there have been fervent addicts of this particular type of hallucinatory literature.

The pleasures of eating food and perhaps particularly of tasting wine are evoked in another type of literature which would again appear to depend on producing at least some of the concomitants of eating and drinking, such as salivation, in their readers; indeed books of wine connoisseurship, attempting to evoke the bouquet of vintages one is never likely to have the opportunity of tasting, would seem to have no other function.[1]

The exercise of the larger striped muscles is another physical sensation which has a large hallucinatory literature devoted to it. Most of the novels about fox-hunting make little sense to those readers who do not know the pleasures of a good run; but hunters can get from them, at least in a diminished form, the physical and emotional sensations that they would have, were they taking part in the activities described. Books devoted to other field sports and games have similar aims; but since to the best of my knowledge they have not produced a writer with even the distinction of Surtees (Izaac Walton is questionably in the same category) the literature is little known except to specialists.

War novels which, judging by the displays in bookstalls, are today very popular reading in England, obviously depend on hallucination for their effectiveness, for the reader's identification either with the narrator or with the general situation; but I would not like to hazard whether it is fear or exercise of the larger striped muscles which is the pleasure invoked by these books. Quite possibly, it is a combination of the two.

There would appear to be two main motives for reading the

[1] When I was studying the character of the Great Russians, one extremely intelligent Russian lady pointed out to me that, in the works of the classical Russian novelists, the descriptions of eating and drinking play much the same role as do love-scenes in the works of Western Europeans. This seemed to me an accurate and profound observation.

literature of hallucination: as a substitute for experience, or to satisfy an insatiable craving. Young men, for example, might read war books in an endeavour to anticipate what the thrills and perils of war might be like; older men who had enjoyed war (in comparison with their later civilian life) might try to recapture and recreate these experiences through hallucinatory literature. There are physiological limits to the amount one can actually eat or drink; but if gourmandise or wine connoisseurship are sufficiently strong passions, one can get at least some of the same satisfaction from reading of dishes one has enjoyed in the past or not yet tasted, trying to learn from the ecstatic author what can have been the bouquet of pre-phylloxera claret. As far as I can see, pornography, as literature, is parallel with the other literatures of hallucination. In all of them, the qualities of style, characterization, insight, wit, plot and so on which grace the main body of literature are, as it were, irrelevant; an Edgar Allan Poe may write horror stories, a Surtees may write hunting stories, a John Cleland or Andréa de Nerciat may write pornographic stories, a Saintsbury may write on wine, but these are happy accidents. The vast majority of all hallucinatory books have no qualities beyond those necessary to produce their effects. If they fail in this, they have no qualities at all.

iv

In all literate societies, pornography has been both legally forbidden (save for a few years in revolutionary France) and obtainable through certain channels. This apparent paradox is explicable by a number of hypotheses. First, the complete control of the dissemination of printed or otherwise mechanically reproduced matter was technically impossible before the twentieth century; and even today it can only be attempted by very highly policed states where there are no printing presses or supplies of paper outside government control, where all mail, whether internal or external, is liable to inspection and censorship, when homes and luggage can be visited by the police without warning or explanation.

## The Uses of Pornography

Secondly, until the twentieth century, the only potential purchasers of pornography were the literate minority, the educated classes. Even if the poor could read, and most of them couldn't, they lacked spare money for literature of any sort. Most authorities are more indulgent towards the peccadilloes of people 'of our own sort' than towards the crimes of the public at large. This is illustrated today in Great Britain (and other countries) by the lenience usually displayed towards the crimes committed by motorists.

Thirdly, the actual, in contrast to the proclaimed, aim of most enforcers of morality legislation has been to channel counter-mores behaviour into circumscribed areas, rather than to attempt the impossible task of stamping out counter-mores behaviour completely. The exceptions to this generalization have been theocratic puritan communities—such as Calvin's Geneva—where continuous supervision of each inhabitant was possible, and practised; and secondly those religious communities which have believed that counter-mores behaviour on the part of individuals would call down on the whole of the community supernatural punishment. Incest is the most common cause of supernatural anger; sodomy is much more uncommon. When these acts are thought to be supernaturally dangerous, the whole population will collaborate with the police or other law-enforcement officials in seeing that they are not exposed to risk.

Fourthly, all the historical literate societies have placed an exceedingly high valuation on the virginity of well-born girls. The preservation of this virginity (and in most societies of the chastity of the wives) had been the typical excuse for the toleration of brothels and prostitutes; and, it should be recalled, pornography is, literally, writing about prostitutes. It has been tolerated in the same way, and very often procurable in the same quarters; or else the area dealing in such literature—as for example Holywell Street in nineteenth-century London—has had much the same seclusion and protection as the brothel areas. From the point of view of the police, a confined nuisance is a controllable nuisance.

It seems probable too that from the point of view of the consumer the illegality of pornography is part of its attraction. The great majority of literate societies have had strict rules of sexual decorum; any sexual activity (with the possible exception of that subsequent to properly arranged marriages) has entailed the breaking of formal rules, of laws; and this technical law-breaking is not only inevitable, but part of the 'thrill' of extra-marital sexuality. In so far as the enjoyment of pornography is one form of extra-marital sexual activity, the infraction of the laws in obtaining the material is part of the inherent pleasure.

v

Apart from aesthetic arguments of taste and style, the reasons behind the legal prohibitions of pornography appear to be based on two apparently contradictory fears: that the readers (or consumers) will be excited to proceed to execute in real life the activities they have been reading about or viewing; and, alternatively, that they will not do so, finding sufficient pleasure in their fantasy stimulation. The second fear seems to me to be the more realistic.

The connection between any sort of fantasy in any medium of communication on any material and the subsequent activities of individuals who have been exposed to these fantasies is of the greatest obscurity. The evidence that anybody has carried out in real life activities which would previously have been repellent or forbidden or dangerous, because they have seen, heard or read of them in some work of fantasy or imagination is exceedingly tenuous. Magistrates or reformers with bees in their bonnets can frequently get juvenile delinquents to admit exposure to whatever form of mass communications they themselves hold in abhorrence (older readers may remember the period when juvenile delinquency in England was blamed on the pernicious influence of the B.B.C. radio serial *Dick Barton*); but the evidence of corruption is unclear. It is at least as likely that the youngsters listened to *Dick Barton* (or watched 'violence' on television or read horror comics) because these were congruent with their existing and conscious interests and preferences, as that the fantasies suddenly evoked wishes which had been unconscious before, and led to conduct at complete variance with their conduct before exposure. In *The Picture of Dorian Gray* Oscar Wilde described this as taking place (the corrupting book being apparently a reminiscence of Huysmans' *A Rebours*); but this can hardly be regarded as evidence, though I think the implications of Wilde's fantasy have been influential.

It is curious to speculate why pornography is considered especially likely to stimulate its readers into performing the activities described. The literature of murder is a vast one, particularly in the English language; enormous ingenuity is expended by writers in devising techniques for killing people, and these techniques are described with the greatest possible realism. The motives which would make murder desirable or profitable are so elaborated that they could easily persuade a reader into whose hands these books would be likely to fall that their case was parallel with that described in the book so that their problems could be solved in the same way. But I have never seen it seriously suggested that the literature of murder—detective stories or crime stories—tended to deprave and corrupt, or would incite weak-minded or immature readers into carrying out in reality the activities described in the fantasies. On the contrary, the literature of murder is considered particularly 'healthy' and desirable; and in England representatives of all the most respected professions have stated that detective stories are among their favourite reading. Musing about murder is apparently 'healthy'; musing about sexual enjoyment is not. No one, it is apparently assumed, will commit a murder because he spends his leisure reading about other people committing murder; but there is a grave danger that anybody will commit illegal sexual acts because they read pornography. A considerable number of thrillers have no more literary merit than the better-written type of pornography.

This belief in the inciting effect of pornography tells us something about the minds of legislators and the respectable people who support them; for them, apparently, illicit sexual indulgence is a temptation so near the surface that it will erupt into action if the possibility is ever put into people's minds. There seems to be no evidence to support this hypothesis that I know of.

I have already written that one of the reasons for reading any of the literatures of hallucination is insatiability; and it seems probable that one of the markets for pornography are the insatiable lechers, those people whose enjoyment of sex is limited by their physiological capacity, but whose interest in the subject is not satisfied by the physiological limits. It is possible that such people may derive suggestions of novel sexual techniques, positions or combinations from pornography, though I do not think this can happen often or importantly. The practical variations are so limited that anybody with a mildly licentious imagination can work them all out for him- or herself. A lot of pornography, perhaps particularly the Asian, describes positions or combinations which demand trained acrobats for sex-partners if they are to be successfully executed.

What is perhaps rather more important is the likelihood that some seducers have used pornography as one of their techniques of seduction. Casanova somewhere describes employing an illustrated edition of the *Sonnets of Aretino* for this purpose. But he also successfully accomplished a great number of seductions without this adventitious aid. One would suspect that the impact of pornography was marginal, compared with the other techniques available to the seducer; but this would seem to be the only documented situation in which pornography has had an inciting effect.

It seems probable that the real (though unexpressed) fears of legislators is that pornography will be used as a substitute for action, rather than as an incitement to action, that the readers will find sufficient stimulation in the 'impure and lustful' thoughts and images evoked by pornography for complete gratification. In other words, it is feared that the consumers will find so much satisfaction from masturbation that they will fail in their heterosexual duties.

Since masturbation is predominantly a private and unwitnessed activity, our knowledge of its incidence and effects is very patchy. The evidence suggests that it is prevalent among young males in all human societies that forbid or put difficulties in the way of sexual intercourse in the first years after physiological puberty. It is also general among young primates. It is, apparently, much less common among females; the greatest incidence is reported among the co-wives of polygynous men, women of the harem and the like.

Once the age has been reached at which the society permits heterosexual intercourse, it seems likely that masturbation no longer plays a major role in the sexual life of most men under normal circumstances; it is always available, and apparently generally employed, in situations in which adult men are temporarily or permanently separated from women, in armies, prisons and the like. In simple societies which make marriage difficult and have no prostitutes or other easily available women, such as the Tikopia, it is apparently resorted to without much shame or anxiety; similarly in age-grade societies which demand that the young warriors be chaste.

In all complex societies, including our own, masturbation is considered unsuitable and shameful for adults, and there is an elaborate mythology concerning its evidential value as a symptom and its probable effects if persisted in. If masturbation remains the preferred mode of gratification when sex with a partner is available, this can almost certainly be interpreted as neurotic, as a failure to achieve the degree of psycho-sexual development general within the society. As such, the masturbator probably suffers from deep feelings of inadequacy; but I know of no evidence that he does himself more harm by indulging his wishes than he would by resisting them. To society at large, he would seem today to do no harm at all. In the past it could be argued that all forms of sexuality which did not potentially result in producing children were harmful to society. But today, when one of the dominating problems of the world is overpopulation, this argument has no longer any validity; indeed if any society were to take seriously this serious problem, it would encourage by all legal and fiscal means celibacy and childlessness. The only sexual misdemeanours which would be reprobated would be those which resulted in children or caused bodily harm to the partner.

If masturbators prefer to derive their exciting fantasies from pornography rather than developing their own, this would seem to be exclusively their business. I cannot think of a logical argument which would justify the state interfering; though there are clear theological ones which should be applicable to practising Christians.

There does however remain the danger that through pornography the immature will be precociously excited into sexuality. The development of complex literate civilizations does depend on prolonging social childhood for several years beyond physiological childhood; the more complex the contents of necessary education, the longer this social prolongation has to be. Social childhood is not necessarily defined by complete sexual abstinence, though it is noteworthy that in every society that is approaching or has achieved universal education the 'age of consent' has been continuously and progressively raised. But sex should not (in the opinion of all complex societies) be a preoccupation of the young of either sex while they are still in the process of formal education.[1]

Nobody I think can say what effect exposure to pornography might have on the socially or physiologically immature; but it is feared lest its effects might be over-stimulating. No one knows whether naive youngsters would be more stimulated by complete pornography ('pure filth') than by the suggestive semi-pornography which is so widely available; but I do not think any responsible person would countenance putting the two forms of literature in the hands of a properly selected sample of youngsters to test their reactions. This is however the only way in which the issue could be scientifically decided. Since the experiment is inadmissible, we have to fall back on hunch and preference; and both prudence and tradition suggest that it should be made (at the very least) extremely difficult for youngsters to acquire pornography.

[1] The acceptance, and increasing numbers, of married undergraduates in British and United States universities is one of the most striking changes between pre-war and post-war university life in the two countries. It was started by the late entry of students into the universities after service in the forces; and has presumably continued on the hypothesis that it is better to marry than to burn. But the tradition up to 1945 firmly insisted that education and a continuous sex-life were incompatible.

## The Uses of Pornography

In my view, this is the sole area which makes pornography a proper matter of public concern. As a matter of public policy, its circulation should be restricted, its acquisition demand a certain amount of 'knowing the ropes'. The pattern of nineteenth-century England or France is probably a perfectly satisfactory one. We may think it a pity that some people are dependent on this fairly shoddy type of stimulation, as most people think it a pity that some people drink to excess, and can only find bliss in an alcoholic stupor. But total prohibition does not seem the appropriate answer in either case; and moreover it has never worked.

# PART FOUR

*Books and Writers*

## XXI

## The Erotic Myth of America
### (1950)

How our grandfathers used to snigger and wink among themselves, or look vaguely disapproving if ladies were present, at any mention of France or Paris. The adjective 'French' appended to the most innocuous words—postcard, letter, kiss, love—loaded these neutral terms with meanings which ranged from the suggestive to the obscene. The word could not be used as a verb or verbal noun. Even today this aura of naughtiness still clings around the adjective for the elderly; the late Mr. Ernest Bevin was able to raise titters in the House of Commons by retorting to the serious demand of a University member for the freer import of French books, 'if only the honourable member knew what I was thinking!'

During the nineteenth century, and for the greater part of the twentieth, untravelled Englishmen and Americans have pictured Paris in particular, and generally France as a whole, as though it were a sort of erotic Elysium, with all the women as lascivious as civet cats, ready to commit fornication or adultery at the drop of a handkerchief, and where all the literature was pornographic, all the humour sexual, and all art erotic. Even today Americans who have burlesque shows in many towns still get a thrill from a visit to the infinitely more sedate Folies-Bergère, or find innuendo in a copy of *La Vie Parisienne* which they would never discover in *Esquire*. This myth of an erotic Elysium was perpetuated in an endless flood of pornographic or pseudo-pornographic novels and novelettes with such titles as *Alone in Paris*; and these seem to have had sufficiently wide circulation so that during both wars naïve English and American soldiers made improper advances to the most respectable and carefully brought-up French wives and daughters and these resulted in a considerable worsening of international relations.

This myth seems to have derived, at least in part, from some aspects of French literature and French plays, such as the various vaudevilles and Palais Royal farces, which do picture almost non-stop adultery. Although precise figures are quite impossible to obtain, I have the impression that less pornography is produced and sold in France than in the United States (or England of the mid-nineteenth century); but it is made more easily available to foreigners who don't know the ropes in Paris or Marseilles than in any English or American town, with the possible exception of New Orleans, which trades on its 'French' tradition.

The myth of France is an old established one which I imagine has seen its best days; what I wish to discuss here is a new myth which is growing up in Western Europe, and which dates almost entirely from the last decade; this is the myth of the United States as a sort of Abbaye de Thélème, in which there are endless opportunities to indulge not only all one's erotic, but also all one's sadistic daydreams. I have the impression that this myth is one of the more important components in the fear which many Europeans feel concerning the spread of American culture and influence.

Since the myth is still very young, it is possible to trace at least some of its sources. American movies of course play an important role, but it seems as though American novels have been even more influential, in particular the works of Faulkner, Cain, Hammett, Chandler, Hemingway and their imitators and followers. All these authors have had considerable success in England and the Continent, in many cases (as, for instance, Faulkner) comparatively greater than in the United States. They represent, to a greater or lesser extent, a new technique of writing, and they depict a very strange society in which violence is normal, and normally unpunished (except for the 'criminal' in the detective stories); where the forces of law are weak, or corrupt, or both, and where taking the side of virtue means taking a great deal of 'punishment', and where female chastity, when encountered, is promptly dealt with by rape. The corn-cob in Faulkner's *Sanctuary* might almost be the emblem of the myth. European readers cannot of course place these stories in any sort of context.

This myth is producing its own literature, the pendant to *Alone in Paris*; although on not quite such a low level as the earlier works, it is extremely unpleasant reading. Two authors in particular have achieved enormous sales for their dreams of Thélème in the United States: René Raymond, writing under the pseudonym James Hadley Chase in England,[1] and Boris Vian purporting to translate a fictitious American author 'Vernon Sullivan' in France. Their work is curious enough to discuss in some detail.

Both write in the first person, as one would expect from dreams: Chase in a most curious lingo which is intended to be American, but which, despite a little obsolete American slang, could never be written or spoken by any living person, Vian in fairly racy and economical French with a good deal of argot. Chase would appear never to have set foot in the States, and he is extremely careless in his geography, flora and fauna (he plants mangrove swamps in California!). Vian probably has spent a few days or weeks in New York, for *Les morts ont tous la même peau* (the only novel of his I have read set in that city) contains no very obvious blunders, though the California of *Et on tuera tous les affreux* is, in every way, a very odd state.

In both authors all the women are on heat, from barely pubescent schoolgirls to dowagers, just as in the 'France' of the earlier daydreams. Mr. Raymond's protagonists, however, nearly always resist their improper advances—the most alluring women are likely to be murderesses. Monsieur Vian's heroes, on the other hand, tend to respond with equal fervour and superhuman potency, each fornication described in minute detail; but their lust is not disinterested.

The first, and most scandalous, of Monsieur Vian's books, *Je cracherai sur vos tombes*, reads rather like a paradoxically luscious communist tract. 'I' am a white-skinned Negro, who

[1] Much of the material on 'James Hadley Chase' is based on G. Legman, *Love and Death*.

has moved into an unidentified small Midwestern town after the lynching of my younger brother in the South for his attempted marriage to a white girl. 'I' intend to revenge my kid brother by seducing the most desirable and socially prominent women available, telling them when they are 'in love' with me that I am a Negro, let them suffer from their revulsion for a little, and then murder them *à la* Jack the Ripper. 'I' succeed with two millionaire's daughters, and then am myself caught and lynched. To earn my living while carrying out my plan, I take a job in a book-store, which gives me excellent possibilities of discussing the lack of intellectual culture among white Americans, with discursive comments on the mass manufacture of best-sellers, and so on. This also puts me in contact with the junior high school kids, all of whom (of both sexes) try to seduce me; I sleep with all the girls, but they are too insignificant for my revenge.

The theme of the 'white Negro' recurs also in the second book, *Les morts ont tous la même peau,* but in reverse. 'I' am a barman and chucker-out in a New York bar, and believe myself to be a Negro passing as white. I am married to a white woman and have a young daughter. A black man whom I believe to be my brother comes and starts trying to blackmail me; I follow him to Harlem, and there sleep with a black woman, after which I become impotent with my wife (who says 'If you were to leave me alone for a week I'd either have to take sedatives or sleep with another man'). I then proceed to murder, first my supposed brother, then a whole group of witnesses or possible witnesses, finding out after I am caught that I am completely white, an adopted foundling.

*Et on tuera tous les affreux* is more in the nature of a farce, set in California, about a 'mad scientist' who has perfected a method of developing embryos *in vitro* and bringing them to maturity in a very short time. His plan is to kill all the ugly people in the world and replace them with synthetic supermen. 'I' am 'Mr. Los Angeles', of overwhelming beauty and strength, aged nineteen and a half, and have taken a vow to remain virgin until I am twenty; consequently I am unwilling to be a donor for the mad scientist, though the most desirable society girls and film stars are eager to act as recipients; and I become involved in a most complicated cops and robbers chase, strewn with corpses, ending up on the scientist's private island in a nonstop mass orgy. 'I' abandon my vow about a third of the way through the book, and thereafter make up for lost time. The book is not without humour, the finale demonstrating how, in a world of beauty, ugliness and deformity become desirable; the final sentence has a Navy lieutenant generously offering to introduce me to his secretary, 'who is absolutely hideous, and has a wooden leg!'

Vian's major model is obviously Cain, and to a lesser degree Chandler; the implicit sexuality in the models is made pornographically explicit; what is novel is the overt sadism. Lust murders are gloatingly described in detail, including the physical enjoyment of the murderer. When the hero of *Je cracherai sur vos tombes* is tormenting the elder sister, prior to murdering her, he shows her the murdered younger sister's wrist-watch and then tells her 'he was sorry he hadn't been able to bring one of her sister's eyes, but they were in too poor a condition after the special treatment he had given them'.

Luckily it is not necessary to detail the plots of Mr. Raymond's work. The notorious, and vastly successful, *No Orchids for Miss Blandish* follows fairly closely the plot of Faulkner's *Sanctuary*; *Twelve Chinks and a Girl* that of Hemingway's *To Have and Have Not*, and the later works novels by Hammett and Chandler. The characters are reduced to pasteboard, the plots are coarsened, vulgarized and complicated, but the original pattern is generally discernible. In these books the sadism is chiefly homosexual; men torture and mutilate other men at the slightest pretext, and incidentally to the action, 'I' being the chief aggressor. Thus in his book *You're Lonely when You're Dead*, the narrator breaks into a gambling club, where he is stopped by a couple of bouncer-guards. After being held prisoner for half an hour, he is let go, without suffering any ill-treatment:

He (one of the guards who was showing him out) was beginning a slow leering smile when I hit him. I didn't give him a chance to duck. The punch travelled about four inches and it had all my weight behind it. My fist bounced against the side of his jaw with a crack like the snapping of dry wood. As he began to fall I slammed in another punch to the same spot and stood back to watch him fold on the floor. Then I grabbed his arm and rolled him over on his back. I had to work fast. Gates (the other guard) might come out to see what the row was about. When I had him on his back, I placed the heel of my shoe squarely on his nose and mouth and put my weight on it.

Later in the same book 'I' and an associate use a blowtorch on the feet of a minor witness to make him talk. When he had told the little he knew, my associate and partner 'shoved the flame of the blowlamp in Louis', (the witness') face'.

These books, it must be repeated, are enormously popular. They must represent fulfilments of deeply felt but furtive wishes. But the thought of gratifying such reprehensible wishes must also arouse a great deal of guilt. During the heyday of Victorian morality, the prostitutes who gratified (true, in more concrete fashion) the reprehensible wishes of respectable gentlemen, were accused by the respectable gentlemen of being the source of their sin. The psychological mechanism of projection worked efficiently. In much the same way, it would seem, American culture is thought to be the source of the imaginative sins which the readers of these novels commit during their solitary orgies. For most of them, the United States is the land where these things happen, happen continuously, for they have no facts to set against the falsification of the writers; were American influence to spread, It Could Happen Here; the temptation and the remorse would both be intolerable.

I think it is certainly purely coincidental with Raymond, and probably so with Vian, that their fantasies are almost completely congruent with the anti-American propaganda put out by the Nazi and Soviet Propaganda Ministries. And there is just enough truth for the picture to appear convincing. Compared with their European opposite numbers, young Americans (whether in Armies of Liberation or Occupation) do seek pleasure in sex and alcohol with great openness and publicity. Lynchings do occur;

## The Erotic Myth of America

Negroes are discriminated against; the police in most American cities do tend to greater brutality and greater corruption than most European police.

These facts, I think, are not so disconcerting to European 'liberals', most of whom, like 'liberals' everywhere, find sufficient object of hatred in their own governments, as to the non-political who see lynching not so much as a horror but as an almost irresistible temptation, just as the street-walker aroused the indignation of the respectable, not the libertine. To use a psychoanalytic metaphor, this myth of the United States represents the disreputable forces of the id in opposition to the restraints of the super-ego. The super-ego has a hard enough battle to wage already, in the moral breakdown of a great deal of contemporary Europe; any notion or set of circumstances which promises greater gratification to the id evokes panic and repudiation from the super-ego. To the extent that America seems to offer greater freedom from restraint, greater possibilities of gratification, it is seen as a more serious threat to personal integrity than the severe and puritanical restraints that a dictatorial regime would impose. The quasi-masturbatory daydreams of the novels show the nature and danger of this imagined threat. The spread of American influence is terrifying because in America 'anything goes'; I should torture and lynch and fornicate to my heart's content, and I should hate myself for doing so. Better a police state, which will stop me misbehaving.

## XXII

## *The Perils of Hypergamy*
## *(1957)*

NOW I'M PRACTICALLY sure of it. *Lucky Jim, Look Back in Anger* and all that lot roused my suspicions; and the clincher has come with John Braine's *Room at the Top*, which tells much the same story all over again, brilliantly and bitterly. The curse which is ruining, in fantasy if not in their own lives, these brilliant young men of working-class origin and welfare-state opportunity is what anthropologists have dubbed male hypergamy. It is a new pattern in English life, and apparently a very distressing one.

In any society stratified by caste or class—and this means all complex societies, all societies composed of more than one ethnic group when the groups are distinguishable by appearance or speech, and all societies colonized or missionized by Hinduism—the great majority of marriages or socially recognized sexual relationships take place within the caste or class. This is to say that the caste or class tends to be endogamous, by definition where caste is concerned, by custom with class. But even in the most rigid societies, even in Hindu India or the southern United States or South Africa, some marriages across class or caste barriers do occur or, where such marriages are forbidden by civil law, become established and public irregular unions.

When such cross-class or cross-caste unions do occur, the society has to decide to which social position the couple shall be assigned. Probably the more common is for the higher status partner to be degraded to the lower status, to 'lose caste' or 'become déclassé' in the precise meaning of the common phrases; but there are situations where the lower class or caste partner

## The Perils of Hypergamy

is raised to the higher status of the spouse, and this is technically called hypergamy, marrying upwards.

In most societies status or prestige tends to be connected with one of the sexes rather than the other, a facet of what is popularly (and inaccurately) called patriarchy or matriarchy; in 'male prestige' societies a woman's status is derived from her father and her husband; in 'female prestige' societies a man's status will be related to that of his mother, his sister and his wife. It seems fairly simple for the person of the sex which carries esteem to give status to a lower-class partner; King Cophetua could raise the beggar-maid; or, to come nearer to our own time, any number of chorus girls could be raised to the peerage. Female hypergamy fits fairly well into English society, and has informed the dreams of any number of unprivileged girls, from *Jane Eyre* to most of the serials in most of the current women's magazines.

As far as we know, male hypergamy has always been a relatively uncommon arrangement, though it has taken place regularly in some matrilineal societies, notably some of the tribes and castes of southern India. There seem to be two general, though not universal, reasons for this; in most societies property (other than title to land) is usually gained and held by men, and although wealth and high status never completely coincide, the former is very often a prerequisite for the latter; and leisured men seem to find the manipulation of symbols more congenial than do leisured women; and status, as much as the arts, is to a very great extent dependent on the proper manipulation of symbols.

These are generalizations, not universals. In the contemporary United States, the symbols of high status have been almost entirely left in women's hands—an application for inclusion in the *Social Register* must be accompanied by letters of recommendation from two women who are already included; and in the United States male hypergamy is a recognized technique for the advancement of an able, ambitious but lower status man; 'marrying the boss's daughter' is the way this step is usually described. In the novels and films elaborating this theme, the hero's happiness is rarely shadowed.

In *Lucky Jim, That Uncertain Feeling, Look Back in Anger,*

*Room at the Top* (to mention no others) the hero, of working-class origin, is married to, or involved in a public liaison with, a middle- to upper-middle-class woman and doesn't really enjoy it at all, in the long run. He thinks he is 'destroyed' by her, or would be 'destroyed' by her if he didn't return to his proper working-class environment, or both are reduced to mutual misery and recrimination. These cross-class unions, with male hypergamy, don't work out, we are told with humour and anger and passion and sentimentality; and yet it is implied, if not stated, that it is only among women of this higher social class that these bright young men can expect to find wives or mistresses.

It is perhaps necessary to enter a *caveat* that I am talking about works of fiction, not about the authors, of whose personal lives I know nothing at all. The fantasies underlying these fictions are realistic enough and coherent enough so that they can be treated as referring to contemporary English life, even if it be impossible, or at least very ill-mannered, to identify specific instances of such unions.

The records are sparse, but it seems as if, before 1939, the higher-status Englishwoman was declassed to her lower-status spouse; when a school teacher married a miner, she became a miner's wife, not he a teacher's husband; the fictions of D. H. Lawrence have several examples of the lady marrying downwards (hypogamy, in anthropological vocabulary). The problem, therefore, is why male hypergamy has suddenly become at the least a possibility to be considered, and why it is felt to be so inevitably destructive by the young men to whom it might occur?

The English class structure has never been really rigid or impermeable; but, in the past, upward mobility—the moving from a lower class to a higher one—was a relatively slow process, the penetration of the upper middle or upper classes usually taking more than one generation. Typically, a man of the middle or working classes made a fortune and provided his children with the type of education which would train them to move in a social class in which he and his wife would never be at ease. Both real life and fiction abound with examples; it was one of

## The Perils of Hypergamy

Thackeray's favourite themes (the Osbornes in *Vanity Fair* make all the points).

The 1944 Education Act, and its sequels, have enormously speeded up this process, so that the university education which was formerly the culmination of two or three generations of earnest striving on the part of the whole family, is now available to the sons (apparently much less to the daughters) of working-class families if they are bright enough, persistent enough and tough enough. Although higher social class has not been determined entirely by education in England, it is probably the single most important component of class position between the ranges of the upper working and upper middle classes, that is to say for something like a quarter of the English population; and anybody who completes a university education has the qualifications for a profession in which most of his colleagues will be of middle- or upper-middle-class status.

These bright young working-class lads jump three or four social classes (in the English seven-class social hierarchy) in the second decade of their lives. At the end of that period their intellectual interests, their social horizons, and almost certainly their accent and vocabulary—the chief stigmata of social class—are much nearer to those of their fellow graduates than they are to those of their parents or their less bright brothers and sisters. But because this process of social mobility has started so relatively late (probably after the 11-plus examination) when the main lines of their character are already established, their emotional values, their type of sex identification and their patterns of domestic life are all rooted in the sub-culture of the English working class, nostalgically for Mr. Richard Hoggart, more or less defiantly for the heroes of the novels and plays I am discussing. They are, quite inevitably, divided men unless (as in *That Uncertain Feeling*) they decide to reject all the opportunities a grateful state has given them.

The further you go down the English social scale the greater the contrast made between the typical and expected behaviour, and even voice pitch, of male and female. It is very much easier for a working-class man to imperil his status as a male than it is for one of the upper middle class. A light tenor voice, a la-di-da

(B.B.C. standard English) accent, an extended vocabulary, restraint in the use of expletives, all carry the stigma of being cissy or pansy; and not one working man in a hundred but would be ashamed of being caught by a mate in doing the sort of housework and child-tending which is taken for granted by young fathers of the professional classes today.

In their secondary school days the future university students are likely to have undergone a good deal of mockery and self-questioning for their studious abstention from the pursuit of money and pleasure which their mates enjoy from the age of fifteen; and consequently they feel driven to emphasize their manliness in such ways as are open to them, perhaps by surliness or pugnacity, but certainly by frequent copulation or attempts thereat. There is no reason to suppose their physiological urges are stronger, or less strong, than those of their contemporaries who have not moved in social class; but their psychological urges are much more over-determined.

This is where the trap of hypergamy opens. Casual intercourse with tarts is likely to be inadequately satisfying (to say nothing of the expense). One wants to be able to talk to the girl as well; and girls still in the working class have no conversation which is satisfying for any length of time to a newly-educated man. Presumably the happiest marry girls as mobile as themselves or foreigners, but they haven't so far written books or plays, or even appeared in them. The others get involved with upper-middle-class girls, with the comically tragic results we read about.

The assured status of the upper-middle-class girl is intellectually seen as desirable, indeed as an emotional reward for all the hard work, so that it would not be satisfactory if she abandoned her manners and habits and became a working-class wife; but the upper middle classes and the working classes have very different models of ideal masculine and feminine, husbandly and wifely behaviour, and each is seen as destructive to integrity and self-respect by the member of the other sex and class. The working-class husband expects, and most of the time gets, far more service and subservience from his wife than does a man of the upper middle class (whose wife would complain that she is being turned into a drudge); an upper-middle-class wife gets far more

## The Perils of Hypergamy

consideration and physical help, where there is no money for servants, from her husband than does a woman of the working class (whose husband would complain that he is being unmanned, turned into a cissy). If both are strong characters—and both are likely to be, the man to have fought his way to his present position, the girl to have defied conventions so far—conflict would appear theoretically almost inevitable; and the books and plays tell us what forms these conflicts take.

In this English pattern, there is a much better fit with female hypergamy, for both sexes feel themselves indulged; and, as far as I know, chorus girls were happy, and made their well-born husbands happy, in the old Gaiety days.

## XXIII

*Poor Honey*
*Some Notes on Jane Austen and Her Mother*
*(1957)*

'She deserved their pity, more than she hoped they would ever surmise'—*Mansfield Park*, XVIII, 170.

ONE OF THE constant themes in Jane Austen's novels is the damage which, wittingly or unwittingly, parents, or people standing in the position of parents, do to the happiness of their children, nieces, wards. In two of the novels, General Tilney in *Northanger Abbey*[1] and Sir Walter Elliot in *Persuasion*, the father is the cause of the daughter's unhappiness; but in all the novels except the youthful *Northanger Abbey* the mother, if she is alive, or the mother substitute, if the mother be dead, is the cause of unnecessary suffering. Probably the most attractive mother figured in the novels is Mrs. Dashwood in *Sense and Sensibility*; but she is shown to be the direct cause of Marianne's misery, first by encouraging and exacerbating her daughter's sensibility and, above all, by failing in her maternal duty to clarify the ambiguous relationship between Marianne and Willoughby. In *Pride and Prejudice*, Mrs. Bennet is shown to be directly responsible both for Jane's temporary unhappiness (by disgusting the Bingleys and Darcy with her vulgarity) and for Lydia's disgrace. In *Mansfield Park*, Fanny's real mother is heartless, her Aunt Norris a persecutor, her Aunt Bertram a cypher; and these two latter make for the disgrace of their own daughter and niece. Emma's ill-considered friendship with

---

[1] I am using the abbreviations employed by R. W. Chapman in the Oxford editions of the novels and letters. All page references are to these editions.

## Poor Honey—Some Notes on Jane Austen and her Mother

Harriet and her dangerous flirtation with Frank Churchill are encouraged by Mrs. Weston; and much of the plot turns on Mrs. Churchill's pride and malice concerning her adopted son. It was Lady Russell in *Persuasion* whose well-meaning advice caused Anne her nine years' misery. Finally, in the minor works, *Lady Susan* is Jane Austen's one attempt to paint an unrelievedly evil character (Mrs. Norris is given her due) and it is as a heartless mother, even more than as a heartless flirt, that she shows her wickedness; and in *Sanditon* Lady Denham promises to be one more monster.

So recurrent a theme suggests a personal involvement; and it seemed to me that it might be interesting to discover what one could of the character of Mrs. Austen and her relationship with her daughters. This I knew would be little and inferential; the Austen family piety and Cassandra's drastic censorship of the letters would have let little survive which could reflect on the character of any of the family; it was a question of paying attention to each phrase, of following out each faint clue. In going through the correspondence and memoirs for this purpose, I found that my view of Jane Austen's circumstances—to a lesser extent of her character—were considerably modified.

I imagine I have not been alone in considering Jane Austen's life to have been not unlike the genteel and elegant life she portrays in most of the canonical novels; not as grand, of course, as life in *Mansfield Park*, but perhaps not unlike what we can guess of Kellynch Lodge. I have now reached the conclusion that, if Jane Austen anywhere portrays her own way of living, it is in the chapters on the Price family in Portsmouth. From her father's retirement, and even more from his death, until the move to Chawton in 1809 she lived in poverty, misery and no little squalor.

Only fifteen letters survive from the unhappy Southampton years; but they contain a number of parallels with the nine Portsmouth chapters in *Mansfield Park*. The following are some of the most striking:

> Her father asked him to do them the honour of taking his mutton with them and Fanny had time for only one thrill of

horror, before he declared himself prevented by a prior engagement.... To have had him join their family dinner-party and see all their deficiencies would have been dreadful! (M.P., pp. 406–7.)

She was so little equal to Rebecca's puddings, and Rebecca's hashes, brought to table as they all were, with such accompaniments of half-cleaned plates, and not half-clean knives and forks.... (M.P., p. 413.)

He (Captain Foote) dined with us on Friday, and I fear will not soon venture again, for the strength of our dinner was a boiled leg of mutton, underdone even for James; and Captain Foote has a particular dislike to underdone mutton; but he was so good-humoured and pleasant that I did not much mind his being starved. (Letter 48: January 7, 1807, p. 172.)

You will be surprised to hear that Jenny is not yet come back; we have heard nothing of her since reaching Itchingswell, and can only suppose that she must be detained by illness in somebody or other, and that she has been each day expecting to be able to come on the morrow. I am glad I did not know beforehand that she was to be absent during the whole or almost the whole of our friends being with us, for though the inconvenience has not been nothing, I should have feared still more. Our dinners have certainly suffered not a little by having only Molly's head and Molly's hands to conduct them; she fries better than she did, but not like Jenny. (p. 174.)

Jenny and Molly (Jane Austen could not like anybody of that name, cf. letter 141) correspond with the 'trollopy-looking maidservant' and the 'attendant girl, whose inferior appearance informed Fanny, to her great surprise, that she had previously seen the upper servant' (M.P., pp. 377, 383) and seem to have been the total staff of the Southampton household; later there was apparently a man-of-all-work for 'We have been obliged to turn away Cholles, he grew so very drunken and negligent, & we have a man in his place called Thomas'. Apart from the Prices, the poorest family in the canonical novels are the Dashwoods;

their household by Elinor's wisdom consisted of 'two maids and a man' (S.S., p. 27); but the Dashwoods were somewhat richer than the Austens; they had £500 a year, Mrs. Austen and her two daughters £460 a year between the three of them, even with the brother's contributions. Neither Edward Ferrars nor Elinor were 'quite enough in love to think that three hundred and fifty pounds a-year would supply them with the comforts of life.' (S.S., p. 369.) They, the Edward Ferrars, were going to live rent-free in the parsonage; Mrs. Austen had to pay rent.

Our changed attitude towards the employment of domestic servants tends to make us consider the employer of even two incompetent domestics as fairly well off; but this was not the case at the end of the eighteenth and beginning of the nineteenth centuries. They were quite essential to any claims of gentility; their presence indicated that their employer had not quite fallen below the poverty line; Mrs. Smith 'was . . . living in a very humble way, unable even to afford herself the comfort of a servant, and of course almost excluded from society.' (P., p. 153.) Note the 'even', note the 'of course'.

The Austens were not excluded from society even in Southampton, but their domestic comforts were meagre indeed.

> There will be green baize enough for Martha's room and ours;—not to cover them, but to lie over the part where it is most wanted, under the Dressing Table. Mary is to have a piece of carpet for the same purpose; my Mother says *she* does not want any;—& it may certainly be better done without in her room than in Martha's & ours, from the difference of their aspect. (Letter 50: February 20, 1807, p. 184.)

> Our dressing Table is to be constructed on the spot, out of a large Kitchen Table belonging to the House. . . . (Letter 49: February 8, 1807, p. 174.)

> Could my Ideas flow as fast as the rain in the Store Closet it would be charming.—We have been in two or three dreadful states within the last week, from the melting of the snow &c.—and the contest between us and the Closet has now ended in our defeat; I have been obliged to move nearly

everything out of it, and leave it to splash itself as it likes. (Letter 65 : January 24, 1809, p. 256.)

It is cold enough now for us to prefer dining upstairs to dining below without a fire, & being only three we manage it very well, & today with two more we shall do just *as* well, I dare say. (Letter 56 : October 17, 1808.)

Where the fire was upstairs is not stated; but I feel pretty confident it was in Mrs. Austen's dressing room. It was certainly not in the sisters' room; like Fanny, Jane Austen was always very conscious of the luxury of a fire in her own room—'very snug, in my own room, lovely morning, excellent fire, fancy me' (Letter 91 : November 6, 1813; see also Letter 25 : November 8, 1800); and I think she suffered a great deal from cold. Similarly, she rejoices every time she has a decent-sized room to herself in one of her brother's houses :

I am in the Yellow room—very literally—for I am writing in it at this moment. It seems odd for me to have such a great place all to myself. . . .

Yes, I enjoy my apartment very much, & always spend two or three hours in it after breakfast. (Letters 51, 52 : from Godmersham, June 15 and 20, 1808.)

Jane Austen had very little money of her own, and the letters are full of economic contrivances—dresses dyed or remade and the like. At a party in Southampton on October 7, 1808 'There were two pools at Commerce, but I would not play more than one, for the Stake was three shillings, & I cannot afford to lose that, twice in an evening'. (Letter 56.) And in 1814 'I suppose my Mother recollects that she gave me no Money for paying Bracknell and Twining; and *my* funds will not supply enough.' (Letter 94.) I think Bracknell and Twining were the tea merchants. In the letters there are frequent references to the settling of small accounts between the sisters or between mother and daughter, but never for more than a few shillings. A brotherly present of £5 is something to dwell on at length.

## Poor Honey—Some Notes on Jane Austen and her Mother

There is no reason to suppose that this poverty ended with the final move to Chawton; the house was probably less uncomfortable—though, in bad weather in March, 1816 'our walls are damp' (Letter 125)—but there was the very material difference that the place was relatively quiet. I think Jane Austen had abnormally sensitive, as well as abnormally accurate, ears and that loud noises were particularly painful to her. She hated thunderstorms:

> We sat upstairs and had thunder and lightning as usual. I never knew such a spring for thunderstorms as it has been. Thank God! we have had no bad ones here. I thought myself in luck to have my uncomfortable feelings shared. . . . (Letter 72 : May 29, 1811.)

Jane Austen does not use 'Thank God!' loosely. And I don't think she was altogether joking when she wrote, from Bath:

> . . . even the Concert will have more than its usual charm with me, as the gardens are large enough for me to get pretty well beyond the reach of the sound. (Letter 20 : June 2, 1799.)

The two heroines with whom Jane Austen seems to identify herself most nearly, 'my' Fanny Price, and Anne Elliot, both share this horror of noise :

> The living in incessant noise was to a frame and temper, delicate and nervous like Fanny's, an evil which no superadded elegance or harmony could have entirely atoned for. It was the greatest misery of all. (M.P., p. 391.)

> Everybody has their taste in noises as well as in other matters; and sounds are quite innoxious, or most distressing, by their sort rather than their quantity. When Lady Russell, not long afterwards, was entering Bath on a wet afternoon . . . amidst the dash of other carriages, the heavy rumble of carts and drays, the bawling of newsmen, muffin-men, and milkmen, and the ceaseless clink of pattens, she made no

complaint. No, these were noises which belonged to winter pleasures; her spirits rose under their influence; and, like Mrs. Musgrove, she was feeling, though not saying, that, after being long in the country, nothing could be so good for her as a little quiet cheerfulness.

Anne did not share these feelings. She persisted in a very determined, though very silent, disinclination for Bath. . . . (P., p. 135.)

'It will be two years tomorrow' Jane Austen wrote on June 30, 1808, 'since we left Bath for Clifton, with what happy feeling of Escape!' (Letter 54.)

It seems to me not improbable that it was the removal from the noise of Southampton—the 'greatest misery of all'—which decided Jane Austen to resume writing, rather than the supposed recovery from the grief of the death of a 'nameless and dateless' young man.

I have not quite done with poverty yet, for it seems to me basic to an understanding of much of the novels, particularly the emphasis given to the fortunes of the heroines and of their admirers. This has been resented by most of Jane Austen's hostile critics, at any rate the male ones, as crass, gross and unromantic. I question whether any of these gentlemen had the 'comforts of their life' so drastically curtailed by poverty as she did.

At the turn of the nineteenth century the only alternatives to poverty at home for an unmarried woman of good family were to go as governess or schoolmistress. In *Emma*, Jane Austen spoke her thoughts on the governess-trade (chapter XVII, p. 300), putting the words into the mouth of a character to whom she gave her own Christian name, Jane Fairfax. I do not know any other major novelist who gave his or her own name to a subsidiary character (as opposed to the narrator); Jane Bennet may have been so named to put people off the scent of the authoress's identity; but by the time Jane Austen started writing *Emma* in 1814 her anonymity was pretty transparent. Her notion of being a schoolmistress was voiced in the unfinished *The Watsons*, Jane Austen's unique attempt at depicting people as poor as herself:

## Poor Honey—Some Notes on Jane Austen and her Mother

Poverty is a great Evil, but to a woman of education & feeling it cannot be the greatest.—I would rather be a Teacher at a school (and I can think of nothing worse) than marry a Man I did not like.—I would rather do any thing than be a Teacher at a school—said her sister. I have been at school, Emma, & know what a life they lead; you never have. (p. 318)

Jane Austen too had been at school. The alternatives to genteel poverty were not possible. 'Single women have a dreadful propensity for being poor,' she wrote to her niece, Fanny Knight, a few months before her own death (Letter 141 : March 13, 1817); and in *Emma* she elaborated the point :

A single woman with a very narrow income, must be a ridiculous, disagreeable, old maid! the proper sport of boys and girls ... a very narrow income has a tendency to contract the mind, and sour the temper. Those who can barely live, and who live perforce in a very small, and generally very inferior, society, may well be illiberal and gross. (E., p. 85.)

A few months before penning these lines she had written to her sister :

By the bye, as I must leave off being young, I find many Douceurs in being a sort of Chaperon for I am put on the Sofa near the Fire and can drink as much wine as I like. (Letter 91 : November 6, 1813.)

The Sofa brings us to Mrs. Austen with a vengeance, for it was Mrs. Austen's nearly permanent place from before she bore Jane Austen to many, many years after she buried her; and it is also a link with the Austen poverty. Even during Jane Austen's last illness, when she was so weak that she could neither walk nor sit up much, it was apparently never considered feasible to buy a second sofa for the invalid's use.

The sitting room contained only one sofa, which was frequently occupied by her mother (Mrs. Austen) who was more than seventy years old. Jane would never use it, even in her mother's absence; but she contrived a sort of couch for herself with two or three chairs, and was pleased to say this arrangement was more comfortable to her than a real sofa. Her reasons for this might have been left to be guessed, but for the importunities of a little niece, which obliged her to explain that if she herself had shown any inclination to use the sofa, her mother might have scrupled being on it so much as was good for her. (*A Memoir of Jane Austen* by J. E. Austen Leigh, 2nd edition, 1871, p. 156.)

One of the few really cross remarks in Jane Austen's letters to her sister occurs in a letter from Godmersham about events at Chawton:

> Mary P. wrote on Sunday that she had been three days on the Sofa. . . . How can Mrs. J. Austen be so provokingly ill-judging?—I should have expected better of her professed if not her real regard for my Mother. Now my Mother will be unwell again. (Letter 84: September 23, 1813.)

Shortly after Mrs. Austen's marriage:

> . . . the family moved from one residence to the other in 1771. . . . Mrs. Austen, who was not then in strong health, performed the short journey on a feather-bed, placed upon some soft articles of furniture. . . . (Memoir, p. 8.)

And the last glimpse we have of her is characteristically similar. Her grandson, Jane Austen's biographer, recounts:

> She once said to me, 'Ah, my dear, you find me just where you left me—on the sofa. I sometimes think that God Almighty must have forgotten me; but I dare say He will come for me in His own good time.' She died and was buried at Chawton, January 1827, aged eighty-eight. (Memoir, p. 11.)

It seems clear that Mrs. Austen was a highly developed hypochondriac; whether she also suffered from ill-health, other than frequent colds, during Jane Austen's lifetime, is much less clear.

## Poor Honey—Some Notes on Jane Austen and her Mother

I do not think Jane Austen believed that she was ever seriously unwell; nearly every letter, when she was with her mother and her correspondent absent, contains bulletins on her mother's health; and although Jane Austen had far too strict views on filial piety to criticize her mother in so many words, little turns of phrase, even if we did not have the novels, suggest that she considered her a *malade imaginaire*.

My Mother continues hearty, her appetite and nights are very good, but her Bowels are still not entirely settled, & she sometimes complains of an Asthma, a Dropsy, Water in her Chest and a Liver Disorder. (Letter 14: December 18, 1798.)

She (my Mother) is tolerably well—better upon the whole than some weeks ago. She would tell you herself that she has a very dreadful cold in her head at present; but I have not much compassion for colds in the head without fever or sore throat. (Letter 18: January 21, 1799.)

. . . now indeed we are likely to have a wet day—& tho' Sunday, my Mother begins it without any complaint. (Letter 55: October 1, 1808.)

For a day or two last week, my Mother was very poorly with a return of *one* of her old complaints—but it did not last long, and seems to have left nothing bad behind it.—She began to talk of a serious illness, her two last having been preceded by the same symptoms; but—thank Heaven! she is now quite as well as one can expect her to be in Weather, which deprives her of Exercise. (Letter 64: January 17, 1809.)

I am sorry my Mother has been suffering, & am afraid this exquisite weather is too good to agree with her. (Letter 118: December 2, 1815.)

There are more quotations in the same vein; despite the dutiful care and attention with which Mrs. Austen's complaints are detailed, I do not think there is much doubt that Jane Austen thought most of these complaints unjustified.

There are a number of hypochondriacs in the novels; with the exception of Mr. Woodhouse, and his elder daughter, who are treated with tenderness, Jane Austen does not show much sympathy with them. Mr. Woodhouse is exceptional among the hypochondriacs in that he shows real and continuous consideration for others; he 'enjoyed' ill-health, but it is never suggested that he manipulated his health either to vent his anger or to gain his own way. Far different are the other hypochondriacs—Mrs. Bennet ('When she was discontented she fancied herself nervous'), Mrs. Churchill, Mary Musgrove, Mrs. John Dashwood and the quite ferocious picture of the three Parkers in *Sanditon*. (These last were drawn when Jane Austen was herself desperately ill, and this may in part explain the savagery of the satire. But it has always seemed to me that *Sanditon* was meant to be a savage book, a gallery of fools, dupes and monomaniacs, not too unlike the novels Peacock was shortly to write.)

For Jane Austen the novelist, hypochondriacs use their imaginary ailments to increase their own self-importance, to get their own way, to bend others to their will, as a sort of sanctified selfishness. And such a belief was not confined to the novels. To her brother Francis she writes:

> They (The Bridges) have been all the summer at Ramsgate, for *her* health, she is a poor Honey—the sort of woman who gives me the idea of being determined never to be well—& who likes her spasms & nervousness & the consequence they give her, better than anything else.—This is an ill-natured sentiment to send all over the Baltic. (Letter 85 : September 25, 1813, p. 339.)

Is it possible that this insight was clouded when Jane Austen thought of her own mother? It was of course never voiced; but 'with a knowledge, which she often wished less, of her (parent's) character' (P. 34) could it possibly not have been felt? And can there have been no echo of personal feeling in the resentment which Anne Elliot felt in having to minister and give way to Mary's 'jealous and ill-judging' claims? Like Mary Musgrove, Mrs. Austen was considerably better born than her husband.

Though the indications are slight, it seems as though Mrs.

## Poor Honey—Some Notes on Jane Austen and her Mother

Austen was adept at avoiding trouble for herself. Mr. Austen Leigh tells us:

> I know little of Jane Austen's childhood. Her mother followed a custom, not unusual in those days, though it seems strange to us, of putting out her babies to be nursed in a cottage in the village. The infant was daily visited by one or both of its parents, and frequently brought to them at the parsonage, but the cottage was its home, and must have remained so till it was old enough to run about and talk; for I know that one of them, in after life, used to speak of his foster mother as 'Movie', the name by which he called her in his infancy. . . . Jane was probably treated like the rest in this respect. (Memoir, p. 41.)

I have no means of knowing to what an extent the custom of boarding-out infants (as opposed to hiring a wet-nurse) was in fact common in the second half of the eighteenth century, though I should question whether it were ever general. It is obviously an arrangement which avoids a great deal of work and trouble for the mother and, one would think on *a priori* grounds, one liable to diminish the deepest emotional bonds between mother and child. For what the observations are worth, I do not think there are any foster-relations in the canonical novels, even though it was potentially a useful device; the relationship between Darcy and Wickham, for example, could thus have been given a simpler explanation. But though there are no foster-relations in the novels, most of the heroines have a second woman *in statu matris* —Mrs. Jennings, Mrs. Allen, Mrs. Gardiner, Mrs. Weston, Lady Russell; although some of these are less well-born or well-connected than the real mother, they tend to be kinder and more indulgent, less demanding.

Mrs. Austen had to be spared, spared worry and spared discomfort:

> I have just received a note from James to say that Mary was brought to bed last night at eleven o'clock, of a fine little boy, and that everything is going on very well. My Mother had desired to know nothing of it before it should be all over,

and we were clever enough to prevent her having any suspicion of it. . . . (Letter 11 : November 17, 1798.)

Surely it is a rather odd mother who requests that she shall be told nothing of the birth of her eldest son's first child. Apparently she was (like her sister-in-law Mrs. Leigh Perrot) one of those women who spend their time expecting the worst:

> Indeed I shall be glad when the event at Scarlets is over; the expectation of it keeps us in a worry, your Grandmama especially; she sits brooding over Evils which cannot be remedied & conduct impossible to be understood. (Letter 142 : March 23, 1817, p. 142.)

She was, we are told by W. and R. A. Austen-Leigh:

> Always ready to contemplate the near approach of death both for herself and others; for in July 1811, after buying some bombazine in which to mourn for the poor king, she said : 'If I outlive him it will answer my purpose; if I do not, somebody may mourn for me in it; it will be wanted for one or the other, I dare say, before the moths have eaten it up.' As it happened, the King lived nine more years, and Mrs. Austen sixteen; and it was the lot of the latter to lose two children before her own time came. (Jane Austen—her life and letters, p. 257.)

As so often happens with this type of mild melancholia, Mrs. Austen was much less distressed by actual misfortune when it occurred, than by the anticipation of possible disasters. All the Austen women were deeply disappointed at having been forgotten in their uncle's will, and Jane, who was within three months of her death, was thrown into a relapse. She writes to her brother Charles:

> I am the only one of the legatees who have been so silly, but a weak Body must excuse weak Nerves. My Mother has borne the forgetfulness of *her* extremely well;—her expectations for herself were never beyond the extreme of moderation. . . . (Letter 143 : March 26, 1817, p. 491.)

## Poor Honey—Some Notes on Jane Austen and her Mother

Hypochondriac, and possibly also an invalid, slightly melancholic, demanding protection—what other traits can be deduced? They are not many. A love of putting things in order, keeping them tidy, locking them up can perhaps be seen in the following quotations:

> The Pembroke has got its destination by the sideboard, & my Mother has great delight in keeping her money and papers locked up. (Letter 25 : November 8, 1800, p. 83.)

> As you have been here so lately, I need not particularly describe the house or style of living, in which all seems for use and comfort; nor need I be diffuse on the state of Lady Brydges's bookcase and corner-shelves upstairs. What a treat to my Mother to arrange them! (Letter 46 : August 27, 1805. p. 165.)

And just as Mrs. Price was discomposed if she saw 'Rebecca pass by with a flower in her hat' (M. P., p. 408) so apparently was Mrs. Austen put into a taking by her maid Mary being unsuitably dressed for her station :

> Mary's blue gown! My Mother must be in Agonies.—I have a great mind to have *my* blue gown dyed some time or other—I proposed it once to you and you made some objection, I forget what. (Letter 87 : October 14, 1813.)

She was apparently a competent house-keeper, when she felt up to it: the letters contain many references to the making of jams, home-made wines, etc. 'My Mother has undertaken to cure six Hams for Frank;—at first it was a distress but now it is a pleasure.' (Letter 55 : October 1, 1808.) She enjoyed working in 'her' garden on occasion. She was proud of her domestic economies. She was a strong-minded woman, and spoke her mind: 'I like the gown very much and my Mother thinks it very ugly' (Letter 23 : October 25, 1800)—not the most endearing remark to a daughter who had just got a new dress.

What does not occur in the records is an account of a single good-natured or spontaneous action, any lovable behaviour. All that the dutiful Mr. Austen-Leigh can say in her favour is:

> She united strong common sense with a lively imagination, and often expressed herself, both in writing and in conversation, with epigrammatic force and point. (Memoir, p. 11.)

Even as a betrothed girl when 'a little before her marriage [she] was shown the scenery of her future home she . . . thought it unattractive. . . .' (*op. cit.* p. 19.)

Mrs. Austen may well have been—probably was—an intelligent, sensible woman; but there is not a detail which suggests that she was lovable, or even likeable. She was probably not as disagreeable as her sister-in-law Mrs. Leigh Perrot, who (I think) may well have furnished the characteristics for Mrs. Norris; but the picture which emerges is of a domineering old lady, fussy and querulous, making the whole tiny household revolve round her comfort and her health, using the threat of disease to avoid or prevent anything which did not please her. It is not an uncommon picture even today, the widowed lady of straitened means, dominating and almost devouring her spinster daughter. But the spinster daughter seldom turns into a writer of genius.

Jane Austen had some alleviations. The task of caring for her mother was shared, not only with her sister Cassandra but also with a spinster friend Martha Lloyd, who lived with the family; although Cassandra seems to have avoided the heavy work involved with their fairly numerous changes of residence quite consistently, Jane was able to go for long visits to her prosperous brothers and the other friends who must have provided the settings for most of her novels (if nothing more); from time to time she could live a life of elegance and comfort, enjoy the 'luxurious sensation' of 'sitting in idleness over a good fire in a well-proportioned room'. (Letter 25 : November 8, 1800.) When she finally got away from the misery of the noise, discomfort, and poverty of Bath and Southampton, and had resigned herself to being no longer young and (as a portionless woman) extremely unlikely to marry, she felt able to resume the writing which had been the source of such pleasure and amusement when she was

## Poor Honey—Some Notes on Jane Austen and her Mother

young and relatively carefree, when she still had some hopes of 'this world'.

I think it clear, though I do not remember ever having seen it stated, that in the last years of her life, after the return to Chawton, Jane Austen found increasing comfort in the practice of her religion, and, indeed became increasingly severe in her notions. There is the famous letter to Fanny Knight: 'I am by no means convinced that we ought not all to be Evangelicals, & am at least persuaded that they who are so from Reason and Feeling, must be happiest & safest' (Letter 103: November 18, 1814); and these sentiments come out in very small phrases in the later novels, apart from *Mansfield Park* where the edification is open. Thus, for example, when Anne Elliot is trying to discover the past behaviour of W. W. Elliot she learns that 'there had been bad habits; that Sunday-travelling had been a common thing' (P., p. 161); but in *Northanger Abbey*, written thirteen years earlier, the fact that Catharine was made to do her unescorted journey from Northanger to her home on a Sunday (N.A. p. 224) is not considered to add in any way to General Tilney's monstrous behaviour, and is not necessary to the plot; turned out at dawn on the Monday she still would not have seen Henry. The obvious conclusion is that between 1803 and 1816 the author's views had become much more strict.

The religion was not merely formal. After she had become re-united to Captain Wentworth Anne Elliot returned home:

> An interval of meditation, serious and grateful, was the best corrective of everything dangerous in such high-wrought felicity; and she went to her room, and grew steadfast and fearless in the thankfulness of her enjoyment. (P., p. 245.)

Similarly, when Emma is considering the future after she has accepted Mr. Knightley during a sleepless night:

> With respect to her father, it was a question soon answered. She hardly knew yet what Mr. Knightley would ask; but a very short parley with her own heart produced the most solemn resolution of never quitting her father.—She even wept over the idea of it, as a sin of thought. (E., p. 435.)

Except for the hypochondria, there is as little resemblance between the parents to whom the daughters were devoting their lives as there was between the circumstances of Emma and Jane Austen; but Jane may well have had the same temptation, the same contrition, and the same support.

The phrase 'poor Honey' occurs twice in the letters, and was apparently either a slang phrase, or a family phrase, for an invalid. In one of the last letters she wrote, to her niece Caroline Austen, Jane Austen applied it to herself:

> I have taken one ride on the Donkey & like it very much.—& you must try to get me quiet, mild days, that I may be able to go out pretty constantly.—A great deal of wind does not suit me, as I have still a tendency to Rheumatism. In short I am a poor Honey at present.' (Letter 143 : March 26, 1817.)

I have chosen this phrase as a title for these notes because, in its modern connotations, it seems to be very applicable. Jane Austen was poor, almost desperately poor financially, poor in being tied to such a mother and having to spend so many years of her short life in the most uncongenial surroundings; and her sweet character, to which all the records of her family bear testimony, as well as many of her letters, the fact that she never became embittered or sour, makes the endearment, Honey, appropriate, if perhaps a trifle familiar.